BRITHOP

Brithop

THE POLITICS OF UK RAP IN THE NEW CENTURY

Justin A. Williams

OXFORD
UNIVERSITY PRESS

Oxford University Press is a department of the University of Oxford. It furthers
the University's objective of excellence in research, scholarship, and education
by publishing worldwide. Oxford is a registered trade mark of Oxford University
Press in the UK and certain other countries.

Published in the United States of America by Oxford University Press
198 Madison Avenue, New York, NY 10016, United States of America.

Library of Congress Cataloging-in-Publication Data
Names: Williams, Justin A., author.
Title: Brithop : the politics of UK rap in the new century / Justin A. Williams.
Description: New York : Oxford University Press, 2021. | Includes bibliographical references and index.
Identifiers: LCCN 2020005423 (print) | LCCN 2020005424 (ebook) |
ISBN 9780190656805 (hardback) | ISBN 9780190656812 (paperback) |
ISBN 9780190656836 (epub) | ISBN 9780190656829 | ISBN 9780197531372 | ISBN 9780197520321
Subjects: LCSH: Rap (Music)—Political aspects—Great Britain—History—21st century. |
Rap (Music)—Great Britain—History and criticism.
Classification: LCC ML3918.R37 W513 2020 (print) | LCC ML3918.R37 (ebook) |
DDC 782.4216490941—dc23
LC record available at https://lccn.loc.gov/2020005423
LC ebook record available at https://lccn.loc.gov/2020005424

9 8 7 6 5 4 3 2 1
Paperback printed by LSC Communications, United States of America
Hardback printed by Bridgeport National Bindery, Inc., United States of America

For my daughter, Amy Elizabeth

Contents

Preface and Acknowledgments

WHEN I STARTED THIS book in 2015, the UK political and musical landscape looked very different from what it is now four years later at the time of this writing. Rappers Akala and Loki (Darren McGarvey) had not yet released their own books, the latter of which received the Orwell Prize for *Poverty Safari* (2017), and Sleaford Mods were an obscure band. The Grenfell Tower fire had not happened, drill music had not reached the mainstream, and then–Prime Minister David Cameron had not yet called a referendum on the UK leaving the EU. This book essentially begins with The Streets's *Original Pirate Material* and ends with responses to Brexit and Grenfell, a fifteen-year period from 2002 to 2017. What I hope to show in this book is that UK rappers have something important to say about this landscape, revealing an artistic world worth considering as part of political discourse in the UK and as an integral part of British music history.

This book is very much a personal one, both in the sense that I have felt the "otherness" in Britain first-hand, and that the voices of these artists have affected me on a personal level. My experiences, admittedly, have not been based on race or class, and I have felt isolation and prejudice to a much lesser degree than those marginalized by ethnicity, sexuality, ability, class, etc. I arrived in Britain just as US and British troops were entering the presidential palaces of Saddam Hussein. There was a certain level of (understandable) contempt by the British toward America, in part, given these circumstances. I cannot say that I have felt the "exile" of an Edward Said, or a DuBosian "doubleness," but my positionality has allowed me a unique perspective on British identity—in that sense it reflects how Said writes that exiles are able to be aware of at least two cultures rather than just one. How one is made to feel outside the UK mainstream in different ways, and how it can be celebrated through rap, is one of the ongoing threads in the chapters to follow.

The time period that I investigate in this book mirrors my time as a British resident, and now British citizen. It was The Streets in particular in 2002 and 2003 as a moment when UK hip-hop/dance music started to pique the interest of American college students. Since then, the UK popular music scene has witnessed the rise of grime in the early-to-mid-2000s, a grime Renaissance in the mid-2010s, drill music, further offshoots of electronic dance music, and vibrant pockets of more "traditional boom bap" styles of hip-hop that I discuss in the following pages. No single book would be able to capture accurately the variety of scenes and musical styles found in what could be considered UK rap in all its forms, but I do hope this small offering explores many of the themes that we find in the music's social and political contexts.

This book would not have been possible without the support of the University of Bristol, the music department in particular, and the UK's Arts and Humanities Research Council (AHRC). I was awarded a sabbatical in 2015 as part of a University Research Fellowship from the Institute of Advanced Studies at the University of Bristol; this allowed me the time to start the project. I am also grateful to have been involved with the Being Human/InsideArts Festival in 2015 for which I gave an evening talk at Rise Music that became the overall structural foundations of the book. The AHRC awarded me a Leadership Fellowship in 2016 which enabled me to finish the book, and I thank them for their support.

A number of scholars, artists, and colleagues have offered advice and information for which this book would not have been as cohesive otherwise. Thanks in particular to Nick Braae, Lori Burns, James Campbell at Intellect Books, Carpetface (Adam Russell), Carlo Cenciarelli, Michael Ellison, Steven Gamble, Steven Gilbers, Severin Guilliard, Jonathan Godsall, Loren Kajikawa, David Kerr, Madhu Krishnan, Sina Nitzsche, Laudan Nooshin, Adam de Paor Evans, Cecilia Quaintrell, Florian Scheding, Simran Singh, Tim Summers, David Trippett, Unity (Amelia Thomas), Eileen Walsh, and Polly Withers. As you will see, in addition to the heavy influence from Paul Gilroy, J. Griffith Rollefson's work is a strong presence throughout what follows, and I am grateful to him for our friendship and our long conversations about hip-hop. Aspects of this research were presented at a number of conferences and colloquia, including the Royal Musical Association (Bristol and Liverpool), IASPM (Kassel, Huddersfield), Hip-hop Conference: North and South (Helsinki), Popular Culture Association (Washington, DC, and Seattle), "It Ain't Where You're From, It's Where You're At" International Hip-hop Conference (Cambridge), and the Universities of Surrey, University of Bristol, Hull, Groningen, Nottingham,

Oxford, Plymouth, Wolverhampton, Royal Holloway, King's College London, and University College Cork. Thanks to everyone who invited me and to those who engaged with important questions and comments which helped make my work better.

To those involved in the production of this book: Special thanks to Mary Horn and project manager Anitha Jasmine Stanley at OUP, and especially to Suzanne Ryan who was supportive from the start of the project. It was great working with you! Thanks to the anonymous manuscript reviewers, copyeditors, design team and all those involved in making this happen.

As ever, my students have provided a lot of inspiration and enthusiasm. While space doesn't allow for naming the hundreds of UGs and MAs I have taught over the years, I would like to mention my PhD students Chris Charles, Zach Diaz, Alex Gibson, Marko Higgins, Jon James, Ivan Mouraviev, and Matthew Williams. Chris in particular had the role of helping to format and organize the book manuscript so it was palatable to press. I would like to give a special thanks to those artists and scholars up in Scotland who spent time helping me with my Scottish chapter and saved me from more than a few embarrassing mistakes—Jo Collinson Scott, Paul Harkins, and Dave Hook (Solareye)—thank you.

I am blessed to be a part of a vibrant departmental writing group led by professor Emma Hornby and composed of music faculty, final year PhD students, and post-doctoral colleagues. While we once compared it to "open heart surgery without anesthetic," it is a warm and jovial group of Medievalists, jazz scholars, Russianists, editors, pop scholars, composers, computer scientists, and others who all strive to make each other's work better. I would like to thank Emma, Argun Çakır, Lindsay Carter, Chris Charles (again), David Dewar, Will Finch, Sara Garrad, Kate Guthrie, Sarah Hibberd, James McNally, Peter Relph, Raquel Rojo Carillo, Paul Rouse, Dianne Scullin, James Taylor, and Sarah Thompson. You've all read loads of this already, but I do hope you find the end product satisfying. Thanks to Kawa Morad for the Arabic translations, and thanks to Argun for the recommendation.

James McNally, my postdoc on the wider AHRC project, was simply the best postdoc anyone could ask for. His work on early UK hip-hop is ground-breaking, and his knowledge of the UK hip-hop scene in general is more than impressive. And he's a really nice guy! It was great to work with him and he was really helpful and encouraging with this manuscript. As ever, any errors found within are my own.

A big thanks, as ever, goes to my wife Katherine, who has been unwaveringly supportive over the past decade, and has also been a fruitful collaborator. As ever, we share ideas, and I come to her with a lot of questions and when I get stuck, and I couldn't have done this without her. The past few years have presented a number of unexpected turns, and her heroism in the face of everything has been an inspiration to keep me going.

Brithop is dedicated to my daughter Amy. I started writing this book about a year before she was born, and it is her I thought about most while writing it. "What does it mean to be British?" or "What does it mean to be from cultures across continents?" and "How can we go from critique to change?" are questions I think about since becoming more personally invested in the answers than ever. Can we point to a better way so that she can have the same opportunities, freedoms, and rights that I had? Our two countries are headed in worrying directions, and hip-hop seems to be one of the more positive ways forward. To Amy's new little brother Alexander: thank you for the smiles, and the motivation you also provide in these "interesting times."

As I make the finishing touches to this preface, with the Covid-19 pandemic currently raging, things look even more uncertain than when I completed this book, but I can safely say that recent events have only amplified the political arguments therein rather than discredited or revised them. Rap critiques of the government's failure to take care of its most vulnerable and marginalized people have been proven *in extremis*, while tracks like Lady Leshurr's "Quarantine Speech" (2020) have continued a combination of critique, humor, self-reference, and didacticism around hygiene ("Gotta stay safe / cause I ain't dumb / Got the Lysol with me / I get my spray on") and staying home ("Yo, trust me know exactly how you feel / Now I got to quarantine and chill").

Last but most certainly not least, the rappers that I focus on are of course what make the book, and what I do for a living, possible. I acknowledge that my white privilege has helped in my journey to becoming an academic, a world that may seem somewhat removed from sites of rap performance. In some ways, writing an academic book on UK rap is playing into the "system"—this "output," for example, will no doubt become part of a governmental exercise in an increasingly privatized and neoliberalized Higher Education sector. Despite this, however, I do hope that I let the artists' voices come through, reflecting the high esteem and respect that I have for them, and in concert with my observations as a hip-hop scholar. They are the true authorities, and as we try to include artists and practice into more and more of our academic events, the ethics of artist-academic collaboration are more and more at the forefront of my mind these days. The fact that some of the figures I feature in this book (e.g., Akala, Stormzy, and Loki) have now written their own books goes to show that what they have to say also lends itself to literary treatment, and that artists are having their voices heard through multiple media. Thank you for your music and artistry.

Portions of Chapter 2 appeared in an earlier form as "Performing Multiculturalism in UK Hip-hop: The Case of Riz MC" as part of the discussion forum " 'Who Is

British Music?' Placing Migrants in National Music History" (ed. Florian Scheding), *Twentieth-Century Music* 15, no. 3 (2018): 445–51. © Cambridge University Press 2018. Reprinted with Permission.

Portions of Chapter 3 appeared in an earlier form as, "Rapping Postcoloniality: Akala's 'The Thieves Banquet' and Neocolonial Critique," *Popular Music and Society* 40, no. 1 (2017), and is available in open access form at https://www.tandfonline.com/doi/full/10.1080/03007766.2016.1230457.

A Note on Listening

A PLAYLIST STARTED to emerge in the planning of this book, much of which has stayed the same throughout. As I prefer to allow the music to be central in my writing, it is important to note how critical these tracks are to my thinking and what I want to present to you. For this reason, I highly recommend that you listen to this music alongside reading the book, as it will provide both the sonic and visual complement to the narrative. This playlist is available on the companion website to this book at www.oup.com/us/brithop

The playlist is also available on YouTube at: https://www.youtube.com/playlist?list=PLzUchoqHtqA4dLwodSopKmJwwXZiyDuRI.

1

INTRODUCTION

Rapping Back to the Postcolonial Melancholia

of Twenty-First-Century Britain

BRITHOP INVESTIGATES RAP music's politics in the twenty-first-century United Kingdom. In what follows, I argue that this music is partly an extension of, or often a counter to, political discourses happening in other realms of British society. These rappers are essentially "talking back" (hooks 1989, see also Hutten and Burns 2021) to mainstream Britain's political discourses,[1] as "an act of resistance, a political gesture that challenges politics of domination that would render us nameless and voiceless" (hooks 1989, 8). The rappers in this book critique the UK's more conservative narratives, and they express their relationship to Britain in the politically turbulent climate of the new century, providing valuable perspectives which can go unnoticed by those skeptical of or ignorant of hip-hop culture.

These counter-narratives occur through a range of themes that emerge in the post-1997 UK hip-hop scene: (banal and counter-) nationalism, history, style/subculture, politics, humor, and diaspora/belonging. While my case studies come from a number of UK regions, it became clear during the research that a single book can only scratch the surface of the diversity of hip-hop happening across the UK. A number of artists included in the book are based in London, reflecting the high density of mainstream hip-hop in the capital,

Brithop. Justin A. Williams, Oxford University Press (2021). © Oxford University Press.
DOI: 10.1093/oso/9780190656805.001.0001

but the book also makes wider geographical excursions, starting in Birmingham (Mike Skinner/The Streets), down the M40 motorway to Kentish Town (in North London, home of Akala), up the M1 to Nottingham (Sleaford Mods), then far up the M1-A1 to Edinburgh (Stanley Odd), M8 to Glasgow (Loki), way back down the country via the M6 to Newport, Wales (Goldie Lookin Chain), and then East along the M4 to London (Lowkey, Shay D), where our journey ends.[2] These artists are primarily UK-born yet many of them have heritage that inform their hybrid identities, roots often from regions of the former British Empire: with parents or grandparents from Jamaica (Akala), Ghana (Stormzy, Lethal Bizzle), Nigeria (Skepta), Serbia (Bricka Bricka), Iraq (Lowkey), Iran (Shay D, Reveal), Pakistan (Riz MC), and Palestine (Shadia Mansour).

The following chapters investigate the complex ways in which these rap groups and artists both adhere to and rebel against constructed notions of Britishness. Although the concept of the "Black Atlantic" (Gilroy 1993) no doubt theoretically underpins music of the African diaspora in the UK (such as hip-hop), I also wish to highlight music by those from other diasporas, including South Asian (e.g., Riz MC) and Middle Eastern (e.g., Lowkey, Shay D). In addition to hip-hop's performance of identity politics or a politics of the everyday, I also engage with hip-hop as political protest locally and globally. In Chapter 5, for example, I look at the role of hip-hop in the 2014 "Yes Scotland" (independence) campaign (e.g., Stanley Odd, Loki), but I also investigate rappers who advocate for the Palestinian cause in Chapter 7 (e.g., Lowkey, Shadia Mansour).

Despite a high degree of journalistic attention and institutional backing from national media outlets such as the BBC,[3] rap cultures in the UK are often misunderstood by the wider public for a few reasons. For the uninitiated, UK rap is either conflated with mainstream imagery imported from the US, or in some cases, deemed a lesser version of the "authentic" US original. Furthermore, given that grime in the mid-to-late 2010s has eclipsed most other forms of rap on the UK charts, a distanced onlooker might be led to believe that grime is the only rap style in existence in the UK. Lastly, rap genres can be misconstrued or dismissed in the mainstream in part because many Black, Asian and Minority Ethnic (BAME) rap artists arouse suspicion and skepticism from those who still see British-born, second- or third-generation citizens with African or Asian heritage as "immigrants," rather than as genuinely British (a product of what Gilroy calls "postcolonial melancholia," Gilroy 2004). What Modood and Salt call the "tacit whiteness" of national identity in Britain (2011, 10) means that ethnic minorities may feel outside a sense of national belonging, and subject to racism and other forms of marginalization. In contrast to this conflation of "Britishness" with "whiteness," British hip-hop tells a different story.

***

Rap music in Britain began in the early 1980s through inspiration from US styles yet quickly evolved to be more representative of the local in accents, lyrical references, and social contexts. In 2003, *The Times* described British hip-hop as a "broad sonic church" (Batey 2003). Since then, dozens more offshoots and sub-genres have originated and developed. Influences from the US hip-hop scene as well as earlier UK popular music such as jungle, house, garage, and others have contributed to (or in some cases, been rejected by) the often-hybrid offshoots such as (so-called) trip-hop, grime, dubstep, garage, trap, drill, and road rap, to name a few.[4]

It was grime, and its mid-2010s resurgence, however, that caught outside interest above all other genres. In part an offshoot of garage MCs, the emergence of grime in the early 2000s came from primarily black British adolescents in East London that were using video game and electronic dance music sounds to create a new rap soundscape. Monique Charles defines grime as including, "the juxtaposition of intensely heavy baselines and a vastness of space . . . between 136 and 140 bpm and early use of the PlayStation in music-making contributed to the grittiness of grime's sound" (2018, 41).

MC Wiley's "Eskimo" (2002) and More Fire Crew's "Oi" (2003) were early examples of grime, with genre-defining low-fi sounds, emphasis on low frequency and space in the beats for rapid lyrical delivery. Originally known as Eskiboy, and now considered the godfather of grime, Wiley released "Wot Do You Call It?" in 2004; it was a commentary on what to call this new style of music which was called Eskibeat, sub-low, 8-bar, or garage rap in its earliest days. Dizzee Rascal received national and international recognition through his Mercury Prize-winning *Boy in Da Corner* (2003), and his place in the post-war British music canon was confirmed through his performance at the London 2012 Olympics. The BBC Proms put on a *Grime Symphony* concert in 2015 featuring Lethal Bizzle, Little Simz, Stormzy, Chip, Krept & Konan, and others accompanied by the sixty-four-piece Metropol Orkest, giving the music a new platform while bringing in different audiences into the Royal Albert Hall.

By 2015, grime was not only reaching larger numbers of UK audiences, but was also starting to get recognition from global rap superstars. On February 25, 2015, the annual BRIT awards ceremony (the UK equivalent to America's GRAMMYs) included a performance of "All Day" by internationally successful rapper-producer Kanye West. Alongside him were twenty-five of the top UK artists from the grime rap scene (including Stormzy, Novelist, Fekky, Krept & Konan, Jammer, Shorty, and Skepta). Despite West's performance being heavily censored by the television channel ITV for his lyrical expletives, it was hailed by journalists as a moment of international recognition for the London grime rap scene. Not since 2002, with garage act So Solid Crew, had an "urban" artist performed on the BRIT stage, and many commentators noted that West's performance reflected a "grime Renaissance" in the mainstream (Hancox 2015; Barrett 2015; Mearon 2016; Wiley 2015).

The BRIT awards performance was one sign that American artists were starting to take notice of grime, and that the UK mainstream music scene should as well. US audiences initially tried to understand grime through a US-based hip-hop lens, generating debate on grime's place in relation to hip-hop: was it a subgenre of hip-hop? Or was it its own thing? Grime *was* its own thing, and in fact, grime's unique localisms are no doubt one reason why it has garnered global interest. Kanye's performance offered new visibility to rappers working within the grime genre. Since then, Skepta won the Mercury Prize in 2016 for his album *Konnichiwa*, and the 2018 BRIT awards saw grime artist Stormzy win two awards for his debut *Gang Signs and Prayer*. With Stormzy headlining Glastonbury Festival in 2019, it is undeniable that rappers have become a key component of Britain's mainstream musical landscape.

While rarely used by rappers or journalists (see Youngs 2005 and *VogueVideo* 2017 as exceptions), the term *Brithop* both eschews association with a specific rap genre and also suggests a broad network of rap styles originating from a variety of musical and geographical sources. It is an attempt to acknowledge genres such as grime, but also to highlight the many other varieties of UK rap in existence. Any attempt to map these scenes out geographically, musicologically, or otherwise is far beyond the scope of this project, but it is worth noting the plurality of British rap scenes and the ebb and flow between those mainstream and underground scenes.[5] I note grime's importance to diversifying British identity and its international popularity, and briefly cite examples where most relevant, but the rappers I primarily discuss in this book utilize beats stylistically resembling US-inflected (funk-based and/or "boom bap" style) hip-hop traditions.[6]

From New Labour to Grenfell: Political Contexts (1997–2017)

Despite the fact that the four elements of hip-hop (MCing, scratch DJing, graffiti, and breakdancing) have been in the UK since the 1980s,[7] I choose to investigate the twenty-first century for a number of reasons. First, it is the moment in which UK rap begins to acquire a greater degree of mainstream attention in the UK and abroad. Central to this book are cultural products seen and heard online and elsewhere by diverse audiences. I am less concerned with the "underground-ness" or other indices of authenticity in the UK's rap scenes than I am with the political discourses found within the tracks and music videos. Second, the 1997 election of New Labour after eighteen years in opposition to the Conservatives, and subsequent successful referendums on devolution of powers to Wales, Scotland, and Northern Ireland, were important milestones for considering national identity vis-à-vis "Britishness" as they entered the new millennium. As the Scottish and Welsh were embracing the ramifications of their new political and economic powers, the English were left to search for and explore their own sense of distinctive identity. Many of the artists that I discuss were responding (explicitly or implicitly) to definitions of Englishness and Britishness, many of which were constructed without them in mind. This book reflects an opportunity to study these voices, make them more visible, and discuss them in the wider context of Britain's politics.

The turn of the new century was also a moment when the Labour government's multiculturalism policies were contested by the opposition, and ultimately said to have failed after the 7/7 home-grown terrorist bombings of 2005. This contributed in part to the increasing racialization (and essentialization) of Muslims which had already intensified after September 11, 2001 (Garner and Selod 2015; Hussain and Bagguley 2012; Abbas 2007). One example of Islamophobia can be seen in social media comments that fictitiously tried to link Grenfell Tower victims' families in 2017 to terrorists involved in Manchester and London Bridge (Akala 2018, 20–21). Artists such as Riz MC respond to these sentiments through rap songs such as "Englistan" which discuss the nation's multicultural identity.

Many UK hip-hop and grime artists have commented extensively on key twenty-first-century political events: the Iraq War, the 7/7 bombings, the global financial crisis and an era of austerity, the Conservative-Liberal Democrat Coalition Government (2010–2015) followed by Conservative rule under Cameron, the 2011 riots, the 2014 Scottish Independence Referendum, the 2016 EU referendum, and the Grenfell Tower fire in 2017, which became a symbol of failure of the state as Theresa May's government was criticized for prioritizing neoliberalist ideals over the welfare of its citizens. The fifteen-year period that this book covers, from The Streets's "Don't Mug Yourself" (2002) to Lowkey's "Ghosts of Grenfell" (2017), has been a turbulent time in Britain's history, and I will tell its story through the rappers who have so much to teach us about the complexities of Britain.

Given hip-hop's associations with minority difference, many of the themes in this book deal with racial politics, either as translated from or contesting a certain form of black masculinity imported in part from the US. These are often intersectional with the ever-present class discourse in British counter-hegemonic politics. Hip-hop is often discussed as giving voice to the voiceless, empowering marginalized communities disadvantaged by power inequalities (Mitchell 2001; Williams 2015; Rollefson 2017). But while at once themes emerge which start to create links or narratives which hinge on a reduced notion of "marginal" and "dominant" identities, a more complex picture emerges upon closer investigation. Several hip-hop groups are multiracial, multiaccentual, and polystylistic, and individual identities remain more hybrid and fluid than many commentators and census data suggest. Examples from various artists will show the political in UK rap through discussions of nationalism (Chapter 2), history (Chapter 3), style and subculture (Chapter 4), governmental politics (Chapter 5), humor (Chapter 6), and themes of identity and belonging from rappers of the Middle Eastern diaspora (Chapter 7).

Postcolonial Melancholia in the Twenty-First Century: The Rap Response

In order to understand the rap contexts that I discuss in this book, it is important to outline the conditions to which the artists are responding in more detail, the milieu in which they are negotiating minority difference and their sense of place in twenty-first-century Britain.[8] In his 2004 book *After Empire*, Paul Gilroy outlines a concept he calls "postcolonial melancholia," which he defines as a psychological condition mourning the loss of Empire in an unhealthy manner (Gilroy 2004). For Gilroy, echoing Freud, mourning is healthy and of the conscious mind, but melancholia is when someone grieves for an incomprehensible or unidentifiable loss. Melancholia takes place in the unconscious mind and is pathological. Racism, binge drinking, and neurotic repetition of the (selective) past are symptoms of this condition. For many who lament for an earlier era in British history, WWII becomes an idealized focal point, highlighting past victories fueled by a heritage industry focused on that era and its perceived whiteness—usually, via Hollywood, using World War II as the favored means to find and even to restore an ebbing sense of what it is to be English (Gilroy 2004, 96). There is an obsessive repetition in the continued citation of WWII, but also of key themes in related cultural and political discourses such as invasion, war, contamination, and loss of national identity which reflect this melancholic mood (Gilroy 2004, 15).

The figure of the "immigrant" as an ethnic minority (either from within or outside Britain), according to Gilroy, symbolically lends a sense of discomfort to the nation's postcolonial melancholia. He notes that "The vanished empire is essentially unmourned. The meaning of its loss remains pending. The chronic, nagging pain of its absence feeds a melancholic attachment" (Gilroy 2005). Gilroy writes, "Today's unwanted settlers carry all the ambivalence of empire with them. They project it into the unhappy consciousness of their fearful and anxious hosts and neighbors. Indeed, the incomers may be unwanted and feared precisely because they are the unwitting bearers of the imperial and colonial past . . . The immigrant is now here because Britain, Europe, was once out there" (Gilroy 2004, 110).

After Empire was written in the immediate post-9/11 moment (and perhaps not coincidentally during the birth of grime), and yet, over fifteen years later, the sentiments expressed by Gilroy have amplified with further political consequences. In addition to the outcome of the Brexit referendum, we could also include the UK Home Office hostile environment policy which was promised in the 2010 Conservative Party Election Manifesto, carried out under then–home secretary Theresa May. Shocking, but not surprising, was the cultural amnesia around the immigration status of the Windrush generation, those invited from the Caribbean to fill post-WWII labor shortages (many of whom sailed on the ship the Empire Windrush in 1948). Under the hostile environment policy (2012–), those Commonwealth citizens were unable to prove their right to remain in the UK despite some having lived in the country for half a century, and many who had been British citizens when they arrived in the UK before Jamaican independence (1962). Under May as home secretary, their identity cards had been destroyed in 2010 and various other paper records lost or disposed of, making it difficult to find adequate documentation and in many cases leading to wrongful deportation in 2018.

We can also see anti-immigrant and ethnonationalist anxieties played out by groups such as the English Defense League, a far-right protest movement that vocalizes opposition to what they view as the spread of Islamism and Sharia law in the UK. More recently, political parties such as the British National Party (BNP) and the United Kingdom Independence Party (UKIP) included substantial reduction in immigration numbers as part of their platform. In 2015 and 2016, UKIP's then-leader Nigel Farage was vocal about the "migrant crisis" as a reason to leave the EU, most symbolized by the "Breaking Point" poster which depicted a queue of hundreds wanting to enter the country. The term migrant is, in itself, a dehumanizing term, in contrast to a term like refugee, not to mention the more outrageous comparisons of migrants as "cockroaches" by Katie Hopkins in *The Sun* (Hopkins 2015; see also Williams 2015; Anderson 2017). For parties like UKIP, these outsiders perceivably threaten the sanctity of "British culture," fearing that the spread of multiculturalism will eclipse traditionally recognized symbols of the "quintessentially British" and their taken-for-granted associations with whiteness.[9] Given subsequent reports from the Government's All-Party Parliamentary Group on Social Integration (Grice 2017; Waldron and Ali 2019) and studies such as the one published in *The British Journal of*

Social Psychology (Meleady 2017; Johnston 2017), it is safe to say that a large contributing factor to the "Brexit" referendum in June 2016 was anti-immigrant prejudice (see also Beauchamp 2016; Hall 2016).[10] Additionally, Fintan O'Toole wrote, "The Brexit campaign is fuelled by a mythology of England proudly 'standing alone,' as it did against the Spanish armada and Adolf Hitler," with English leavers aspiring to an English nationalism that ignores the fact that England has rarely "stood alone" historically (not least being part of the UK).

Through discourses of xenophobia and idealization of a mythic past, two main features of postcolonial melancholia, many "leave" voters assumed that Brexiting the EU would somehow bring the country back to an (imagined) past, less saturated with immigrants, or at least a time when only "good immigrants" were tolerated (Shukla 2016). After the referendum, there has been a tripling of hate crimes in some of the most Eurosceptic parts of the UK (Johnston 2017), with xeno-racism targeting Polish migrants in particular in both the right-wing media and as the target of hate crimes (Rzepnikowska 2019).[11]

Responses from BAME rappers to this melancholic anti-multicultural, anti-immigrant narrative are rife in UK hip-hop. For example, Riz MC (discussed further in Chapter 2) advocates immigrant contributions to society as positive factors: "Who these fugees [refugees], what did they do for me / but contribute new dreams, taxes and tools, swagger and food to eat." He continues, "Buckingham Palace or Capitol Hill / blood of my ancestors had that all built." This verse, from "Immigrants, We Get the Job Done" from the *Hamilton Mixtape* (2016), highlights the labor and cultural contributions of ethnic minorities and migrants to both the US and UK.[12]

For many rappers in the UK who represent and enact the consequences of Empire, lyrical content often includes a critique of postcolonial melancholia as part of a more introspective reflection on their own ethnic identities. British-born BAME rappers tell of the lived experience of racism and being made to feel they do not belong. British-Iraqi Lowkey (discussed further in Chapter 7), for example, raps, "Still I feel like an immigrant, Englishman amongst Arabs and an Arab amongst Englishmen." Other rappers, such as Akala (discussed in Chapter 3) and Shay D (discussed in Chapter 7), question the "tick box" categorizations of ethnic identity, acknowledging that their overlapping and intersectional characteristics paint a much broader picture than census data. Some artists use humor to discuss identity: one response to recent xeno-racism is the character Bricka Bricka (played by David Vujanic, discussed in Chapter 6) who plays an Eastern European immigrant laborer who performs all the stereotypes that are expressed in right-wing publications.[13] Punk-rap duo Sleaford Mods (Chapter 4) tackle capitalism, trendiness, the government, and the monarchy with profanity-laden lyrics with echoes of punk.

Scottish rappers like Solareye of Stanley Odd (Chapter 5) question Empire and its legacy (even though Scotland had been actively involved), with pro-independence Scots wishing to move beyond their past and toward a more civic (Scottish) nationalism separate from the UK and England in particular.

To give a more sustained example of rapper response to postcolonial melancholia, Lowkey's "Children of Diaspora" (2010) addresses the quality of "exile" that the children of diaspora feel, using words and sentiments from Edward Said's famous essay "Reflections on Exile," originally published in the *London Review of Books* in 1990. In the music video, Lowkey opens with a definition of diaspora: "The movement, migration or scattering of a people away from an established or ancestral homeland." His video shows community members of all ages and ethnicities, using close-ups of individuals which cut between them not-smiling and smiling. This feels like a conscious attempt to humanize those who are often portrayed as a problem in society. The "day in the life" nature of the video attempts to humanize, perhaps in response to postcolonial melancholia and other anti-multicultural sentiments.

Lowkey opens the song by rapping, "Don't you ever wonder what became of the children of Diaspora?" He raps, "Lost in this city of fog rarely seen by the sun / Just 'cause you're both but neither doesn't mean that you're none / Never captains of the ship but they mistook us for some passengers / Now we're stuck here singing soul music from diaspora." He wonders what became of these children, and discusses those who have suffered the tragic fate of race-driven lynching and murder at the hands of the police (Emmett Till, Stephen Lawrence, Mark Duggan, and others); he also states, "Zaha Hadid was a child of Diaspora so fear not, fear not. Edward Said was a child of diaspora so fear not, fear not . . . Nina Simone was a child of diaspora so fear not, fear not. Frantz Fanon was a child of diaspora so fear not, fear not." He ends the video with the following quote from Said from "Reflections on Exile" scrolling up on the screen in front of a gray background:

> Exile is strangely compelling to think about
> But terrible to experience
> It is the unhealable rift forced between a human
> being and a native place, between the self and its true home:
> its essential sadness can never be surmounted.
> And while it is true that literature and history
> Contain heroic, romantic, glorious, even triumphant episodes
> In an exile's life, these are no more than efforts meant to overcome
> The crippling sorrow of estrangement.
> The achievements of exile are permanently undermined by the loss of
> something left behind forever.

Lowkey's invocation of Said reflects the other side of postcolonial melancholia, the perspective of those who come from diaspora, often as consequence of the British Empire. These rappers essentially enact lyrically what this video also achieves visually: greater visibility for the arguably forgotten members of British society. The chorus states, "We never bow to the Queen, no," which is repeated six times per each chorus, setting in direct contrast to a symbol of British (white) national identity as well as Empire. And although the condition of exile is "unhealable" according to Said, Lowkey says, "fear not," as if speaking to the children in his community, reassuring them that success can come out of this condition. "Children of Diaspora" is one instance of how British rappers can respond to the condition of diaspora and Empire, insert their perspectives into the political discourse, and in some cases try to find a positive way forward.

Spivak famously asked, "Can the subaltern speak?" which became one of the important defining questions of postcolonial studies. In this context, rappers are certainly speaking *for* the subaltern by a mix of those who may identify as subaltern and/or those who sympathize with them. The "cosmopolitan solidarity" in the global response to the Al-Aqsa intifada in Palestine (Gilroy 2004, 89) is one such example where hip-hop has provided a soundtrack to resistance from a global community of rappers who sympathize with a more global humanism, and the internet has helped connect these people together. Hip-hop becomes voice for the voiceless beyond simply essentialized ethnic lines as well: it becomes lingua franca for any marginal identity, which is why Lowkey can speak for Palestinians and the poor of multicultural London, and why white Scottish rapper Loki can also speak for the UK underclass. One's circumstances can shift as well: Akala went from humble origins to becoming a successful owner of many businesses (restaurant, record label, publishing houses), Riz MC is now an international film and television star, and grime rapper Stormzy has formed his own press and scholarships for BAME students who attend Cambridge University. With this comes the issue of access: not only should the question be asked, "who can speak for whom?" but also "who has the platform to do so?" Part of the reason that this is rarely discussed is the assumption in both hip-hop and other forms of popular music that the artist speaks of their own situation as if it is autobiographical, a performance which stages an implicit contract assuming first person authenticity for their audiences. While a deep investigation of the motivations and affiliations behind these artists' work is beyond the scope of this current study, it is safe to say that the work is broadly motivated by a sense of wanting to respond to and critique other more visible stories, to tell other stories, sometimes theirs, sometimes of others. As we see time and time again, it is rap music that becomes the form adopted to tell them.

The rap scenes of multicultural London (Speers 2017, 36–37) and its regional variants are an intersectional mix of racial, gender, and class-based identities that loosely coalesce into an entity concerned with minority difference, social equality, and space to enjoy oneself. This book largely focuses on political elements of UK hip-hop, but this is not to suggest that UK rap styles do not often involve fun, music for dancing, general enjoyment, and/or an element of competition (such as in rap battles). There is a diversity of scenes which include more old school party rap stylings like Def Defiance (crew from Exeter between 1989 and 1991) who still perform the style under different names across the UK (de Paor Evans 2020), and all the grime music making across UK youth centers (Bramwell and Butterworth 2019). White's recent work (2017) has emphasized the notion of entrepreneurship in the UK's post-millennial urban music community, with creative enterprise around genres such as grime as an important social practice and providing a sense of belonging within the informal economies of the urban music scene. Her work deftly navigates both online and offline networks, and the desire for these artists to reach as large of an audience as possible.

Rapping becomes a way to perform individualized experiences while also being part of something more, attaining a form of "cultural citizenship" (Craft 2018) within the imagined community of global hip-hop culture. In this sense, these rappers form a "family of resemblances" alongside hip-hop's minority politics worldwide.[14] Hip-hop therefore provides counter-narratives to seemingly more dominant ideologies such as postcolonial melancholia and what follows in many ways demonstrates the range of responses therein.

Objectifying Rap?: Negotiating Methods, or the *What* of Rap Analysis

In terms of the methods and techniques used for this book, I have tried to balance a compelling narrative centered on and structured around particular themes, rappers, and their lyrics with the complexities of the music and its contexts. The structuralist aim is to create something for audiences that may know less about UK rap than its dedicated fans while engaging with deconstructionist critical theory that opens up the fault lines of the complex intersectional aspects of artist identity. Ultimately, the *what* I am looking at, the objects of my inquiry, are recordings of UK rap rather than a particular scene, audience, or industrial structure.

Furthermore, the focus on lyrics in particular on these recordings (and imagery from music video in some cases) should not suggest that music and other sonic elements are not a part of the meanings communicated. I made that argument forcefully in my book *Rhymin' and Stealin'* (2013) on the back of Krims's pioneering *Rap Music and the Poetics of Identity* (2000). This, rather, is a book about the messy politics of the UK in all its forms, and how the voices of MCs provide (counter-)narratives to various strands of the political economy. In some ways, then, it is not a book about UK rap scenes or genres, but it is a story of the UK in the twenty-first century as told *through* these important voices. It is of course also about these rappers and their communities, but this book shows how *their words reveal complex ideas*. It is for this reason that textual analysis often involves lyrics only, and in some places, imagery from music video. Elements like production and musical structures are left in the background in the interest of teasing out lyrical meaning. This also allows space for important context: both in terms of critical theory and historical contexts of the topic at hand.

Rhymin' and Stealin' (Williams 2013) attempted to place hip-hop's intertextual practices (mostly rap music but could be applied to the other elements) as fundamental to the culture and within a wider history of musical borrowing and Signifyin(g).[15] In keeping the music-centric focus of the book, other aspects such as politics and gender were regrettably less explored. This book attempts to engage with some of those themes more closely, considering how they play out in the UK compared to their rap cousins across the pond.

Given my background as a Californian who has lived in the UK for over fifteen years, my perspective will also be at once distanced and heavily invested in the political debates and the future of the country. I am reminded of the Ann du Cille quote which opens Guthrie P. Ramsey's article on black music, critical bias, and the "musicological skin trade":

> As more and more scholars—male and female, black and non-black—take up the task of reading the work of African-American women writers, *who* reads these texts may have a direct bearing on *how* they are read. In a best of all possible intellectual worlds, where we all had equal access to each other's cultures, the race, gender, and historical experiences of the critic might be irrelevant. (du Cille 1992, quoted in Ramsey 2001, 1)

I have, therefore, tried to bring something to the table from my own perspectives, an awareness that I am not part of these rap communities from an artist standpoint, but have a critical awareness of academic studies of hip-hop while understanding British culture both from the inside and from the perspective of an outsider.

Previous studies of twenty-first-century UK hip-hop have relied on ethnographic approaches. Laura Speers has written comprehensively about the notions of authenticity in twenty-first-century London (non-grime) hip-hop scenes (real and virtual) through interviews and participant observation (Speers 2017). Bramwell takes a similar sociological approach but focuses on grime music's role in the formation of young people's identities in London, looking at live gigs as well as music consumption and playback on mobile phones while riding London's buses (Bramwell 2015). Bramwell and Speers use relevant cultural theory to reinforce their studies, and their work paints a picture of two different rap scenes in London.

As grime has increased in popularity in its mid-2010s resurgence, it has attracted substantial academic and journalistic attention (Collins and Rose 2016; Charles 2016; White 2017; Boakye 2017; Hancox 2018). Journalism has pointed to grime as a quintessentially British sound, similar to punk in its DIY ethos and attempt to capture the sentiments of a particular time and place (Hancox 2018; White 2018; Adegoke 2018). Rapper Akala (discussed in Chapter 3), says this of the moment of British rap visibility in the mainstream: "nationalism is ironically at play in the UK in that I don't think it's a coincidence that part of grime music's recent success has been underpinned by journalists' ability to claim it as an authentically 'British' form of music, even if the 'truly British' status of its dominant practitioners is still in question" (Akala 2018, 260–261). Rappers themselves are starting to tell their stories on the written page as well, most notably the 2018 Stormzy book *Rise Up: The #Merky Story So Far* (co-written with Jude Yawson). For *Brithop* I emphasize the rappers' lyrics in particular, but it is clear that these artist discourses are appearing in other outlets beyond their music, bolstered by the recent interest in UK rap styles.

As opposed to a heavily ethnographic approach, this book's methodology considers the close reading of hip-hop tracks and music videos as having an important sense of agency. Part of this is given my background in (popular) musicology, using recordings as the primary source material, whether on albums, streaming, YouTube, or Bandcamp as a common methodology. Another reason is for the opportunity it affords us to look at elements like accent as well as lyrical and musical content. I therefore foreground recorded texts as primary object of analysis as they circulate in a network of social media, streaming services, etc., prioritizing what the rappers *want* to say (literally) *on record*, and what gets communicated to their audiences via those media.

The fact is that recordings are ever-increasingly culturally influential: the 1.6 million YouTube views of Shadia Mansour's "The Kuffiyeh is Arab," the 1.1 million views of Goldie Lookin Chain's "Fresh Prince of Cwmbran," the 2 million views of Sleaford Mods's "Tied up in Nottz," or the 5.7 million views of The Streets's "Don't Mug Yourself" will attest that a diverse audience are viewing these products and consuming them (not to mention the viral power of grime—Stormzy's "Shut Up" from 2015 now has over 103 million views).[16]

Accent is often neglected in the study of rap recordings, and UK rap is no exception. Linguists have looked at Multicultural London English (MLE) or Multicultural Youth English (MYE) language, a mix of Jamaican, American, British English, etc., which finds itself performed in London grime and a lot of UK hip-hop. MYE or MLE (Kerswill 2013, 2014; Cheshire et al. 2011) is considered a sociolect as well as a dialect, and is reflective of a postcolonial condition that is informed by history, migration, and globalized society. But MLE or MYE is also a resistance vernacular, in direct confrontation with the "accepted" Received Pronunciation accent tacitly associated with British whiteness. MLE has specific systems of grammar and phonology, including fronting of the /ʊ/ vowel in *foot*, and "th-fronting"—/θ/ is fronted to [f] in words such as *three* and *through*, which become *free* and *frough*, and /ð/ is fronted to [v] in words such as *brother* and *another*, which become *bruvver* and *anuvver*. Another feature is "th-stopping" where interdental fricatives can be stopped, and *thing* and *that* become *ting* and *dat* (Cheshire et al. 2011). Loanwords from Jamaican Creole ("wagwan," "mandem") and African American English ("man") are in the mix as well. When sociolinguists look at accent and dialect in general, they tend to operate through observation and interview. It seems rare that sociolinguists look at the cultural products in circulation amongst these speech communities. A study of popular music recordings (online or otherwise) would go some distance to show how these circulated products contribute to the speech communities that linguists study.

Rob Drummond (2017, 2018), who prefers calling MYE Multicultural Urban British English (MUBE), discusses the raised onset and monophthongization of the *price* vowel, and that words like *like, might*, and *try* have a "flatter" vowel with very little movement of the tongue. The pronunciation has moved towards a longer version of the vowel sound in *cat*. There is the extreme fronting of the *goose* vowel in words such as *food, blue*, and *crew*, which is produced further forward in the mouth, approximating the pronunciation of the vowel in the French *tu*. DH and TH stopping consist of words beginning with "th": *they, them*, and *there* are pronounced with a "d" sound *dey, dem*, and *dere*. Words beginning with "th," such as *thing, three*, and *think*, are pronounced with a "t" sound, resulting in *ting, tree*, and *tink*. There is the use of pragmatic marker *you get me?* at the end of a sentence (often said by grime rapper Skepta), similar to the popular *innit*. Right-wing newspapers such as *The Daily Mail* have noted the trend in more affluent areas and often blame immigration for the changes (Clark 2006; Harding 2013). One could say this dialect is yet another reminder of postcolonial melancholia as well as a celebration of localized difference, in active contrast to more mainstream "national" (e.g., "BBC English") accents.

Although a close reading of accent and dialect is more peripheral to my current narrative, accents are an important part of the discussion, not least that these accents contribute to the performative sense of "resistance vernacular" (Potter 1995; Reinhardt-Byrd 2015), adding as much resistant weight to the track as the beat and the lyrics if not more in some cases. MYE or MUBE are in direct contrast to the Received Pronunciation (or Queen's English or BBC English) that represent the mainstream, the elite, stereotypically white upper-class identities that define stereotypical British society. Another effect of these influential recordings is that it contributes to the homogenization of multicultural youth cultures in the UK, a linguistic hybridizing into an "urban" identity which can be used as a marker for marginality and resistance but also for belonging.

To demonstrate the importance of accent with an example, the opening of Skepta's "That's not Me" (feat. JME) from 2014 opens with the lines:

> It's the return of the mack
> I'm still alive just like 2Pac

If spoken with a US accent, this rhyme would not work. The phonetics would read: [ɪts ðə ɹətɜɹn əv ðə mæk aɪm stɪl əlaɪv dʒʌst laɪk tuːpɑk], where the long ɑ (sounding like "ahh") of Pa(aah)c does not rhyme with the æ (sounding like "back") of "mack." However, the UK MLE pronunciation of 2Pac ("tooh pack") rhymes with "back" or "mack," and thus the rhyme works. The phonetics for the MLE accent would be: [ɪts ðə ɹətɜːn əv ðə mæk aɪm stɪl əlaɪv dʒʊst laɪk tʉːpæk], which is far from any RP accent.

RP is often used as the foil to the multicultural urban British accent in grime and other forms of rap. RP is often gendered in rap recordings, feminized as it is used by a female voice. Skepta's grime track "Shut Down" (2015) includes a short interlude of an account by a female voice in an RP accent (heard through some sort of muffled effect as if she were talking through a megaphone): "A bunch of young men all dressed in black dancing extremely aggressively on stage. It made me feel so intimidated and it's just not what I expect to see on prime time TV." This is most likely a reference to the BRIT award performance described earlier in this chapter, referencing the criticism from (perceivably more mainstream white) audiences including ITV's censorship of the expletives in the song. The same voice also opens Skepta's "Ace Hood Flow" (2014) as a BBC 1 announcer, introducing the song: "This film contains graphic scenes of nudity, drugs, and violence. Please switch off now if you feel you're going to be offended. Listener discretion is advised."

KSI's "Keep Up" (2015) frames the male grime lyrics around an ongoing narrative of women with RP accents. It is reminiscent of the "Becky, Look at Her Butt" opening of Sir Mix-a-Lot's "Baby Got Back" (1992) which used the Southern California-associated "Valley Girl" accent to suggest a middle-class whiteness. The opening lines in RP in "Keep Up" are: "What's going on these days? People are get-ting famous from YouTube? I mean, have you heard of that guy, KSI? Apparently, he's got millions of subscribers, and a book . . ." The introduction to JME's version is prefaced with the same girl, "Have you heard of this JME guy? What the hell is 'grime' music? Is it a UK thing?" The contrast in accent sonically performs a divide between those not in the know, and those who are more "on the ground" with refer-ence to grime subculture. MLE and RP perform class, race, and gender that frames and reinforces a notion of black masculinity associated with grime music. In these cases, the gendered RP accent is being used in opposition to the rappers and to rep-resent some mainstream they wish to resist. In other words, there are not only dem-onstrations of resistance in lyrical content but are also performed so through accent. As Dizzee Rascal raps in "Pagans" (2014), "I don't speak Queen's English, but I'm still distinguished."

Hip-Hop Geographies: Nation, Nation-State, City, Region?

Many books on non-US hip-hop have assumed the nation-state as the geographi-cal catchment area for their analysis (Condry 2006; Durand 2002; Moreno Almieda 2017). But should it be the case? Rollefson (2017), in contrast, looks at three cities across nation-states (London, Paris, and Berlin) to investigate minority ethnic difference in rap. James Butterworth and Richard Bramwell use "Englishness" in the title of their studies, which suggest that the nation is the preferred unit, separate from Wales, Scotland, and Northern Ireland. They argue convincingly that the English rappers they interview (from London and Bristol) use the term "UK" as an "unconscious euphemism" for England (Bramwell and Butterworth 2019). Adam de Paor Evans's forthcoming book takes a criti-cal regionalist approach by looking at the rural South West of England where he grew up, and how hip-hop arrives to provincial England in the mid-1980s (de Paor Evans 2020). He, like Bramwell and Speers, weave critical theory and ethnography together to paint temporally and geographically specific scenes. Bramwell's book on grime (2015) and Speers's book on hip-hop authenticity (2017) focus almost exclusively on London. In contrast to these city-based or England-based examples, my study includes examples from England, Scotland, and Wales.[17] Although I do not investigate the fascinating history of hip-hop in Northern Ireland in favor of focusing on the three nations of Great Britain,[18] I do consider my study to engage with Britain as the nation-state[19] (formally named The United Kingdom of Great Britain and Northern Ireland) alongside other regional, national, and multicultural metropolitan geographies.

There is a lot more work to be done in thinking about hip-hop's regional specifici-ties, their rural and urban manifestations, and the playing with national and regional identity that happens in these genres. In the case of de Paor Evans's research (2020), not only does his approach show the intersection between rural, more home-made music making (e.g., bedroom graffiti, bus shelter freestyles, pause-button home mixes) and urban, industry-supported mainstream forms (e.g., McLaren's *Duck Rock, Street Sounds Electro* compilations), but it also shows the migration of indi-viduals to traverse rural contributes not only a unique perspective for not only hip-hop studies, but also for anyone interested in the workings of cultural production and consumption in rural regions.

The idea of a diverse range of individuals using rap music to question mainstream notions of national identity and belonging is by no means a phenomenon that is local to the UK. It is most certainly a global phenomenon ripe for transnational com-parison. Rollefson makes this patently clear: "Through both the political struggle and commercial visibility of hip hop, Senegalese Parisians, Turkish Berliners, South Asian Londoners, and countless others are holding up mirrors to their societies to show their respective nations that they are not who they think they are" (Rollefson 2017, 2). In his study, he argues, "It is the sons, daughters, and grandchildren of set-tlers from the former colonies and peripheries of Europe who are on the front lines and are best equipped to offer new insight into current affairs . . . if we have the sense to listen" (18).

In many ways, the sentiments of this book overlap with Rollefson's main argu-ment, and his book provides an important model for consideration of hip-hop's dou-bleness: hip-hop and/as postcolonial theory, the globalization of African American musics, the art/life dynamics at play as well as the commercialism/politics paradox found in the form. What I hope to expand upon in the following pages, however, is a more varied investigation of minority difference, not only in terms of race and eth-nicity, but also in terms of class and of political minorities (e.g., Scotland). Although Rollefson focuses on how music encodes racial difference, I attempt to look at how music encodes other forms of difference (and how difference encodes music) in cultural products like music videos which can be easily viewed and shared on the internet.

Using the nation-state as a methodological unit of one's field of inquiry, however, risks "methodological nationalism," as Schiller and Meinhof define it, "the tendency to equate nation-state boundaries with the concept of society" (2011, 21).[20] The cri-tique is that such a method reduces actors to a binary of natives or migrants/for-eigners (and always seen through an "ethnic lens"), and risks ignoring some of the transnational and transcultural forces in a given scene. In other words, it does not properly acknowledge the mobility of citizens (and their technologies, I might add).

In the context of this study, however, I am not necessarily dealing with a migrant-native divide, but with a more productive distinction between natives and *natives who are made to feel foreign*, one way or another.

Considering the methodological risks of taking the nation-state as a unit of analysis, I do believe that the UK's media structures have an effect on the music industry for its artists and fans (Cloonan 1999), in counterpoint with some of the more grassroots/local (e.g., SB.TV) and global (e.g., YouTube) media networks: BBC Radio One and Radio1Xtra, for example, dictate a form of "official popular culture" for lack of a better term, or the historicizing of "national culture" through BBC4 music documentaries (e.g., "Jazz Britannia," "Reggae Britannia," "Punk at the BBC") and the like (Long and Wall 2010). France's nationalism-based policies in the 1990s helped support the rise of French hip-hop, as a certain percentage of music on the radio needed to be in the French language. The UK does not have that specificity as so much mainstream pop and hip-hop is from the US (and thus already English-language), but Welsh-language radio and television have helped to support Welsh-language music along similar lines (including hip-hop, see Hill 2007). In the late '00s (pre-"grime Renaissance"), artists like Lethal Bizzle made it their aim to get mainstream radio airplay (not just 1Xtra), and have adopted strategies to try to cross-over into this sphere. Who headlines "rock" festivals like Glastonbury (of which portions are broadcast by the BBC) are often the subject of debate around genre and are often treated as a barometer of popular music tastes in the UK.

Furthermore, the "nation within a nation" status of Scotland and Wales in particular make such a notion of imagined communities along nation and nation-state lines all the more complex. One could go as far to say that the current politics of colonialism are in effect and negotiated daily in the relationship between Northern Ireland, Scotland, Wales, and England via the Westminster-based governmental powers. How these power relations are perceived largely depends on one's situatedness, political leanings, knowledge of history (e.g., Scotland's sense of marginality while nevertheless profiting from Empire), and how one's identities overlap in relation to these communities. What we do find is a complex web of overlapping and intersecting marginal-mainstream considerations along the lines of gender, class, ethnicity, race, citizenship, and more. Rap music has allowed a space to negotiate some of these complexities.

I would also argue that while hip-hop in the UK remains primarily a male space in terms of rappers, there are numerous notable (and arguably more financially successful) exceptions over its history including Mystery MC, Cookie Crew, She Rockers, Lyric L, Est'elle, Floetry, Lady Sovereign, M.I.A., Monie Love,

Lady Leshurr, Shay D, Little Simz, and Speech Debelle, and we must acknowledge how the genres of rap, their accents, performance spaces, and racial identifications are gendered as well. There are important initiatives such as Ladies of Rage in Cardiff and Girls of Grime in London which are trying to include and foster women's creativity in terms of rap, production, graffiti, and other hip-hop forms in the country, and these projects are due to the tireless efforts of rap activists who are putting in work to make visible the creative labor of hip-hop women. This study has included the voices of Lady Sovereign, Shay D, Speech Debelle, and Shadia Mansour but still does not do adequate justice in painting a more gender-balanced picture academically (but is a start).

The rappers explored in this study perform multiple in-between "third spaces" (Bhabha 1994), perhaps reflective of the "broken histories" of exile and diaspora (Said 2002), while often simultaneously communicating clear themes and ideas via the lens of popular culture. In the process of writing this book, I have tried to balance the sanitizing historicism entailed in "writing a book on UK hip-hop" which has clear themes and messages, and the poststructural complexities of the postcolonial condition ("the gritty human realities of postcoloniality," Rollefson 2017, 3). After all, the deconstructionist impulse is strong this side of the pond (not least in continental Europe), as is its desire to dissect grand (American) narratives and canons.

But once everything is deconstructed, what do we have left? Rarely are we left with an alternative picture painted, or even another way forward; we are left simply with a critique of the old way without a replacement. To this end I have tried to tell a story (not *the* story) of twenty-first-century UK rap that teases out shared themes while not trying to suggest they are the only forms and artists that exist in these vibrant and diverse scenes.

Brithop is an investigation of UK rap's politics in the new century, as told through rap recordings and filtered through various musicological, linguistic, and postcolonial lenses. It could also be read as a set of interweaving stories, laced by my desire to find commonalities without trying to reduce the complexities of the music and their creators/performers. My ultimate aim is to share these artistic texts and their contexts with multiple audiences inside and outside the UK, in an attempt to deepen our understanding of them. What it shows is a multifaceted group of voices that reflect the politics of the postcolonial condition of the UK, having the cultural citizenship of the global hip-hop nation and its penchant for talking back to (or even better, rapping back to) dominant discourses, while performing some of the localized particularities of their regional and national circumstances.

Notes

1. The idea of talking back in the context of intersectional feminism is utilized effectively in Rebekah Hutten and Lori Burns work on Beyoncé's "Sorry" from *Lemonade* (Hutten and Burns 2021).

2. My choice in cities and regions are not to suggest that these are the only or most vibrant scenes in UK rap. To the contrary, there are strong scenes in a number of towns and cities not covered in this book (including my own in Bristol).

3. BBC Radio 1Xtra was launched in August 2002 as a digital urban contemporary and Black music radio station which began around the time of grime's emergence and has been generally supportive of the UK's urban music scenes, albeit risking the genre's marginalization from the UK's pop radio mainstream (BBC 1).

4. Rollefson notes the many subgenres of breakbeat musics in twenty-first-century London and that he "came to see London's hyperactive subgenre glands as part of a larger innovation engine powered by the simultaneous attraction to and repulsion from the American black music industry" (2017, 169).

5. As ever, intermediaries label certain rappers in groups together that rarely represent the diversity of their stylistic characteristics, and/or ignore some of the collaborative endeavors between artists not normally considered in the same genre. A given rapper's album might include multiple genres, and collaborations with rappers from diverse scenes, thus complicating the narrative further. Some group all these styles into one large categorization of "urban" music, which is basically synonymous with contemporary black popular music. Urban music as genre categorization has been used to describe not only music, but also how some youth in cities like London categorize their own identities (Song 2010a, 2010b). Critiques of the term from writers such as Kehinde Andrews believe that defining black music by its location "reinforces racial stereotypes and helps white artists profit from them" (Andrews 2018).

6. On a generalized level, the "basic beat" of many UK rap or hip-hop tracks adheres to funk breakbeats associated with "boom bap" styles of hip-hop that proliferated in 1990s East Coast hip-hop but are as varied as beats found in tracks by Nas, Eminem, A Tribe Called Quest, 2Pac, Queen Latifah, and Common. Digable Planets's "Rebirth of Slick's (Cool like Dat)" at 98 bpm or A Tribe Called Quest's "Excursions" at 96 bpm would be representative with US hip-hop of this style using ca. 85–95 bpm. In contrast, grime which involves more synthesized and video game-style electronic sounds is closer to 140 bpm. Its breakbeats have origins in UK subgenres such as garage. "Pow (Forward)" by Lethal Bizzle is 138 bpm, Skepta's "That's Not Me" is at 139 bpm, and Dizzee Rascal "I Luv U" is 136 bpm.

7. The first element to arrive in the UK was MCing, with London's first rap club, the Language Lab, opening in Soho in January 1982 (McNally 2015, 2). While there were brief glimpses of hip-hop in the mainstream in the 1980s (Malcolm McLaren's "Buffalo Gals," Morgan Khan's Street Sounds Electro compilations, channel 4 broadcast of Wild Style), by the early 1990s, UK hip-hop went firmly underground for a number of reasons, not least with the rise of genres such as acid house and moral panics around the music and violence (McNally 2016). Rappers at record labels such as Low Life (1992–2008), YNR (started in 1999), and SFDB (started 2001) such as Lewis Parker, Taskforce, Jehst, and Skinnyman were taking the

genre in one direction (i.e., the more NY backpack "boom bap" style of ATCQ and DJ Premier), and the rise of grime (Wiley, Dizzee Rascal, Jammer, JME, Tinchy Stryder, Lethal Bizzle) was taking their rap in another. Furthermore, the late '90s introduced the label Big Dada (owned by Ninja Tune) which put out artists like Roots Manuva, New Flesh, and Ty, not quite like the rappers in the more backpack-influenced scene nor like the grime MCs. Rather, they performed aspects of their Caribbean heritage in a more forceful way, were more experimental, and at times fused with other popular styles (such as with the early 2000s garage scene).

8. Note that I am using the term *postcolonial* without the hyphen as I am not suggesting a "post-colonial" after-colonialism as a historical period, but to quote John McLeod "as referring to disparate forms of representations, reading practices, attitudes and values" (McLeod 2010, 6). "We might say that postcolonialism does not refer to something which tangibly *is*, but rather it denotes something which one *does*: it can describe a way of thinking, a mode of perception, a line of enquiry, an aesthetic practice, a method of investigation" (McLeod 2010, 6). In other words, postcolonialism does not mean the same thing as "after-colonialism," not a radically different historical era but that "it recognises both historical continuity and change" (McLeod 2010, 39).

9. The UKIP 2015 manifesto, under the category of "British Culture," states: "We will not condone the philosophy of multiculturalism because it has failed by emphasizing separateness instead of unity." Under this heading, we are provided no information about art, music, film, theater, or the like. See "The UKIP Manifesto 2015," available at: www.ukip.org/manifesto2015.

10. "EU migration into the UK was a key issue in the EU referendum debates in 2016. The Leave campaign used the anti-immigration discourse claiming that the main cause of all the UK's issues, including housing shortages or the strained National Health Service (NHS), is 'uncontrolled mass immigration' caused by the right to freedom of movement within EU member stages. The Leave campaign argued that exiting the EU would allow Britain 'take back control of its borders'—the slogan previously used by UKIP" (Rzepnnikowska 2019, 65).

11. The term "xeno-racism" or xenophobic racism, refers to racism not just directed toward those with darker skin and/or from former colonials, but a newer category of displaced whites: "It is a racism in substance but xeno in form. It is a racism that is meted out to impoverished strangers even if they are white" (quoted in Rzwpnikowska 2018, 63).

12. The track features a global lineup: Riz MC (Pakistani-British, discussed further in Chapter 2), Snow tha Product (Mexican-American), Residente (Puerto Rican), and K'naan (Somali-Canadian). They discuss the hidden labor of their national economies, rapping on behalf of these marginalized and hidden figures (Williams 2018).

13. In terms of humor around some of the race and class expectations of the rap persona, Dr. Syntax and Pete Cannon in their track "Middle Class Problems" (2014) take the trope of rapping about problems of underclass disenfranchisement and translates it to the white British middle class and their problems, highlighting their triviality or banality. Mr. B the Gentleman Rhymer is another example, espousing white Victorian middle-class stereotypes through rap and his banjo + ukulele hybrid the "banjolele." He calls his style of rap "chap hop." Thanks to Tom Attah for bringing Mr. B and the style to my attention.

14. The term was used by George Lipsitz with reference to Hispanic musicians in Los Angeles (Lipsitz 1997). Sarah Hill discusses the hip-hop nation as a family of resemblance, writing with respect to Welsh rap (Hill 2007).

15. Signifyin(g) is a concept theorized at length by Henry Louis Gates Jr. in his 1988 book *The Signifying Monkey*. To Signify is to foreground the signifier, to give it importance for its own sake. It comes from the language of the Signifying Monkey from African folklore; playful and intelligent language used to trick and outwit others in the jungle. It has been applied to African American forms, and hip-hop, to point to the use of double and triple entendre, repetition with difference, sampling and other forms of borrowing, "riffing on" things that came before (Williams 2013, 3–4). The use of the (g) is to make distinct from a simpler one-to-one use of semiotic signification ("this means this"), incorporating the semiotic concept with signifyin' from African American vernacular folklore. For the purposes of this book, I am pointing out that rappers both signify simply as a strategy of popular music communication and Signify in more complex ways simultaneously.

16. In addition to pirate radio and live venues, these virtual scenes were crucial to the rise of grime's new generation, perhaps analogous to pirate radio and Channel U in the earliest days of grime. One of the most important YouTube channels has been SB.TV (Smokey Barz), a company founded by Jamal Edwards which focuses on web-based content of freestyle raps and music videos and has been active since 2010.

17. Given my lack of linguistic knowledge of Welsh and Scots Gaelic, I focus on Anglophone Welsh and Scottish hip-hop in my examples from those regions.

18. For those looking for more information on the rich and vibrant history of hip-hop in Northern Ireland, see the documentaries *Bombin', Beats and B-Boys* (dir. Chris Eva) and *Together in Pieces* (dir. Eileen Walsh and David Dryden). It was the Belfast City Breakers who started the scene with breaking, graffiti, MCing, and DJing (Meredith 2018), and key members include Micky Rooney, Damian McIlroy, Anto Lynn, Stevie Copeland, Kevin McKenna, Tommy Wilson, the Madden Twins, Sconey, Boo, Matchy, Paddy G, Stev McFall, Aidy McLaughlin, Caig Leckie, Keith Connolly, and Colin Elemental Kent and their MC Geoff Allen. Graffiti artists included Keith Connolly, Glen Molloy, Kev Largey, and VERZ. My thanks to Eileen Walsh for providing this information.

19. As will be explained in more detail in Chapter 2, the United Kingdom of Great Britain and Northern Ireland is the official title for the nation-state, but also comprises the nations of England, Wales, Northern Ireland, and Scotland, some powers of which are devolved to the non-English nations (with assemblies in Cardiff, Stormont, and Edinburgh, respectively), yet are governed by the powers in Parliament based in Westminster. It is a parliamentary democracy led by a Prime Minister and has a constitutional monarch. I engage with Britain as a unit of analysis because I believe it affects citizens from the level of everyday banality to larger procedural decisions about who can be here. Importantly, Britain has a mythology and a complex semiotic network of references and associations which are in the minds of citizens, residents, and international audiences. It is "Britain" as both idea and as governing force which rappers live out, critique, question, and express a sense of belonging (or not) alongside other notions of community (ethnically, nationally, socio-economically, etc.).

20. To provide their definition at length, "methodological nationalism is an intellectual orientation that (1) assumes national borders define the unit of study and analysis; (2) equates society with the nation state; and (3) conflates national interests with the purpose and central topics of social science . . . it normalizes stasis in a conceptual move that denies that movement has been basic to human history" (Schiller and Meinhof 2011, 22).

2

NATIONALISM

"My England": Banal Nationalism, Discourses, and Counter-Narratives

THE 1997 DEVOLUTION of powers to Scotland, Wales, and Northern Ireland was a moment which helped to intensify national identities vis-à-vis the UK. But what about England, the nation treated most synonymously with the wider nation-state? As commentators have noted (Alabhai-Brown 2015; Kumar 2006, 2010), devolution became a moment for England to explore its own identity, one whose nationalism never fully developed like those of its neighbors.[1] Musically at this time, mainstream pop and pop-rock bands associated with "Cool Britannia" (e.g., The Spice Girls, and Britpop groups like Blur and Oasis) were said to reflect the national zeitgeist, but some felt this neglected a broader diversity of musical styles (e.g., the hybrid styles of Asian Dub Foundation or Fun-Da-Mental) nor did it represent the wider ethnic makeup of the country (Collinson 2008).

Questions around English nationalism—what are English values? who should be defined as English? by what (and whose) criteria?—are topics encountered implicitly and explicitly in English hip-hop in a variety of ways. While rap music often performs its identities in an overt manner, I also want to address the more subtle forms of nationalism, what Michael Billig calls "banal nationalism" (1995), in rap tracks and music videos. Banal nationalism, the everyday representations of the nation that build a sense of national belonging (e.g., currency, domestic vs. world news, linguistic specificities), is at one end of a spectrum that represents a more subliminal

Brithop. Justin A. Williams, Oxford University Press (2021). © Oxford University Press.
DOI: 10.1093/oso/9780190656805.001.0001

form of nationalism. "Hot nationalism" can be found on the other, the more-flag-waving-type of nationalism we see at international sporting events, royal occasions, and citizenship ceremonies.

In terms of citizenship, an English person's passport carries with it British citizenship rather than English, representative of the nation-state rather than the nation. But I would argue that state citizenship is only one type of citizenship. For many practitioners and fans who feel part of the imagined community of hip-hop fans and/or practitioners, it provides a cultural citizenship separate from more traditional notions of citizenship in the UK and elsewhere. Many youth cultures have turned to hip-hop both to express themselves and to gain cultural citizenship where other forms of belonging have seemed unavailable (Craft 2018; Williams 2018): these alternative voices, while varied and multifaceted, reflect a crucial musical and political voice in the British landscape.

Thinking about citizenship as overlapping imagined communities (hip-hop fandom, racial affiliations, gender identification, national affiliations through heritage, local communities) provides a more complex picture of how hip-hop engages with the concept of belonging. As rappers often discuss their localities, I will also look at how English localism intersects with hip-hop and the national, for example, how depictions of the rapper at home ("dwellingscapes") domesticates the local and projects a notion of the "everyday" that can be a part of (banal) national narratives.

In this chapter, I survey the performance of attitudes towards English nationalism in hip-hop, from banal nationalism to ambivalent Englishness, to the role of history and tradition in constructing the national, to the localism of "hip little Englishness," and finally to multicultural Englishness. Its aim is not to provide a comprehensive listing of references or allusions to the nation, but to offer a way into talking about nationalism and hip-hop within a specific geographical context. The versions of "England" that are referenced, discussed, and dismissed reveal deeper understanding of the way in which they are outwardly projected in the wider cultural sphere. A mainstream, culturally dominant form of English nationalism, tacitly white and often class-based, becomes the foil to present a version of England that better represents the personal situatedness of the rapper: "My England," as rapper Lady Sovereign points out, "Isn't all crumpets and trumpets," talking back to a particular form of England which is exported internationally—the royal family, historical period dramas, horse riding, afternoon tea, and other signifiers of "posh" whiteness.[2] Rapper responses to constructed "official" versions of England complicate these dominant narratives, and often create or build upon others such as English white working-class identity. By looking at these various examples and categories that follow, it provides alternative ways to think about the nation and how it is performed, overtly and subtlety, in twenty-first-century English rap music.

Nationalism and Englishness

Nationalism is a modern concept, and one that intensified with the creation of new nation-states in the eighteenth and nineteenth centuries. It generally refers to groups or individuals working in the best interests of the nation, forging a national identity of shared characteristics, and moving toward self-dependence and self-government. Flags, anthems, myths, and language all contribute forcefully to this idea of nation as an often-taken-for-granted symbol of community and identification. This type of "hot nationalism" suggests an active, patriotic, flag-waving, sport-supporting, or policy-making activity in the national interest.[3] What those interests comprise, what shared values and characteristics, and who belongs in the nation thus becomes a hotly contested topic often based on one's political leanings. A range of academic literature exists on this brand of nationalism, including by Ernest Gellner (2006), Anthony D. Smith (2001), and Timothy Baycroft (2010).

In terms of Englishness more specifically, Krishnan Kumar notes that "the English developed a largely 'non-national' conception of themselves, preoccupied as they were with the management of the UK and the British Empire; the 'Celtic' nations followed a more familiar pattern of developing national consciousness, as shown elsewhere in Europe" (Kumar 2006, 428). Although England is a nation within a larger nation-state, there is often the tacit assumption that the former is synonymous with the latter.[4] There are logical reasons for this, in that eighty-four percent of the UK's total population reside in England (as of 2015), and both England and the wider UK are largely ethnically white and Christian populations. Denials of national identity in public, private, or media discourse, of course, by no means suggests that England is devoid of imagined national characteristics—as the following musical examples will attest, there exist visual and lyrical signifiers, consciously or unconsciously, whose placement in these recordings contribute to the idea of a national landscape.

Research over the past two decades or so has been able to move beyond the idea of nationalism as solely the construction and workings of the official nation-state and has begun to acknowledge how people experience and reinforce elements associated with the national in their everyday lives. Billig's *Banal Nationalism* (1995), for example, investigated the ideological means by which nation-states are reproduced (6). Billig shows how these are habits that are not removed from everyday life and that the nation is "indicated in the lives of its citizenry" (ibid.). Billig study of language use (especially in newspapers) and deixis[5] in particular showed subtle (or at least taken-for-granted) constructions of a national "us," adding that there is no "us" without a "them." The concept has been applied to studies of ESL textbooks in Canada (Gulliver 2011) as well as bilingual road signs in Wales (Jones and Merriman 2009). The latter study is particularly useful for the present purposes as they acknowledge a more blurred set of practices on a hot-banal spectrum than simply a duality in practice.

As Michael Skey echoes and extends Billig's pioneering study, noting the "commonplace perception that equates nationalism with extremely political parties and overlooks the degree to which national symbols and understandings permeate the lives of 'ordinary' people as well" (Skey 2011, 5).[6] For example, newspaper layouts focus on the happenings within the nation (sports, politicians, and man/woman on the street) and emphasize British survivors in international disasters (Skey 2011, 5).[7] Skey looks at the processes of creating a national self and Other in terms of insider-outsider dualities. In hip-hop, we find that some rappers adopt these national symbols unconsciously to discuss their locality or everyday life, some put them on their sleeve when talking about belonging, and others question them or provide new frames of reference.

In terms of hip-hop language's constructions of self and Other, personal pronouns are most prevalent ("I," "me"), and secondary pronouns exist, for example, when grime rappers might address another rapper or critic directly, or when addressing an object of romantic interest. The less prevalent "we" or "us," when used, will inevitably invoke these overlapping communities, and may or may not refer to a national identity. Sometimes "we" references the global hip-hop nation, or the British hip-hop community, or the communities that the rapper feels she/he represents. Accent will do some of this work in terms of locality and regional community, and British Urban Multicultural English (BUME, Drummond 2018) will signify a localized English rap community through its accented delivery. International audiences in particular will pick up on a general accent as national signifier of English rap, while more nuanced interpretive community layers will identify the regional variants in accent and how the two intersect.

Engaging with a discourse analysis of rap lyrics that discuss England—the "we" could refer to the nation, a community within that nation, or a greater transnational humanity depending on context. For example, when Lowkey raps in "Dear England," "But remember these children are all ours," he is responding to the bombing of countries like Syria and those who have been forgotten in the national system, suggesting a greater humanity that transcends nation. When Lady Sovereign raps, "We ain't all posh like the Queen," she is distancing herself from "posh" categorizations, and placing the "we" with more working-class and underclass members of the country. When Roots Manuva raps, "we count them blessings and keep jamming," he is responding to how he (and others) are lucky to have food while the third world is starving. Riz MC opens "Englistan" with "This is England, the bridge we living in," which primarily references "we" as the residents of the multicultural nation, often stuck between two or more worlds.

Rather than deixis, syntax, or word choice as the primary method of my analysis, however, I choose to look at references to objects and concepts that could be construed as representing the nation, in an everyday or more "official" capacity. This is in concert with the tradition of referencing numerous objects and ideas in hip-hop lyrics, but also focuses in on a specific discourse to see the ways that rappers can involve the national. For example, in the context of Welshness rather than Englishness, Goldie Lookin Chain's "Fresh Prince of Cwmbran" (discussed in Chapter 6) shows the intersection of the hyperlocal of hip-hop and the provincialism or regionalism of Welsh towns. In this case, it parodies the expectation for the localness to be drawn from urban African American culture but is instead replaced by rural white Welsh signifiers. It also could be said that the hyperlocal and emphasis on regionalism and the provincial could be seen as a trait of Englishness, "little England" as a rural entity. On a more nuanced level of investigation, however, there are numerous ways that rappers perform the interlocking concepts of locality, regionalism (urban and rural), nationalism, and the global. While an attempt to find a common thread or theme with these groups would be artificial at best, my wider point is that all these artists use the local and/or the national as a topic to engage with the concept of "England," some more consciously than others, and to various ends. Not all references to the national suggest the same attitudes toward the nation, and from here I consider some of those different types of attitudes that references might invoke and evoke.

Englishness in Pop-Rock

In his study of popular music and Englishness, Martin Cloonan categorized English popular music of the mid-1990s into five categories (1997).[8] I use Cloonan's study as a starting point to re-frame this idea for the purposes of analyzing Englishness in lyrics and music videos of early twenty-first-century English MCs. Furthermore, the ambivalence that Cloonan finds in punk music and Morrissey for example (Cloonan 1997, 50) can be found in different form in rap tracks such as in Riz MC's "Englistan" and Dizraeli's "Engurland" and other artists who take the issue of English national identity head on.

Cloonan divides the pop-rock engagement with Englishness into five categories: ambivalent Englishness, overt nationalism, "Hip Little Englishness," "Hip Big Englishness," and "nonarticulated" Englishness. Ambivalent Englishness has been demonstrated by groups such as The Beautiful South, The Jam ("Eton Rifles"), Elvis Costello ("Shipbuilding" and "Pills and Soap"), and the Kinks. Cloonan describes this as "Englishness not as celebration, but as preoccupation" and cites punk as representative. Overt nationalism represents far right groups like Skrewdriver and

No Remorse. Hip Little Englishness lies between ambivalence and overt nationalism, citing Morrissey and Blur in particular. Lines from Morrissey like "England for the English" ("National Front Disco") and "We are the last truly British people'" ("We'll Let You Know") appeals to the more narrow notions of national belonging stereotyped in the "little-England" mentality, calling into question who exactly falls into the "we" that Morrissey's lyrics perform.

"Hip Big Englishness" is often performed from those in a folk troubadour tradition and could be associated with artists with leftist political leanings like Billy Bragg. Folk rock, the narrative ballad, and social realist songs would fall under this category, those who believe England is much more diverse than the tacit white British identity would suggest. Cloonan's final category is called "non articulated" Englishness and comprises forms of English music without lyrics such as jungle and techno yet still perform Englishness through their distinctive musical styles. The last category is less relevant to lyric-based hip-hop; however, many of the garage-based soundscapes which became important to grime could be considered a sonic representation of Englishness, even when grime's lyrics do not overtly reference the nation. In many ways, the national context has shifted since Cloonan's article, nor are we looking at the same genre which will have their own separate concerns and characteristics. Nevertheless, I adapt his categorization as a starting point to think about MCs attitudes toward Englishness in the twenty-first century. It also provides an opportunity to discuss women rappers such as Lady Sovereign and Speech Debelle, whereas Cloonan's categorizations involved only white male artists and groups (which have to do, in part, with the male-centricity of the genres he was investigating rather than an oversight on his part).

Adapting Cloonan's framework, the categories I will discuss with reference to English rap are (1) banal nationalism, (2) ambivalent Englishness, (3) History and (faux) traditions, (4) overt (counter-)nationalism, (5) hip little Englishness (or localism as nationalism), and (6) multiculturalism as "Hip Big Englishness."[9]

Banal Nationalism

Most simply, banal nationalism is a reference to everyday representations of the nation, building an imagined sense of solidarity on a national level. Examples include flags in everyday contexts (rather than ceremonies), sporting events, national songs, money, popular language, national press ("*our* team"), and divisions between domestic and international news in the media. They are often effective because of their repetition and subliminal nature. Billig's project, in other words, divides the everyday elements of nationalism from the more extreme versions. He uses the concept to dispute postmodernist claims that the nation-state is in decline, noting for

FIGURE 2.1 Speech Debelle, "The Key" (2009)

example the hegemonic power of American nationalism. For all the political and "top down" studies of nationalism (Gellner 2006; Anderson 2006; Hobsbawm 2012; Hobsbawm and Ranger 2012), the aspects of the everyday and their contributions to national identity have received less attention.

Because banal nationalism is something we "take for granted," something that we experience subliminally every day in the language of people, print media, etc., I would argue that it can be found less in cultural products whose intention are for us to pay close attention. Items like currency, when Speech Debelle hands the cab driver a twenty-pound note in "The Key" music video (see Figure 2.1), would fall under this category, and for an international audience, the iconic London black cab as synecdoche of Britain. The red London buses and Royal Mail van we see in the background of Lady Leshurr's "Queen's Speech 4" could also be included here (see Figure 2.2). They are not foregrounded in the video; instead, they compose a background landscape that suggests both the local and the national.

Many items we associate with the "everyday" of a nation, including transportation, architecture (residential dwellingscapes or otherwise), roads, food, landscapes, road signs will start to fall into a performance of the national everyday, or even of the local, but it is worth thinking about how some of these taken-for-granted items can find themselves in popular music video. Leshurr raps in an underground car park (Queen's Speech 1), outside residential areas (2 and 3), walking the roads in Greenwich's Millennium Village (4), down in London underground station (6), and perhaps more extraordinarily, riding a camel next to a motorway (7). The lyrics and music videos of Sleaford

FIGURE 2.2 Lady Leshurr, "Queen's Speech 4" (2015)

Mods (discussed in Chapter 4) have elements of this everydayness (e.g., references to Mr. Kipling French fancies, images of terraced houses and buses). It is when artists wear their "ordinariness" on their sleeve or performs the everyday more explicitly that it moves closer to the "hip little Englishness" categorization. In short, banal nationalism in lyrics and music video is when there are elements of the national everyday not as foregrounded as the primary topics at hand.

Ambivalent Englishness: Dizraeli

When English rappers begin to define or discuss Englishness, their performance seems to have a degree of ambivalence, an attitude which could be said to be a defining trait of Englishness. The Bristol-born, Brighton-based rapper Dizraeli's engagement with national identity can be heard on a number of tracks on his 2009 *Engurland (City Shanties)* album but is most forcefully heard on the title track "Engurland."[10] The chorus's melody and harmony uses the "Vindaloo" football chant (from the FIFA 1998 world cup song by Fat Les), both with curry as a national dish and football competition as one way that the nation is most forcefully performed. The chorus is as follows:

Engurland, mingerland, middle fingerland
Footie song singerland

Baddiel and Skinner-land
School dinnerland
Red, white, brown, and gingerland
Imperial hinterland
Perpetual winterland
Where happy pills are in demand
Engurland, engurland, engurland
Are you proud?

The football-chant chorus, while drawing attention to a major part of English culture, performs stereotypes of English identity that have negative connotations. With impoliteness (middle fingerland), mingers (slang for ugly), bad weather (winterland), extensive drug use (happy pills), as well as a mention of Empire and school dinners.[11] The red, white, brown, and gingerland plays on the expectation of the red and white of the English flag, extended to include ethnic minority and "gingers" who are also a subject of ridicule and exclusion at times. Baddiel and Skinner-land is a direct reference to the "Three Lions" video, which features the two comedians performing symbols of national identity (tea, Sun newspaper, etc.). While many of these can be perceived as negative traits, the more rainbow ethnic inclusion could be seen as positive, thus demonstrating a more ambivalent position on the country.

He points out the summer pastime of the "English holiday" and of leisure activities more generally: "people on the beach self-harming to get tanned," "it's a land where families spend holidays in traffic jams and radios play tracks by tragic bands" . . . "Next week, you'll take your first ecstasy pill, nine pints of white lightening and get messily ill, the week after that perhaps you'll get a job in Lidl."[12] Food references like "chili sauce on my cheesy chips" and "bulk orders of baked beans" are coupled with social critique: "'Cos here are three kids, and their mother aged eighteen and they dream of stardom, watching the X-Factory, but they have no garden, and nowhere to practice being. Therefore, they question what they're there for and why there's armed policemen outside Mr. Blair's Door." What begins as humorous references to questionable activities on holiday becomes a scathing criticism of the Blair government and his treatment of the poor. He also attacks lad culture and sexual harassment by portraying someone who feels indignant for being arrested for such behavior: "Bit of a geezer, telling Lisa she's a fitty/grab her tits, and she's throwing a seizure fit/Now I'm sleeping in a cell, police are dicks." The "England are you proud?" lyric that ends the chorus addresses the personified nation while allowing the song to be left open ended despite the critiques within. The singsong nature of chorus, meant to be sung communally, may also point to a "we're in this together" sentiment and may give the impression that the song is more positive than it is. Musically, the song is not a lament like Lowkey's "Dear England" but has a celebratory air to it, which can be read as ironic, but nevertheless the mismatch between lyric and music contribute to a sense of ambivalence. Artists in each of these categories have varying degrees of ambivalence; Dizraeli's work lies somewhere in between a subtle performance of the national and an overt critique of national stereotypes that exclude more diverse English voices.

(Faux-)Traditionalism and History

One way of creating national identity involves the construction of a national mythology, a history and set of traditions. Given England's long history and emphasis on traditions real and imagined (both the problematic history of Empire and the country's cultural contributions and innovations), it is no surprise that artists comment on and play with notions of English tradition.

Mainstream internationally distributed media projections of England place high value on history as a concept and as content (both the number of period dramas and historical documentaries produced by the BBC to use two examples). Like any creation of history, gatekeepers decide what (and who) is included in such depictions of England as historical concept. Rappers will sometimes use these fictions to their own ends, either to resist, question, or to place themselves within.

Traditions can be used to include and exclude others. When an artist places themselves in one, through music or otherwise, the gesture either reinforces or questions that tradition. This was the case in the second English folk revival: Allan Moore writes of "faux traditionalism" in "The Ballad of Bethnal Green" (1959) by Paddy Roberts, a case of the artist placing himself and his locality in a longer tradition for humorous effect (Moore 2016, 62–63). Moore also points out a wider list of singer-songwriters that come out of an older folk tradition and use music and lyrics to place themselves in the lineage ("plethora of faux traditional songs produced"), like Kate Rusby's "I Courted a Sailor" from 2001 (Moore 2016, 63).

Returning to Dizraeli's *Engurland* (*City Shanties*), in a similar approach to "Ballad of Bethnal Green," the album opens with a "city shanty," communally sung about traveling on the (London) underground. The rapper plays with history, not least his name having historical associations (Benjamin Disraeli was prime minister in 1868 and 1874–1880), and referencing the longer musical tradition of the sea shanty (Hugill 1966; Palmer 2001). The concept plays with urban and rural, and of home and away, and incorporates these folk influences into rap styles. This reverse engineering has a degree of ambivalence embedded that we have already seen from

Dizraeli: placing himself within a tradition may suggest a desire to be a part of it, while revealing the cracks and fractures in the idea of tradition as wholly constructed anyway, or tradition as a selective choice on those in power.

Connected to this, while some may reverse engineer themselves into older traditions, others are quick to point out contributions of those who have been white-washed from histories, national mythology, and the construction of buildings which are national symbols. This is related to the advocacy of multiculturalism in a later section, but here I want to point out that rappers often want to educate listeners about the contributions from Empire on current national prosperity.

As mentioned in the previous chapter, Riz MC's verse in "Immigrants (We Get the Job Done)" mentions the multi-ethnic contributions ("blood of my ancestors had that all built") to the construction of Buckingham Palace and Capitol Hill. This also places Riz MC's ancestors as part of a longer heritage than his second-generation status would suggest. His skit on the *Englistan EP* "I Ain't Being Racist But..." also mentions the non-white contributors and players in the nation's history, questioning ethnocentric definitions of (white) Englishness. Akala, discussed at length in the next chapter, also considers a broader multi-ethnic history of England and Britain: how the mass enslavement of Africans contributed to the British Empire and to the birth of capitalism in Western Europe more generally (on his track "Maangamizi," which is a term that translates best to the African Holocaust). Dizraeli places himself within English traditions from an ambivalent perspective. Akala and Riz MC take a more critical stance, acknowledging that history can be white-washed and that traditions, good and bad, need to be acknowledged in the national story.

Overt (Counter-)Nationalism

In terms of overtly nationalistic rap songs about England, one would be hard pressed to find a right wing, (ethno)nationalist rap song, or even a rap equivalent to "Three Lions," for example. But rather than dismiss an overtly national category in English rap, I would argue that there exist examples that counter such mainstream national stereotypes, and often end up creating new ones which diversify what it means to be English.

Rapper responses to the more overt, flag-waving Englishness fall generally under two large-scale responses: either critique of the "hot" national stereotypes (tea, monarchy, St. George's flag, etc.) and/or a subtle re-affirmation of everyday elements that define one's local or national identity, often in opposition to those wider stereotypes.[13]

The music video for London Posse's "How's Life in London" (1993) opens with an image of Big Ben followed a young white male newscaster stating in RP "This is London." The camera then pans back to Big Ben, this time with the Black British members of the group in the foreground. It is a simple and powerful play on assumptions of those who may be associated with London (in particular, for the international viewing audience on an American show like Yo! MTV raps). Big Ben is a national symbol, associated with a (mostly white and male) Parliament and so these young black British rappers subvert our associations and expectations through quick signification.

A lengthier representative example of countering a dominant national narrative would be Lady Sovereign's "My England" (2006). The first non-American female artist signed to Def Jam Recordings, her debut album includes the song which questions the (often internationally perceived) stereotypes of Englishness. "It ain't about tea and biscuits, I'm one of those English misfits, I don't drink tea I drink spirits," she says. She mentions Tony Blair in the chorus ("Now do the Tony Blair, throw your hands in the air now everywhere") and that she does not watch Antiques Road show. She does, however, find a literary character, that more accurately reflects her London heritage: "Big up Oliver Twist, letting us know the nitty gritty of what London really is." And on another track ("Love Me or Hate Me") she states "No! I don't own a corgi / Had the hamster—it died 'cause I ignored it. Go on then, go on report me. I'm English, try and deport me." The soundtrack echoes the "crumpets and trumpets" by having a brass band-sounding track into a looping three-chord progression. It is not triumphant brass, but is lumbering and simplistic. It is mixed with synthetic drum sounds associated with grime and other electronic dance music-based styles. The intro of the song puts the brass in the foreground before the sound of a horse whinny ushers in the first verse (and the brass soundtrack goes deeper into the mix for the verse and chorus).[14]

The strategy of the track is very much one of contrast: Sovereign paints a picture of stereotypical "posh" England, and then contrasts it with her own vantage point:

> Oooh the changing of the Queen's guard
> That's nothing for me to march out of my house fo
> Tra la la, I'd rather sit on my arse,
> and have a glass of Chardonnay,
> nah we ain't all bridget Jones clones who say pardon me/
> More like what's gwanin mate, you get me?

"What's gwanin mate" ("what's going on" or "wagwan") as a Multicultural Youth English slang from Caribbean slang becomes contrasted with a "whiter" ("pardon me") Received Pronunciation language.

By no means the first or only artist to question such stereotypes, it does demonstrate how hip-hop can provide a counter-narrative to more dominant cultural exports (The Royal Family, James Bond, Antiques Road Show, Harry Potter, etc.).[15] It is no coincidence that Lady Sovereign was intended to be exported to an international audience given her Def Jam affiliation, and thus we get a lengthier engagement on what it means to be English that other "domestic" examples. It does, however, help construct and build upon another stereotype, that of the "chav."[16]

While Lady Sovereign discusses the country in the first person as the version of the country that she experiences, Lowkey's "Dear England" (2011) addresses the country that he doesn't feel a part of. It's more of a plea to those in power, so he, unlike Lady Sovereign, is defining the nation in terms of policy makers as opposed to the everyday. He also refers to England as part of the Imperial project that he critiques with the opening lines:

> They say God save the queen, Britannia rules the waves
> Britannia's in my genes, but Britannia called us slaves
> Britannia made the borders, cause Britannia's forces came
> Britannia lit the match, but Britannia fears the flame

Thus, he uses tropes of English identity, as part of a wider British history, to critique it. He rails against the justice system, commenting that "the biggest looters are the British Museum." He criticizes the media and its control over things ("Who runs this country, Cameron or Murdoch?") and the harsh cuts from the recent government ("Downing Street I can find villains, cut education, privatize prisons"). He questions the murders of Mark Duggan and Jean Charles Menezes by the police and states "just relax as we slip into fascism."[17] The soundtrack harmonically laments these developments with a descending minor progression alongside acoustic strings and Mai Khalil on vocals, a common soundscape on this album (covered more in depth in Chapter 7). While the song implicitly defines England as the nation-state, Lowkey's song is to remind those in power that others are also part of the country they should be governing, and that "these children are all ours" not only nationally, but globally.

Localism as Hip-Little Englishness

As many have written (Forman 2002; Mitchell 2001; Bennett 1999), local identity is crucial to hip-hop culture. This has played out in the UK from postcodes in grime music and street names and localities in lyrics and music videos (e.g., Kano's "London Town," Wiley's "Bow E3"). And in many cases, the local does intersect with a particular notion of the national. We might go as far as to say that localism and the attachment to regional identity (e.g., distinctiveness of accents in relatively close geographical proximity) is a particular salient feature of English identity. Kumar writes, "Nationalism, to most English thinkers, always seemed to have something of the provincial about it, something more reminiscent of tribalism than of the outward-looking ideologies that seemed more necessary in the contemporary world" (Kumar 2010, 482). This localism of the everyday is most apparent in the debut album of Mike Skinner, who recorded under the name The Streets.

When the album *Original Pirate Material* by The Streets was released in 2002 (hereafter referred to as *OPM*), the album combined UK garage and rap music alongside one funk-based track and the occasional sung chorus. To non-UK audiences, the local accents, slang, and shout outs to specific pockets of London showed a slice of English life rarely encountered in the global mainstream. The Birmingham-born MC and bedroom producer used his love of artists like Daft Punk and Wu-Tang Clan to create something hybrid and local, opening the door for genres like grime to be accepted on a wider stage internationally and at home.

From an initial glance of album's cover, we see a London tower block (Kestral House in North London) both representative of its locality but intersecting with the US "projects" (project housing) that many rappers came from and rapped about. The logo of The Streets is written on a cigarette lighter. Influenced by garage music as well as US hip-hop, it was a hybrid that was influential for later rap and grime artists (Chip's "School of Grime" remix from 2015 uses the beat from "Has it Come to This?" from *OPM*). A number of song lyrics intersect with everyday Englishness (of a masculine white working-class variety): "Geezers need Excitement" and "Too Much Brandy" discuss pub behavior, drinking too much, and sometimes inciting violence. "Geezers" recounts getting beat up at a "takeaway" (restaurant) after the club closes at 3 a.m., describing the food "finest cuts of chicken from the big spitting stick," as well as owing money to your drug dealer. "Too Much Brandy" discusses a night out, and uses the cockney rhyming slang term "Marlons" (as in Marlon Brando) for brandy. The track "The Irony of It All" is framed as a debate between a lad who drinks numerous pints at the pub versus a less-than-moderate marijuana smoker. "It's Too Late" recounts poor treatment of a girlfriend, when it is too late to recover from the damage. "Weak Become Heroes" looks back on easier times when the protagonist went clubbing and took drugs. The last track on the album, "Stay Positive," discusses moments when people reach their lowest point emotionally (though loss, addiction or otherwise) and urges them to stay positive.

As Kenneth Partridge wrote in a long and insightful review of *OPM* in 2015, the album is a "perfectly credible regional rap record" in the traditions of Outkast or

FIGURE 2.3 The Streets, "Don't Mug Yourself" (2002)

N.W.A. talking about their localities of Atlanta and Compton respectively (Partridge 2015). Unlike acts associated with just one city (like Liverpool, Manchester, or Bristol), Skinner grew up in Birmingham yet finalized a lot of work on *OPM* in London (and conceived a lot of the tracks on a one-year trip to Australia, see Skinner 2013). Despite the dual-city influence, lyrically, localism reigns supreme on the album. It is safe to say many of the themes and ideas represent a notion of "little England" with its emphasis on quintessentially English things: drinking tea, supporting football, going to the pub, eating takeaways, etc. This depiction is part of a longer history of English social realism (kitchen sink dramas, Alan Stillitoe, John Osborn's *Look Back in Anger*, Shane Meadows films like *This is England*) and part of a post-WWII culturalization of the white British working class.[18]

Of all the tracks on *OPM*, his lyrics and music video for "Don't Mug Yourself" most convincingly highlights the everyday laddism of white English masculinity: full English breakfast (see Figure 2.3), cups of tea which morph into pints of ale in the evening followed by a game of darts in the pub at night. The music video emphasizes these elements which form a consonance with the song's lyrics. It is the performance of banal nationalism, everyday Englishness put at the forefront of the song's lyrical themes:

> A new day another morning after
> Leanin' back on my chair in a greasy spoon cafeteria
> Last night was some beer-lairy-ness done our way
> But again, we're back in the light of day

> Chattin' shit, sittin' at the wall table, telling jokes
> Playin' with the salt, looking out the window
> Girl brings two plates of full English over
> With plenty of scrambled eggs and plenty of fried tomato

Skinner proceeds to get his phone out to text a girl that he had a nice time the previous night when his friend proceeds to tell him to not get too committed. The chorus takes up this cause as the primary theme, with the term "don't mug yourself" as urban slang for not shooting yourself in the foot, which the friend (Cal) implies he would do by over-committing to this girl he just met. When the banal is performed it becomes less taken for granted, and one can see how such a depiction was popular with both natives who could relate and for outsiders who wanted a voyeuristic invitation into these lifestyles. This is not dissimilar from how Andy Bennett discusses the common thread of *Sgt. Pepper's Lonely Hearts Club* as the "commentary on aspects of British social life" (Bennett 2000, 193).[19]

Like punk in a sense, listeners are able to accept Mike Skinner as "the voice of authentic Britain" (Boayke 2017, 79) as some audiences would for Lady Sovereign as well.[20] The difference between the two is that for *OPM* he becomes a storyteller, and narrator of "real" England and for "My England," Lady Sovereign uses her position as a foil against some constructed assumed notion of dominant Englishness. And though Lady Sovereign might provide some gendered alternative to male working-class masculinity, her rap persona very much adopts the same posturing as her male counterparts.

A year earlier than *OPM*, black British rapper Roots Manuva was also describing similar signifiers of Englishness. On the track "Witness (1 Hope)" from the album *Run Come Save Me* (2001), he raps, "Breakneck speeds we drown ten pints of bitter" . . . "I sit here contented with this cheese on toast" . . . "I stay top shelf material, jerk chicken, jerk fish/Breakaway slave, bliss." We get food references to cheese on toast as well as more multicultural cuisine reflective of cuisine of his parents' home country of Jamaica (and very much a part of urban England's foodscapes). The Streets and Roots Manuva provide everyday references to English foods and drinks, perceivably multicultural or otherwise, that represent the national everyday. This hybridity of objects said to belong to exotic (outsider) England and traditional (white) England is arguably a feature of English culture more widely, from food to art to literature to language: "Exclusive England and exotic England are conjoined twins, symbiotically linked. Most migrants to the UK choose to live in England, which could not purge them without destroying its own body and soul" (Alibhai-Brown 2015, 11).

On Manuva's third album, *Awfully Deep* (2005), the track "Colossal Insight" is accompanied by a music video where Manuva works at a chicken shop. We see him rapping behind the counter, while looking at images of men eating fried chicken. He cleans the tables, then gets ready to ride the bus to a gig where he is a ventriloquist. There is a lot to say about this video, but for the purposes at hand we see images of everyday British life: Manuva as one of the crowd on the bus, and the disjuncture between his young black British identity and the gig audience, old white patrons that one would not expect for a rap audience. He's heckled and told to go (apart from a friend he made at the chicken shop), which could be a wider commentary on critics' behavior.[21]

As hip-hop often depicts the local through the convivial meeting spaces of the neighborhood, we do sometimes get a glimpse inside the "home life" of a rapper, a domesticated and often highly gendered space. For example, in the US context, the music video Dr. Dre's "Nuthin but a G Thang" (1993) depicts the "day in the life" of Compton's post-riot youth. More generally, Tim Edensor writes on national identity and everyday life and the importance of home and dwellingscapes to such identities. He defines dwellingscapes as where "familiar space forms an unquestioned backdrop to daily tasks, pleasures and routine movement" (Edensor 2002, 54). He continues, "For national space to retain its power, it must be domesticated, replicated in local contexts and be understood as part of everyday life" (65). As he reminds us, home can equally refer to house, land, village, city, district, county, or indeed the world (57), but the home or the street is often where we find the landscape of the rap video.

Edensor writes of the home, "As a way of making spatial sense of the nation then, home is able to link these spatial levels together, from the small-scale domestic to the large-scale space. 'Home' conjoins a myriad of affective realms and contains a wealth of transposable imagery" (2002, 57). The opening of "G Thang" shows how gendered home dwellingscapes can be, depicting clearly who takes care of the children and who goes out to socialize, and as genre is often gendered it may be no coincidence that my pop rap example occurs in the home environment and the grime example happens outside the home, on the street. In music video, the setting or settings will say a lot of how the artist or group wishes to place themselves within a local, national, or other type of context. For our purposes, I will look at a few home dwellingscapes as a grounding for the local.

Rizzle Kicks's "Mama do the Hump" (2011), produced by Fatboy Slim, represents a brand of pop rap whose music video depicts the home life of one of the duo's members. No doubt partly inspired by the song's title, both rappers are there and play a recording of the song to their parents. The rappers are mixed race, as is made more evident by seeing their white mothers and black fathers. It, in itself, feels like an important gesture, the mothers lip-syncing their sons' lyrics while the family drinks, dances, and enjoys themselves. The end of the video introduces another house guest, celebrity James Corden, whom they greet enthusiastically, followed by Corden dancing alongside the others to end the video.

The presence of family also suggests background/roots and a groundedness of home life or at least community. In grime music, Stormzy's "Know Me From" (2015) depicts the rapper walking down the street in his neighborhood with various friends as well as his mother (Figure 2.4). In this case, we do not get the dwellingscape of the home interior, but we get the street and its locality, as grime rappers are often ethnographers of their local conditions (Barron 2013). Grime's preoccupation with the everyday and the local may contribute to Boakye's observation that grime as a genre is "allowed to be British" (2017, 31). Family also plays a role in Speech Debelle's "The Key" when she raps about her aunt's house and her "day in the life" music video features what feels like a regular family gathering where the auntie makes food on the weekend for her and other relatives. In an extended example to follow, Riz MC's "Englistan" depicts him drinking tea with family around a sofa in a small house, layering both South Asian and English traditions of tea drinking. Such visual gestures signal a groundedness of values, common stereotype of English tea drinking, and the visible presence/performance of heritage via the rapper's family members. Family at once represents history and the everyday, two elements very intertwined in the concept of nation.

I would also point out that the little England found in some of these localisms are far from "hip" in the sense that they are cool, or necessarily to be desired. And it is precisely the un-hipness of the mundane which also contribute to

FIGURE 2.4 Stormzy, "Know Me From" (2015)

signifiers of everyday nationalism that then define and redefine the national in these examples.

Hip Big Englishness: Multiculturalism

Hip Big Englishness as defined by Cloonan falls into a folk tradition of leftist politics and music. In hip-hop it can very much manifest itself in the previous critiques of Empire as well as the whiteness of dominant English narratives. But rather than look at the past, or at direct critiques, I want to look at multiculturalism as an example of hip big Englishness. Rappers who tout multiculturalism will be likely to hail from large urban centers, especially London.

The term "multiculturalism" refers to an ethnic pluralism within a given community or population. It can occur organically or through governmental policy (such as immigration laws or placing official documents in multiple languages). In the UK, multiculturalism began to be discussed in the 1970s, but as a policy occurred on local levels from the 1980s followed by a national-level approach by the New Labour government in 1997 ("Multiculturalism" BBC 2011). Critics of multiculturalism see it as a policy that encourages separateness rather than integration, as a barrier in society which fosters separate communities based on ethnicity or religion.

Since the rise of New Labour, multiculturalism as policy received increasing levels of backlash from right-leaning voters and politicians. In part this backlash has been fueled by specific incidents: clashes between BAME Muslims and whites in Northern cities in 2001, home-grown Islamic terrorism of the 7/7 bombings in 2005, and the 2011 riots across the country (Skey 2011; Thapar 2014; Meer and Modood 2014; Mathieu 2018). In many ways this backlash came to a head in 2011 when Prime Minister David Cameron said in a Munich speech that "state multiculturalism has failed," adding that it "encouraged different cultures to live separate lives, apart from each other and apart from the mainstream." In his speech, Cameron advocated for a stronger national identity to prevent people from turning to extremism ("State multiculturalism" BBC 2011). Others have argued that the success of the 2012 Olympics, both as host and in the ethnic diversity of its home-grown winners show that multiculturalism has been a success (Grove 2012).

Those who musically perform "Hip Big Englishness" advocate for a more diverse vision of England than more politically conservative entities advocate. I focus here on multiculturalism as one element of this diversity which is tied up with public policy and political debate. I would argue that the racial diversity of English rappers

helps to give an air of hip-hop multiculturalism as in part reflective of multicultural urbanity and through their visibility. Rizzle Kicks's mixed-race identity is on
example of sharing spaces and becoming visible through performance in addition to
their lyrical content, delivery, and beats.

Actor-rapper Riz MC (Rizwan Ahmed) has been featured in numerous television series and films including *Four Lions* (2010), *Nightcrawler* (2014), *Jason Bourne*
(2016), *Rogue One: A Star Wars Story* (2016), *Girls* (2017), and he won an Emmy
in 2017 for his work on the show *The Night Of* (2017). One of Riz MC's earliest
forays into music was the song "Post 9/11 Blues" (2006, under the name MC Riz),
which was deemed too controversial for commercial radio airplay (O'Keefe 2006),
but was a scathing critique of Bush and Blair's involvement in the Iraq War and the
new climate of racial profiling after the terrorist attacks of September 11 in New York
City and 7/7 in London. In addition to his solo rap career, he also forms half of
the duo the Swet Shop Boys with American-Indian Himanshu Suri, a.k.a. Heems.[22]
In March 2017, he gave a speech to Parliament on the importance of representing
minorities in the media: "what people are looking for is a message that they belong,
that they are part of something, that they are seen and heard and despite, or perhaps
because of the uniqueness of their experience, they are valued. They want to feel
represented" (Ahmed 2017).[23]

As Riz MC is Pakistani-British, he belongs to one of the UK's five main minority
groups (in addition to Indian, Bangladeshi, black Caribbean, and black African) and
thus has experienced being central to the debates around British multiculturalism.
As a product of the consequences of Empire, he speaks to the multicultural situation in England—celebrating multicultural London while acknowledging the hate-
ful intolerance and resistance to it. Such a dual perspective (the "green and pleasant
land" and "mean and pleasant land" of England) could be perceived as an ambivalence akin to the '90s pop-rock stars Cloonan outlines.

The *Englistan EP* was released on St. George's Day (April 23, 2016), with its title
track released as a music video on the Muslim holiday Eid al-Fitr (July 6, 2016, celebrating the end of Ramadan). The cover of the EP immediately puts into focus a
sense of duality: wearing a cricket jersey with his back to the viewer, we see "Engl"
of England on the left and the "istan" of Pakistan on the right (see Figure 2.5). The
cricket jersey is a visual reminder of the doubleness of his identity, the perceivably
separate nature of the two worlds. Themes on the album include multiculturalism ("Englistan"), banking scandals ("A Few Bob"), mental health ("Sunburnt"),
honor killings ("Benaz"), the double lives of many second-generation immigrants
("Double Lives"), and the fallacy of a mono-racial British history ("I Ain't Being
Racist But . . ."). Riz MC describes his EP as a mixtape "all about our society and trying to find a place in it" (Bulut 2016) and has advocated for a "new national story"

FIGURE 2.5 Riz MC, "Englistan" (2016)

FIGURE 2.6 Riz MC, "Englistan" (2016)

to be updated from the one which doesn't represent the true diversity of the nation (Ahmed 2017).

The title track, "Englistan," highlights England's dualities, the good and the bad, the "politeness mixed with violence" that defines his country. He raps of the "green and pleasant land" and the "mean and pleasant land"—that these two sides of English identity go together. To cite one of the many food references in the song, he raps, "Racist beef [disagreement], cakes and tea, all go together like a do-re-mi." Multicultural England is described as a "kicharee" (Hindi for mixture), a mix of rice, daal, vegetables, and numerous spices: "This is England, the bridge we living in, a kicharee simmering, women in hijabs, syringe popstars and the promise of a Patel as a Man U star." When he raps "Big up the Queen's Christmas speech and all the shit her kids get for free" one can hear the hybridity of "big up" (Caribbean patois) mixed with a seemingly pro-monarchy sentiment followed by a critique of it. This is an example of code combining, rather than code switching, something that Nabeel Zubieri discusses with British MC culture in particular (Zubieri 2014). The end of each chorus has a sampled-sounding voice saying "This is England" in a South Asian accent, questioning RP's dominance of a national accent.

The music video shows a range of the everyday in local, multicultural London, demonstrating the "conviviality" of cosmopolitan London that Gilroy discusses in *After Empire* (2003). It opens with a mosaic of recent anti-immigrant newspaper headlines (including, for example, those from the *Daily Express*: "Send in Army to Halt Migrant Invasion," "No End to Migrant Crisis," "Soaring Cost of Teaching Migrant Children" (Figure 2.6). A news commentator speaks over images of these headlines: ". . . if it's the referendum or whether it's the barrage of anti-immigrant media coverage in the run up to it, for some, the result has compounded a feeling of isolation, a sense of disconnection from the country they moved to." The video then opens to a large park with Riz MC wearing his Englistan shirt, isolated in the large field, then the camera quickly switches to a residential area with terraced brick houses and children playing in the street. Video settings include a mosque, a synagogue,[24] a pub, a white pensioner in his house (surrounded by memories and decorations from military service), his family's house (with the rapper having tea with them), a kebab shop (Figure 2.7), a petrol station, and other settings of everyday life

FIGURE 2.7 Riz Mc, "Englistan" (2016)

in England. Musically, we hear a bansuri, a side-blown flute found in Hindustani classical music as part of the beat to add a sonic signifier of Eastern exoticism. The beat is therefore a mix of Western and Eastern sounds that can mirror the lyrics and visual content from the music video. Ultimately, like many pop songs about England, ambivalence comes to the fore rather than a flag-waving patriotism or a scathing disavowal/critique: "Is Britain great? Well hey don't ask me/But it's where I live and why my heart beats."

In one interview, Riz MC states that "*Englistan*, as a mixtape, is about stretching the flag so that it's big enough for all of us. It's about identity—from what it means to be English today, to what it's like growing up living a double life, or feeling like you don't fit in" (Bulut 2016). Sonically, hip-hop becomes an important form to say, "we are here." In terms of ethnic marginality and hip-hop, Rollefson notes this about European hip-hop: "hip hop is claiming its seat at the table and having its cake, not to eat it—it doesn't have much of a taste for that cake—but simply to have the cake it was promised. For it turns out that you can have cake—or mithai, or baklava, or flan—and eat it, too, if you aren't beholden to the notion that there is only one true cake at the table" (Rollefson 2017, 227). Hip-hop can navigate both resistance and belonging, as hip-hop has been a mouthpiece for counter-narratives and marginality around the globe, forming a family of resemblances that spans beyond the level of the national while also making it a safe space to discuss issues of the national. Because of hip-hop's embrace of the marginal, rappers provide not only a visual reminder of what England looks like, but they provide vast lyrical commentary on it from their own interpretive vantage points as well.

Conclusion: Performing (or Countering) "Englishness"?

I have shown and categorized several ways that English rappers perform, discuss, and critique aspects of so-called Englishness. Sometimes this is overt lyrically (the "full English" breakfast, "We ain't all posh like the Queen"), and other times it is more subtle but nevertheless present (e.g., Debelle's twenty-pound note). Sometimes it is a scathing critique ("Where there's poison in the food and chlorine in the water"), a reminder of past multicultural contributions to English history ("blood of my ancestors had that all built"), and other times it presents an alternative or parallel to dominant narratives ("This is my England I'm letting you know now"). These categories necessarily overlap, and I wouldn't advocate for a central concept of Englishness, but some shared themes do emerge. Tea and pints of lager become symbols in the already acknowledged bank of national objects, for example. What many of these songs do is to assert belonging in these national communities and conversations (such as the "Englistan" track and music video), questioning previously assumed ideas around mainstream Englishness.

Citing rappers with names like Dizraeli, Lady Sovereign, and Lady Leshurr and her "Queen's Speech" series at once shows how English rappers engage and Signify on symbols of the nation. Their attitudes toward Englishness vary on a spectrum rather than set and fixed categories, and they often overlap: while "Englistan," for example, talks about multiculturalism, there is a heavy level of ambivalence in its lyrics. These categories therefore necessarily overlap, not least to mention that once interpretive vantage point will influence the interpretation.

As others have noted, defining Englishness is difficult to impossible (Kumar 2010, 472). Kumar says, "'English nationalism' is an odd thing, hard to say with a straight face" (2010, 470). This is for reasons already stated, but despite the messiness of what Britain and England means, and despite hip-hop's emphasis on the local, national themes, symbols, and responses to them are very much existent in certain English hip-hop discourses. Thus, the complexity of the rapper's engagement with nationalism (banal to hot, and everything in between) mirrors the complexity we find in their social and political contexts.

Although categorizing a racial divide between the small sample I have discussed in this chapter would be fictitious at best, many of the non-white artists seemed more aware of discussing colonial contributions, critiquing Empire, and going against dominant forms of white Englishness and celebrating the diversity of English everyday life than were their white counterparts. White working-class forms of Englishness were reinforced by rappers such as Mike Skinner, Lady Sovereign, and, as we will see, the Sleaford Mods. This echoes the "glamorization of plebean life" that Cloonan discusses in his own categorizations for rock-pop Englishness (1997, 64). In other words, we now have working-class kitchen sink dramas updated for the grime generation (Kate Tempest's *Everybody Down* [2014] and Plan B's *Ill Manors* [2012] would fall under this tradition, providing less "glamorous" portrayals than The Streets, Lady Sovereign, or Sleaford Mods do). What has become apparent is that there are two streams of English stereotypical identity which artists either engage with or reject: the posh and the working class. Both are cultural stereotypes projected internationally, and one reason they become fodder for rappers' critique.

These examples have shown that English rap is an important forum in which national identity is discussed, and is one which has real consequences: Through the diversity of voices in hip-hop, rappers are re-inscribing the nation so that its projected identities better reflect the lives of its inhabitants.

Notes

1. Kumar writes that "Englishness never evolved into a true nationalism, if by that we mean a well-defined sense of national identity similar to that of its continental neighbours" (Kumar 2010, 470).

2. "Posh" is a term to refer to upper classes, and often those removed from wider social realities. Though there is little to no evidence that it originated with the initials of port out starboard home (the better accommodation on ships between England and India), this is a commonly believed origin of the term.

3. For more on sports and nationalism see Hoberman 1984, Cronin 1999, Allison 2000, Bairner 2001, Seippel 2017 to name a few.

4. The full name of the nation-state is the United Kingdom of Great Britain and Northern Ireland. "Celtic fringe" nations like Scotland and Wales have more fully developed nationalisms, strong differing identities similar to "nation within nation" regions like Quebec, Brittany, Catalonia, Sami, and elsewhere. See Chapter 5 for how this plays out in Scottish hip-hop.

5. Deixis is a linguistic term which refers to words and phrases, such as "me" or "here," that cannot be fully understood without additional contextual information.

6. Skey's research engaged with twenty-one interviewees about what they associate with England, and their answers included the NHS, monarchy, parliament, BBC, tolerance, reserved disposition, sense of humor, polite, pessimism / cynicism, resilience, food (fish and chips, tea, curry, beer), red buses, pubs, Queen, football hooligans, Churchill, Blair, diversity, countryside, Stonehenge, seaside, villages, queuing, sport, binge drinking, weather / rain, and history (2011, 41). When such symbols of national identities were discussed, many of the interviewees then proceed unprompted to discuss anti-immigrant discourse (61), how newer arrivals were not adopting such symbols.

7. Britain has the second largest newspaper readership in the world, and thus such an activity could be interpreted as a national characteristic it itself.

8. Cloonan is swift to point out that references to the quintessentially English do not begin in the 1990s, but is part of a larger tradition: he points to The Beatles, The Kinks, Sex Pistols, Clash, and Smiths before a wider discussion of '90s Britpop groups like Blur and Oasis (Cloonan 1997, 48–49). He discusses Britpop songs like "Country House" and "Roll with It," "Parklife," "Tracy Jacks," "Clover over Dover," and "Bank Holiday" and suggests that popular music was defined in overtly nationalist terms in the mid-1990s (52). Andy Bennett's article on Britishness in '60s and '90s pop (2000) also discusses references to English everyday life (and while his examples focus only on England, he prefers to use the term "Britishness," though this goes unexplained). He acknowledges that while '90s Britpop groups do not address multiculturalism in any way, he prefers to see more multicultural groups as an alternative form on nationalism that listeners can choose to adhere to.

9. As with Cloonan's categories, these are more fluid than any rigid mapping would suggest and will also depend on how overt or not someone finds such lyric or visual references. For example, a lyrical reference draws more attention to an item than say a passing background image in a music video. However, if the visual element matches the lyrical reference, then such a reference (e.g., pint of beer, cup of tea) is even more articulated and foregrounded. Thus, my categorization hinges on both lyrical reference and often (in the case of The Streets's "Don't Mug Yourself") in music video

where one exists. Therefore, I have used personal judgement in what might be considered fore-grounding and background in these examples, acknowledge both that such an interpretation, and its categorization, will be less rigid than any analysis on paper would provide. The blunt instrument of a systematic approach like this will, however, allow us to draw conclusions on English rap and attitudes to English nationalism.

10. Laura Speers notes how Dizraeli's performance of multiple stylistic worlds places him outside of stereotypical notions of rappers, and is sometimes excluded from such a distinction (she makes a distinction between "rapper authenticity" and "hip-hop authenticity"). For more on Dizraeli, see Speers 2017, 38–39 and numerous quotes from him are provided throughout her book.

11. This reference to "school dinners" may be pointing to free school meal programs for the growing impoverished in the country, and often the target of government cuts under Tory policies.

12. The Lidl is a discount chain grocery store which has been referenced in a number of rap songs, including "One Day I went to Lidl" by Afrikan Boy in 2007.

13. This may be done by juxtaposing the rapper's identity with signifiers of dominant culture: MC Sway (and author Patrick Neate) construct an MC named Nobody for a music video entitled "Jerusalem" (2009), which utilizes the Parry hymn, sung (badly) by a black school child to an audience of his peers and Queen Elizabeth II (played by an actress). In the video, three men in balaclavas abduct her, put her in a van, and give her a tour of "real England": grocery stores, council houses, riding on double decker buses and the London tube, pie shop, playing fruit machines and having pints in the pub, and making her own cup of tea in a council flat.

14. The use of the horse as symbol of the establishment and mainstream white England can also be seen in Dizzee Rascal's "Sirens" (2007) music video. The video depicts Rascal running from police sirens in an urban landscape, but instead of policemen, he is chased by foxhunters on horses who chase him through his house and in the streets, eventually killing him in an alleyway.

15. A parallel, for example, could be made in pop with the Spice Girls' debut music video "Wannabe" (1996, released in 1997 in the US), which depicts the young girls gatecrashing the St. Pancras hotel, interrupting old white aristocratic types with their dancing and singing. In other words, "Old England" becomes the foil for what was sold as fresh, hip, and new.

16. Originating around the turn of the twenty-first century, the word became widespread where it began to be added to dictionaries around the period 2004–2005 (and was the *Language Report*'s word of the year for 2004). *Oxford English Dictionary* defines chav as "a young lower-class person who displays brash and loutish behaviour and wears real or imitation designer clothes." It is used pejoratively, and has been parodied such as for the Vicki Pollard character of the *Little Britain* television series. See also Jones 2011.

17. Mark Duggan was shot and fatally wounded by the Metropolitan Police in 2011 in Tottenham and the official account of his death by the police was inconsistent. Protesting his death led to riots in Tottenham and across England. Jean Charles Menezes was a Brazilian electrician killed by the Metropolitan Police at the Stockwell tube station in 2005 after he was wrongly identified as having been involved in the failed terrorist attacks on the tube the previous day on 21 July (and two weeks after the 7/7 bombings).

18. His second album, *A Grand Don't Come for Free* (2004), arguably takes this everyday narrative further, disrobed as a "concept album" about one man's search for a missing £1000 set in an urban British environment and all the encounters that come with it (Barron 2013, 536; Slater 2011)

19. Bennett quotes Stuart Maconie's observation that the post-1966 pop music of the Beatles, the Kinks, and the Small Faces became the focus of "a kind of wry vaudevillian chronicling of . . . ordinary post-war (British) life" (2000, 193).

20. Boakye writes that "his [Skinner's] nervous brand of street wisdom is an easy sell, and that his whiteness is important and acceptable because "we aren't as conditioned to see whiteness and invulnerable" (2017, 79). He continues that Skinner "Makes a virtue of all those things that would detract from Skinner's credibility [as a grime artist]: his whiteness, his non-Londonness, his lack of polish as a lyricist, his mundane, middle-class-disguised-as-working-class existence, his disinclination towards violence, his introspective musings, his muted braggadocio. Skinner is the very opposite of the reactionary masculinity I spoke of earlier, in a field that, by 2001, was becoming characterized by male invulnerability. It's weird but he flipped every expectation of urban masculinity just before Grime would define the rules of urban masculinity for the next 15 years" (2017, 78–79).

21. Rollefson quotes Manuva's resistance to pigeon-holing in terms of UK rap, and spends some time outlining the "ever diversifying" UK rap scene, focusing in particular on the Birmingham-based rapper Juice Aleem (Rollefson 2017, 164–225).

22. One example is their track "T5" (2016), which discusses their experiences of racial profiling at New York City's JFK airport terminal.

23. He advocates for the use of the term media "representation" over the use of "diversity" in the media, and argues that if people aren't represented in radio, television, and film, people can switch off and gravitate toward other fringe narratives (including religious extremism). He also continues, "I think we need to take a leaf out of the book of our music industry: drum and bass, grime, dubstep, these are world-conquering musical genres that are only possible by tapping into our multiculturalism" (Ahmed 2017).

24. Riz MC raps in Sandys Row Synagogue in the East End of London, established in 1766, which is the oldest active synagogue in the UK.

3

HISTORY

Rapping Postcoloniality: Akala's "The Thieves Banquet"

and Neocolonial Critique

Yinka Shonibare's Britannia

After the redevelopment of the London-based Tate Britain art museum in 2001, artist Yinka Shonibare MBE was invited to costume the statue of Britannia in front
of the original façade of the building. Maev Kennedy, reviewing the event for the
Guardian newspaper, acknowledged the complex roots and routes (Gilroy 1993) of
such a project: "He chose to reflect the colonial antecedents of a gallery founded on
the Tate and Lyle sugar fortune, and has dressed her in streaming banners of brilliant
'African' textiles—manufactured in Holland and England for export to Africa but
bought at Brixton market in south London" (Kennedy 2001).

Shonibare is a British-Nigerian artist associated with the "Young British Artists"
of the 1990s (e.g., Damien Hirst, Sarah Lucas, Tracey Emin). His work is often characterized by re-creating scenes or paintings using "African" textiles or Africanizing
sculptures with "African Clothing" (Schneider 2015, 5–8), pastiching Gainsborough
in *Mr and Mrs Andrews without Their Heads* (1998), depicting the Berlin Conference
in *Scramble for Africa* (2003), or re-staging historically white British paintings with
Black ethnicities, for example, in *Diary of a Victorian Dandy* (1998), based on the narrative works of William Hogarth. His artworks try to redress the cultural amnesia of

Brithop. Justin A. Williams, Oxford University Press (2021). © Oxford University Press.
DOI: 10.1093/oso/9780190656805.001.0001

empire, colonialism, and slavery head on, and the "African-ness" of his textiles tells of a much more complicated situation than a simple signification would suggest. Shonibare's work attempts to question the notion of essentialized ethnic origins and to unravel the idea of a racially or ideologically fixed nation. *Britannia* at the Tate acknowledged the role that Africa played in the British Empire, re-contextualizing Britannia from the colonized perspective.

Like Shonibare, London-based rapper Akala attempts to "decolonise the mind" (Ngũgĩ 1986) through his art, espousing a postcolonial worldview that reinserts African[1] historical contributions, critiques past injustices, and addresses current inequalities. His lyrics often reflect a historically fueled didacticism around pan-African solidarity and revolution that encourages his audience to help create change. This chapter focuses on a particular track, "The Thieves Banquet," from Akala's eponymous 2013 album, and its critique of neocolonialism. His theatrical performance on these tracks, with their use of multi-accentuality and code combining with elements of Western classical music, creates a multi-layered and intermedial hybrid text. As Black vernacular forms such as hip-hop have become a powerful site of (capitalist) critique (Gilroy 1987, 155), Akala's performative skills as a rapper allow him to present a complex and didactic allegory informed by imperial history, the literature of the global south, and the global financial crisis. It also points a way forward for the study of accent in hip-hop as well as looking more closely at a performative approach to rap music that acknowledges its inherent theatricality.

Akala, Shonibare, and other Black British artists that negotiate multiple ethnic and/or national identities reflect what Joseph Roach has described as "countermemories, or the disparities between history as it is discursively transmitted and meaning as it is publicly enacted by the bodies that bear its consequences" (quoted in Tolia-Kelly and Morris 2004, 155). As Robert Young argues, "Postcolonialism names a politics and philosophy of activism that contests that disparity [of global economic inequality between Western and non-Western continents], and so continues in a new way the anti-colonial struggles of the past" (2003, 4). Shonibare and Akala want to raise awareness of Britain's colonial past in a way that, as Angela McRobbie describes Shonibare's work, enables "a return to history" (1998, 57). As members of the Black Atlantic, they share the social memory of slavery from the standpoint of the colonized and enslaved. In this sense, Akala applies postcolonial thinking to lyrics that espouse pan-African traditions and protest past imperial atrocities and current neocolonial conditions. His music shows what happens when the empire comes home, carrying reminders of the past that contribute to "postcolonial melancholia" and the artistic responses to it (Gilroy 2004, 99). Akala's message is an attempt to awaken listeners to history and current inequalities, and to leave Plato's cave more enlightened. The links between past (colonialism and slavery) and present (neocolonialism) capitalist exploitation become a juncture in which Akala stages his performative critique showing that, for Akala, knowledge is power.

Akala

Rapper, public speaker, journalist, graphic novelist, and founder of the Hip-hop Shakespeare Company, Akala (b. 1983) is one of the MCs at the forefront of the UK's thriving hip-hop scene. Born Kingslee James Daley, the London-based rapper chose the stage name Akala because it is a Buddhist term meaning "Immovable." His father is a British-born child of two African-Jamaican migrant workers who came as part of the Windrush generation, and his mother is an army child (of a Scottish mother and English father), born in Germany, who spent her infancy in Hong Kong before moving to the UK (Akala 2018, 2). As a child, Akala went to a Pan-African Saturday school called the Winnie Mandela School in Camden (along with his sister Niomi, a.k.a. MC, singer, and producer Ms. Dynamite), and his stepfather was stage manager of the Hackney Empire, the leading African-Caribbean theater at the time. He started his rap career as a grime MC, but as time passed, his lyrics became more politically and socially conscious. He released his first album *It's Not a Rumour* (2006) followed by *Freedom Lasso* (2007) and *DoubleThink* (2010). He gained further notoriety on BBC Radio 1Xtra in 2011 for his "Fire in the Booth,"[2] a freestyle that can be heard on his first mixtape *Knowledge is Power Vol. 1* (2012). His albums have highlighted numerous themes: the dystopian qualities of British society, racial inequality and stereotypes, the commercialism of US rap music, global wars, the importance of education, the prison industrial complex, Britain's colonial past and the slave trade, Black revolutionaries, capitalist corruption, inequalities of power, and the need for self-reliance. He owns his own record label, Illa State Records, so he is under little pressure from major record labels to perform in a particular way, on or off stage. His studio albums often include live bands drawing from a range of genres, and this polystylism arguably helps him avoid any subgeneric pigeonholing by the rap music industry.

His pan-African education, in particular about the transatlantic slave trade and revolutionary leaders such as Marcus Garvey, Malcolm X, and Jean-Jacques Dessalines, informs his lyrics on tracks such as "Maangamizi" and "Malcolm Said it" (both on *The Thieves Banquet*). Black nationalism was a prominent influence in the 1980s and early 1990s US rap scene, when groups like the Jungle Brothers (e.g., "Acknowledge Your Own History"), others associated with the Native Tongues collective (Queen Latifah, A Tribe Called Quest, and De La Soul), groups like Public Enemy and X Clan, and UK artists such as Black Radical Mk II and Katch 22 drew from Black nationalist imagery: pan-African flags, graphics of the African continent in pan-African colors, African clothes, and iconography and teachings from strong Black revolutionary leaders. Black nationalist hip-hop and the results of his own pan-African educational background are therefore prominently foregrounded and convergent influences on his musical style. As Akala raps, "Come to my shows and some cry tears / It mean that much to 'em, it's a movement! / I don't speak for myself but a unit" ("Fire in the Booth").

He often shows his music videos at live shows. "Malcolm Said it," for example, is rife with imagery of Black revolutionary leaders (none of whom are not part of history curricula in the UK), adding a visual dimension to his didacticism. As stated in his BBAF Mandela lecture, one purpose of his lyrics (and his lectures) is that the younger generation are taught these less sanitized histories and that they do not learn to idolize colonizers and imperialist history. He states, "The way we view and understand past injustices unquestionably colours the way we perceive and thus interact with today's politics; and by exalting the resistance of everyday people, instead of colonizers by making plain, that unspeakable brutality of the world, we can push these same young minds to interact hopefully in ways that are less complicit with injustice" (Akala 2014).

To this point, Britain's history of colonization and actor in the slave trade is a period that some would like to leave unremembered. From around 1400, as European powers expanded their control across the world, the mass enslavement of Africa began, mining resources and using unpaid labor treated more as property than human. At the height of colonialism in the nineteenth century, nine-tenths of the entire world was controlled by European or European-derived powers (Young 2003, 2). Furthermore, colonial and imperial rule was legitimized by anthropological theories which portrayed the peoples of the colonized world as inferior, childlike, or feminine, incapable of looking after themselves, and the basis of these theories formed the development of race as a concept. Slavery's legacy in Britain is perhaps more hidden than in the US. To quote David Olusoga:

> Slavery resurfaces in America regularly. The disadvantage and discrimination that disfigures the lives and limits the life chances of so many African-Americans is the bitter legacy of the slave system and the racism that underwrote and outlasted it. Britain, by contrast, has been far more successful at covering up its slave-owning and slave-trading past. Whereas the cotton plantations of the American south were established on the soil of the continental United States, British slavery took place 3,000 miles away in the Caribbean.

That geographic distance made it possible for slavery to be largely airbrushed out of British history, following the Slavery Abolition Act in 1833. Many of us today have a more vivid image of American slavery than we have of life as it was for British-owned slaves on the plantations of the Caribbean. The word slavery is more likely to conjure up images of Alabama cotton fields and white-washed plantation houses, of *Roots*, *Gone With The Wind* and *12 Years A Slave*, than images of Jamaica or Barbados in the 18th century. This is not an accident. (Olusoga 2015)

Most of postcolonial theory, and postcolonial thinking, in effect, is to deal with the legacy of colonial rule, and those who suffer most directly from its consequences. Racism, both everyday racism, and structural and institutional racism, is a legacy of the colonial era, and its consequences still ring throughout the world. As Gilroy writes, "Our postcolonial environment reverberates with the catastrophes that resulted from the militarized agency and unprecedented victimization of racial and ethnic groups" (Gilroy 2004, 31). Many of Akala's tracks try to address the cultural amnesia of Britain's role in the slave trade and other aspects of the imperial project.

Akala's track "Maaganamizi" refers to the enslavement of the African people and the ensuing destruction. A Swahili expression which translates as "destruction," "doom," and/or "annihilation," it is appropriated to these purposes to speak to a broader continuum of injustice, exploitation, and abuse. "Maangamizi" discusses the African holocaust, forced migration, torture, and slavery in raw, powerful terms. He concludes that these injustices will only stop when current institutions of unequal power relationships cease to exist:

> When we put a stop to false charity
> That gives with one hand and bombs with the other
> When the IMF and World Bank, along with their puppets
> No longer strangle our nations.
> When the invaders don't have military bases
> In so many places
> When the jail cells are not packed with Black backs
> And the gats and the crack are no longer factors
> When we celebrate true self-determination
> Not a few token bit part actors
> When the truth is told and there is
> The dignity to remember the dead
> Because as long as they are distorting the past
> It means they have the intention of doing it again.

Like Shonibare, who "explores the problem of historical omission and recurrence" (Schneider 2015, 5), Akala addresses African genocide as well as forced migration and displacement and links them to the recurrence of exploitation in the prison industrial complex; guns, drugs, and the culture of military intervention; and the corrupt relationship between national governments and international financial organizations.

The first verse opens with, "Maangamizi, meaning African hellacaust / Because we paid a hell of a cost / And don't really know what was lost / And the process ain't ever stopped." He cites atrocities including the torture of Black men and women, rape, and the use of Black women for gynecological "research" (without anesthetic) as well as later developments such as Jim Crow and apartheid. Akala also questions educational systems that ignore these histories and Black revolutionaries, figures such as Haiti's Jean-Jacques Dessalines, who led the first successful slave revolution in 1804; Nanny of the Maroons, who escaped her plantation in Jamaica and started a community and helped to free over eight hundred slaves in thirty years; and Paul Bogle, a Jamaican Baptist deacon, who led the 1865 Morant Bay protest against widespread poverty, prejudice, and the lack of voting rights for Black men and women. Additionally, Akala highlights the ongoing racial inequality and the continuing dependence of "third world" nations ("They changed that much? Are you so sure? The world's darker people still the most poor?"). This overt link between past and present forms of imperialism, while questioning the "independent" status of "third world" nations references writers such as Frantz Fanon and Ngũgĩ wa Thiong'o and leaders such as Kwame Nkrumah since the 1960s. Akala updates the neocolonial critique presented by earlier thinkers, making the argument for liberation as pressing as ever. While "Maangamizi" is the most lyrically overt example of this past-present link on *The Thieves Banquet*, the album's title track most theatrically demonstrates it.

Neocolonialism and "The Thieves Banquet"

Neocolonialism, a term coined by Ghanaian president Nkrumah in *Neo-Colonialism, the Last Stage of Imperialism* (1965), is defined by John McLeod as "the perpetuation of a nation's subservience to the interests of Europe, supported by an indigenous elite, after colonialism has formally ended" (2013, 108). While a postcolonial state may look independent politically, it may still be controlled by outside forces, usually economic ones. In *The Wretched of the Earth* (1961), Fanon wrote of his concern that the newly independent nation could be compromised by what he called the educated national middle class who pursue their own interests rather than help their country's people (Akala 2014, 120–21). Akala cites the examples of South Africa and

Haiti, two countries with celebrated revolutions in different eras. In post-apartheid South Africa, the South African Central Bank became independent, but it continued to be run by the same man in control under apartheid. The Bank's debt had to be serviced by the new African National Congress, as he has explained elsewhere, "to the tune of 4.5 billion US dollars per year" (Akala 2014). Haiti staged the first successful slave revolution (1791–1804), yet under the threat of re-invasion from France in 1825, had to pay 91 million francs "from a loss of property" and the former slave colony labored to pay the debt to its colonizers until 1947 (Akala 2014).

The literature of the global south had a direct influence on Akala's work. For example, the story of Akala's "The Thieves Banquet" was inspired by Kenyan writer Ngũgĩ wa Thiong'o's *Caitaani Mũtharaba-inĩ* (*Devil on the Cross*, 1982; see Edwards 2013).[3] The novel tells of a student witnessing a banquet in a cave hosted by the Devil for local and foreign capitalists in Kenya who have mortgaged the nation to foreign capital, and become fat, wealthy, and boastful. The novel is a Marxist critique of postcolonial Kenya, its new leaders, and corruption under capitalism, as well as middle-class intellectualism. The wealthy elites under capitalism believe in "the democracy of drinking the blood and eating the flesh of workers and peasants" (Ngũgĩ 1987, 89), and they "encourage the growth of a class of eaters of other people's products . . . a class of man-eaters—in our own land" (Ngũgĩ 1987, 168). The book is also a political satire of neocolonial Kenya, addressed to "all Kenyans struggling against the neo-colonial stage of imperialism" (Ngũgĩ 1987, 1). In the novel, the masses unite against injustice and chase the capitalists out of the cave, pointing toward the possibility of revolution.

Akala's track provides a more global allegory devoid of specific geographical location in terms of city or country, but we can deduce from the introduction that we are talking about our own planet: "Once upon a time in an obscure part of the Milky Way Galaxy, there was a spinning ball of water and rock ruled by the forces of evil." The narrator goes on to explain that the Devil decided to hold a banquet for the greatest thieves of the world:

> He sent invites to thousands of the greatest murderers, rapists, and general-assorted scum, inviting them to attend his palace at the dawn of the new moon. Each thief would be given a chance to stake his claim as the greatest messenger of murder upon the planet, and the Devil himself would then decide who should be crowned king.
>
> After many days of deliberating, all of the petty thieves, such as street criminals, have been found far short of the required level of wickedness and there were just four sets of thieves left in the competition.

They were: the monarchs of empire, a cartel of bankers, the heads of religious orders, and the third-world dictators. Each set of thieves appointed a spokesman to give his case to the Devil. We have recorded these events for posterity.

Akala, as narrator, frames the story from the outset, and then performs as the different characters using a different English accent for each. Similar to Uganda's President Idi Amin, Akala's Dictator of the Third World nation brags in an African English accent that he came to power in a military coup, can murder his people at will while telling them to worship colonizers, and has a bank account in Switzerland. The verse is accompanied by Romantic-style piano phrases over the song's basic beat. The Monarch of Empire asks, "who do you think . . . trained these amateur dictators to act this way?" The Monarch brags of the death, mass enslavement, and deliberate starvation of whole nations. The thieves don't have to touch money; it is all handled for them ("So blingin' out of control you would vomit / Don't even touch dough, but my face is on it!"). Strings accompany this verse. The third thief, a "pervert hiding under the cloak [of] the clergy," brags that despite widespread pedophilia, no offender has been jailed. With church organ (stereotypically) accompanying the next verse, the priest boasts about these crimes, committed with the blessing of the church.

The last thief is the head of a cartel of bankers, bragging in a Received Pronunciation accent and accompanied by a female operatic voice in the background:

> I think I'm the biggest sinner
> All of those three depend on me
> All they ever do is defending me
> Cos I paid for all of the things they have
> Of course, and all of the lives they lead
> Paid for the guns, bombs and the tanks
> That's why you see, there is always more
> Never fired a gun but millions die because of him, no one
>   knows what he looks like . . .
> I hold the keys to every single door
> Sell sex and drugs, profit and lies
> Earth and skies, I'll even sell life
> I'll even sell freedom for the right price
> But no one is smart enough to ask me nice
> So Mr. Devil, give me the medal
> Don't be biased
> If you don't give it to me
> I'll just BUY IT!

The Devil declares the last speaker the winner, suggesting that Akala finds those who control economic power and help create inequality in the world to be the evilest. In addition to past economic exploitation during the slave trade and the corruption outlined in *Devil on the Cross*, one cannot help but think that the 2008 financial crisis also influenced Akala's critique. Caused in part by a lack of financial regulation on property mortgages (and the greed and exploitation inherent in loans such as sub-prime mortgages), this economic crisis was then lessened by bailouts from national governments. The track clearly demonstrates the link between politics and capitalist interests. Furthermore, the album's artwork depicts the all-male guests at the banquet feasting on severed human heads and limbs, visually depicting Ngũgĩ's "man-eaters" surrounded by images of poverty, war, and money. Unlike Ngũgĩ's novel, however, "The Thieves Banquet" includes no collective representation of the masses. The final track of the album, entitled "The Thieves Banquet Part II (bonus track)," describes the end of the banquet: the Devil decides to retire and all the thieves make a pact to work together, while dining on a final course of murdered children, drinking the still-warm blood, and laughing and toasting to their future success.

Akala's performative role of narrator and also the four other characters in the story might suggest his self-construction as an African-based trickster figure (as some suggested about Eminem's triple persona; see Nielsen 2006). Indeed, Akala's performance demonstrates an ability to play multiple roles with adept authenticity and virtuosity. Given Akala's emphasis on didacticism in his work, however, the performance is perhaps best considered an allegory that reflects the "national allegory" of *The Devil on the Cross*, echoing writers such as Fredric Jameson who believe that all "Third World" texts are allegorical (1986, 69).[4] Akala's allegory, in contrast, resists time and place in the interest of a more globalized critique while being firmly embedded sonically in the world of Western popular and classical music. The relationship between the Monarch of Empire and Third World Dictator addresses the issue of "mimicry" ("Who do you think trained this amateur dictator to behave this way?"), most eloquently expounded by Homi Bhabha in his essay "Of Mimicry and Man," where the colonized mimic aspects of the colonizer as a "form of colonial discourse" (1994, 89). Furthermore, the banker as "winner" in the banquet echoes the Marxist critique in Ngũgĩ's novel. The line "no one knows who I look like" could also echo Nkrumah's comments that neocolonialism is the worst type of colonialism because it accepts "power without responsibility" (1994, x). It is not a coincidence that the accent used is that of Received Pronunciation, representing standard "Queen's English" with its associations with the wealthy elite. The four accents, as well as Akala's own voice as narrator, provide an example of Voloshinov's concept of "multi-accentuality," the idea that language

TABLE 3.1

Formal Structure of "The Thieves Banquet"

Formal unit	Character	Accent	Musical features
Introduction (0:00–1:36)	Narrator	Multicultural Youth English (MYE)	Strings
Verse 1 (1:37–2:30)	Third World Dictator	African English	Romantic-style piano
Chorus (2:31–2:44)		Backward vocal placement (heavy throat tone)	English choral technique Keyboard upbeats
Verse 2 (2:44–3:32)	Monarch of Empire	Received Pronunciation (with some slang and MYE elements)	Violoncello
Chorus (3:32–3:44)		Backward vocal placement (heavy throat tone)	English choral technique Keyboard upbeats
Verse 3 (3:44–4:33)	Head of religious order	Breathy Received Pronunciation	Church organ
Verse 4 (4:34–5:28)	Head of banking cartel	Received Pronunciation (most theatrical delivery)	Operatic voice in background
Double Chorus (5:29–6:36)		Backward vocal placement (heavy throat tone)	English choral technique Keyboard upbeats Caribbean MC singing in outro

produces different meanings dependent on how it is "accented" by those who utter it in a given context (Procter 1994, 31). These utterances, as always, will be fully decoded by those with knowledge of the varying English accents and their connotations.

Multi-Accentuality and Multicultural Youth English in
"The Thieves Banquet"

The accents in "The Thieves Banquet" are different from Akala's standard idiolect when rapping, what linguists call Multicultural Youth English or Multicultural London English (MLE; see Kerswill 2013, 128–64). Akala's Third World Dictator's accent resembles the dialect of African English, and the clergyman uses Received Pronunciation with a breathy, villainous delivery (like the British-accented villains of Hollywood film). The banker has the most theatrical and performative form of Received Pronunciation which is markedly different from that of the Monarch of Empire. For example, the Monarch uses colloquial phrases such as "blingin out of control" and pronounces "things" as "tings." The use of Black vernacular cultural codes within these stereotyped accents not only represents the presence of linguistic traces from the history of Empire, but also what Nabeel Zubieri calls "code combining" rather than code switching for UK-based MCs (reminiscent of '80s MCs like Smiley Culture; see Zubieri 2014, 191). MLE is in itself a combination of elements, representative of the hybridities of multicultural Britain. The banker, who does pronounce the "<u>th</u>" in "things" ("Cos I paid for all of the <u>th</u>ings they have"), may be more distanced from historical reality and his accent adds to his "invisibility."[5] The exaggerated nature of these accents also add an element of satire and humor, juxtaposing "high" and "low" forms and accents, in addition to a strong notion of theatricality in his virtuosic performance.

The use of MLE, like Stylized Turkish-German or African American Vernacular English, can be perceived as a resistance vernacular (Mitchell 2000, 41–54; Reinhardt-Byrd 2015, 292–93), in opposition to prestige varieties such as Received Pronunciation. In a sense, Akala is rejecting the stereotype of MLE given the high intellectual content of lyrics spoken in an accent associated with a less educated class. Associated with a migrant language, the language of Jamaican immigrants primarily, it is perhaps predictable that articles in the *Daily Mail* express anxiety that MLE has spread well beyond the perceived "Other" (Harding 2013). The theatrically "over-the-top" Received Pronunciation accent that uses phrases from Black vernacular is analogous to Shonibare's paintings, a switch in codes which resists and disrupts stereotypes, showing perspectives from the other side of the power relationship, thus demonstrating that the two are inextricably intertwined. This hyperbolic performativity resists the everyday performative, pedagogic (Bhabha 1994, 209), nationalist, and other essentialized dominant discourses in both Britain and wider international communities.

While the soundscapes of a number of tracks on the album interrogate distinctions between elite and vernacular vocalizations and represent a polystylism that makes it difficult to pin down an overall musical style, the allusion to Western classical music on "The Thieves Banquet" demands further investigation.[6] The multi-tracked singer of the chorus is clearly alluding to the British "choral tradition" in chant, religious choral music, or other forms of "early music," a style that has developed, in particular, in post-WWII Britain (Day 2019). Examples of this style in popular music include the chant in the opening of Enigma's "Sadeness" (1990) and the unnamed, possibly sampled, singing voice at the opening of Justin Timberlake's "Cry Me a River" (2002). This choral style is defined by backward vocal production rather than "forward singing," through the backward placement of the singing voice and vocal production with a heavy throat tone (Coward 1914, 39). It also has sonic associations with what Melanie Lowe calls the "gothic choral aesthetic" (e.g., Verdi and Mozart Requiems), often used for an "epic" sound in film music. And yet, we should not read the notion of "classical music" too literally here, as we are dealing with a pastiche of the Western classical style. As in Shonibare's work, Akala's track echoes the artist's own assertion that "my work remains critical of the relations of power through parody, excess and complicity" (quoted in Tolia-Kelly and Morris 2004, 155). Writers such as Amiri Baraka have long dealt with the trope of white appropriation of Black forms such as jazz, rhythm and blues, and hip-hop (e.g., Paul Whiteman, Elvis, Eminem). Akala, in contrast, performs and considers the appropriation of European music, flipping historical notion of cultural-economic appropriation and empire on its head. Such a reading, however, may be too simplistic considering Akala's sonic message, and cannot be solely based on notions of appropriation. The beat is extremely hybrid. The sound of the whip which forms part of the "basic beat" configuration is powerful in itself, but the choruses see it combined with reverb-laden keyboard upbeats reminiscent of dub and reggae, and there is a Caribbean MC-style voice at the end of "The Thieves Banquet," and a female operatic voice in verse four. The beat of the track, moreover, is a musical analogue for the code combining in the lyrical delivery.

The European classical choral voice obviously represents the soundtrack of the elite, alluding to a compositional style of Western European classical works that were written at the height of colonialist territorial expansion and are firmly associated with high art. The soundtrack could be said to represent the music of the thieves (and the enemy),[7] but it is also the medium that conveys Akala's message. There may be an inherent tension between the critique of empire and the pleasures of the music, but protest songs have always dealt with such tension. In fact, such a tension may be reflective of the ambivalence inherent in postcolonialism itself (Bhabha 1994, 85). As numerous cultural studies theorists have noted, popular culture can never be fully separated from the dominant institutions and cultures that helped to shape it (Procter 1994, 45–46), and Akala's powerful critique of capitalism on a for-profit popular music recording demonstrates this contradiction. As Hall reminds us, culture is a crucial site of social action, a site of ongoing struggle where power relations are formed, critiqued, and potentially unraveled. Akala's counter-narratives of dominant forms of history and storytelling are necessarily hybrid, necessarily ambivalent in their pleasure and discomfort, musically navigating the same routes and roots that London's global citizens negotiate daily.

Hip-Hop, Performance, and Theatricality

The Thieves Banquet was launched on April 26, 2013, at the Tate Modern with a live performance by Akala and his band, and a digital art installation of the cover art for the album by Japanese artist Tokio Aoyama. Like Shonibare's work at Tate Britain, these artists rewrite, or create a palimpsest over the imperial-funded institutions in Britain, producing another site of postcolonial ambivalence, akin to artists who receive Royal honors such as an OBE (Officer of the Most Excellent Order of the British Empire) and MBE (Member of the Most Excellent Order of the British Empire). To refuse such a title (as did poet Benjamin Zephaniah) is to reject publicly Britain's Imperial heritage and its consequences.[8] To accept it (as did Shonibare) is to acknowledge that the individuals' contributions to and membership in the British Empire (and the UK) go beyond a (tacit) identification with white ethnicity. This acceptance/refusal dichotomy is, however, far too reductive for postcolonial Britain, a Britannia draped in "African" textiles. The "graffiti" around the Edward Colston statue in my hometown of Bristol, England, paints an even more apt picture. Born in Bristol, Colston was a member of the Society of Merchant Venturers in the seventeenth and eighteenth centuries, and helped eradicate the London-based monopoly on trade, opening up ports like Bristol and Liverpool to global goods, including slaves. In recent years, the statue has included someone scrawling "slave trader" under his list of achievements, using dripping red paint to signify blood, and a shackle around Colston's wrist and gold chains around his neck. These interventions, or the rewriting of dominant history within the dominant forms themselves, may be likened to protest art that uses the Western forms of the novel, the commercial music recording, or the art gallery. It reminds us of the syncretic connection of past and present, history as less distanced than is presented in more mainstream narratives.

In a review of *The Thieves Banquet* in 2013, Killian Fox writes that "Nuance is sometimes sacrificed for theatrical effect, particularly on the title track, but Akala's intricate flow is so engaging it rarely matters." It is worth acknowledging the theatricality of the album and "The Thieves Banquet" in particular, and its consequences for thinking about hip-hop's music-lyric dichotomy. Rarely do hip-hop scholars consider "performance" or the fact that rappers often play a role, even if their own persona is loosely based on real life. The theatricality of hip-hop as a performance art, not only for hip-hop theater (Persley 2015, 85), but also for hip-hop culture as a whole, is an important element for "The Thieves Banquet" and its critiques. Furthermore, if a concept of "theatricality" is the key to analyzing the relationship between music and lyrical delivery ("beat and flow"), as in theater or a radio play, the music becomes crucial to meaning, but also incidental. Not all rap music, I would argue, has an unequal relationship between music and lyrical delivery—in some cases, there is an equal relation, or at other times the music/beat is foregrounded (in music produced for club dancing, for example), and much of this interplay is dependent on the listener. "The Thieves Banquet," in contrast, places an emphasis on "staged" performance (a sonic stage, but a stage nonetheless). In a didactic allegory, highlighting the lyrics is what matters, and the music can add a sense of drama without "getting in the way." Akala's awareness of theatricality is not absent in this track or elsewhere, as founder of the Hip-hop Shakespeare Company is one of the many accomplishments in his rich and varied career. Lastly, the satirical aspects of such a performance not only add to its theatricality, but also allow for such a caricatured portrayal to be possible. Humor through excess, as we will see further in Chapter 6, allow these important meanings to be communicated in direct and overt ways.

Conclusion: Decolonizing the Mind through Rap Music

Akala inherits the legacy of the pan-Africanist movement and uses a notion of Black nationalism to educate listeners on the atrocities of empire, past and present. He adapts and translates allegory from literature of the global south such as, in particular, Ngũgĩ's Marxist critique of neocolonial Kenya in *Devil on the Cross*. Akala's didactic revolutionary rhetoric falls into the "knowledge rap" (Krims 2000, 79) tradition from several US hip-hop artists and groups that are often labeled "conscious" rap artists, given that Afrika Bambaataa dubbed "knowledge" as the "fifth element" of hip-hop (Gosa 2015, 56). Akala shares such an approach with Black British artists like Shonibare who re-inserts African contributions into narratives of the British Empire and reflects Black Atlantic perspectives so eloquently explored by Black British intellectuals such as Hall and Gilroy, though I would argue that Akala's strategy is much more essentialist than Shonibare's. Akala's provocative counter-narrative complicates race-based notions of Britishness, itself an elusive concept given Britain's imperial past. Akala retrieves forgotten or neglected histories, expressed in the Black resistance vernacular of Multicultural Youth

English, reclaiming identity in light of the "postcolonial melancholia" felt by those who lament the loss of empire.

Akala notes that the paradoxes and contradictions of British history are what made him: "I am partly a product of Britain's injustices, of its history of class and race oppression, but also its counter-narrative of struggle and the compromises made by those in power born of those struggles. I am a product of the empire, and also of the welfare state" (Akala 2018, 16).[9] To the former, postcolonial discourses can be used to tease out these invisible histories of empire while using a Black vernacular critique of current social and economic inequalities. Such counter-narratives are in fact too integrated to be separate from more dominant ones. What Akala presents in his rap music, among other things, echoes Gilroy's observation that "We may discover that our story is not the *other* story after all, but *the* story of England in the modern world" (1990, 52).

Notes

1. I use the term "African" throughout this chapter, while I am consciously aware that many thinkers use "Afrikan" instead of "African" to echo activists who believe Africa is a European imposed construction of the continent rather than an Afrika-centered perspective.

2. "Fire in the Booth" is part of BBC Radio 1Xtra's The Rap Show hosted by Charlie Sloth.

3. In an interview with Simone Elesha Edwards, Akala states that the title of *The Thieves Banquet* "came about as I was reading a novel by a Kenyan author which was called Devil on the Cross" (2013). Numerous tweets from his twitter account (@Akalamusic) in March 2013 praise Ngũgĩ's novel for its insight and humor.

4. Jameson's "Third-World Literature in the Era of Multinational Capitalism" is not without important problematizations of his rhetoric. See Ahmad 1987 for an important critique.

5. The banker's RP accent is similar to that of Akala's character Pompous Peterson, who introduces himself thus: "My name is pompous Peterson and I am heir to the 'Print Money When You Like—Fund Genocide at Will' Banking Dynasty." He also briefly appears at live shows, signified by the accent and his costume of a white dress jacket and cane, and proceeds to chastise any "immigrants" and "chavs" in the audience. A promotional video for *The Thieves Banquet* entitled "Pompous Peterson freestyle" goes into more detail on how to become an excellent thief: "Speak proper English, you'll go further, The accent of legitimate murder." Available at: https://www.youtube.com/watch?v=L6GOoWtECFA.

6. This is not the only instance of Akala sampling or borrowing from Western classical music. The track "Psycho" (from the 2010 album *DoubleThink*), presents the complexity of his feelings, and makes a direct association with classical music and the violence undertaken by Western European empires: "I know what it is that's got me feeling so violent lately. It's all this classical music I've been listening to"; then we hear a harpsichord phrase with four chords arpeggiated (no doubt reversing the often-cited critiques that "Black" rap music is harmful for [white] youth to listen to because it promotes violence). On the track "Educated Tug Shit," on *Knowledge Is Power 1* (2012), he samples Antonio Vivaldi's Concerto No. 4 in F minor, Op. 8, RV 297, III. Allegro

"L'inverno" (Winter), in which the sample is performed at a different tempo from the rest of the beat, creating a disorientating effect.

7. Classical music has been used to represent villainy in other contexts, as written about by Carlo Cenciarelli for the use of Bach's "Goldberg Variations" by Hannibal Lecter in *Silence of the Lambs* (2012, 107–34).

8. Black British dancer, MC, spoken-word artist, and director Jonzi D was offered an MBE in 2011 for services to British dance. His decision to accept or reject became a piece of choreopoetry called "The Letter": 45 minutes of solo dance, monologue, and mime, weighing up the different perspectives. In the end, he rejects MBE given the legacy of empire.

9. The history of Britain, as Akala himself notes, has been paradoxical with positive innovations as well as negative actions: "Britain has two competing traditions—one rooted in ideas of freedom, equality and democracy, and another that sees these words as mere rhetoric to be trotted out at will and violated whenever it serves the Machiavellian purposes of power preservation" (Akala 2018, 10). He points to the fact that the UK can have the largest demonstrations against the invasion of Iraq and have a government that ignores such protests as one example of this paradox.

4

SUBCULTURE/STYLE

Punk Aesthetics in Sleaford Mods and Lethal Bizzle

IN HIS BOOK *The Black Atlantic*, Paul Gilroy states, "The hybridity which is formally intrinsic to hip hop has not been able to prevent that style from being used as
an especially potent sign and symbol of racial authenticity" (1993, 107). Rap's relation
to "blackness" has influenced the production and reception of hip-hop worldwide,
and UK rap is no exception. Prior to this, one of the most important and influential
pop cultural developments in post-WWII Britain was the development of a punk
subculture which became coded as signifying "whiteness." This was reflected in the
demographic of most punk groups, their fans, institutions (record labels, shops),
and journalism, and thus Gilroy's comments about racial authenticity might as well
apply to the whiteness of punk as much as to the blackness of hip-hop. This association of punk culture with (perceivably working-class) whiteness was there from the
onset, as the earliest foundational studies of punk observed (Hebdige 1979, 64).[1]
What happens, then, when these two genres converge musically?

UK hip-hop's intersection with a "quintessentially English" musical pop style,
that of punk,[2] forms the subject of this chapter as a case study of cross-genre interaction. Both hip-hop and punk were born in the 1970s and continue to represent
the voice of the subaltern in different ways. Although the term "punk" reflects
a set of highly diverse musical styles in reality, in this context, I am primarily

Brithop. Justin A. Williams, Oxford University Press (2021). © Oxford University Press.
DOI: 10.1093/oso/9780190656805.001.0001

concerned with the codification of British punk aesthetics, its key tenets, and features that are integral to the subculture.

This chapter focuses on the punk-rap duo the Sleaford Mods and grime-pop rapper Lethal Bizzle, artists who appropriate and translate punk aesthetics via different means to varying consequences.[3] What follows examines the result of combining aesthetics from an older genre with newer developments, highlighting the racialized identities that often exist within these genres. While punk is not the only musical genre utilized in hybrid UK hip-hop styles, it nevertheless lends particular sonic and ideological meanings to English rap music, meanings which complicate an already multifaceted history of racially essentialized categorizations of the music industry and their listeners. The perspectives and methods of this chapter are indebted to the "Birmingham School" of the Centre for Contemporary Cultural Studies, in particular, Dick Hebdige and his 1979 study of punk in his groundbreaking book *Subculture*.[4] Hebdige's account of British punk, which some have criticized for its monolithic treatment of the scene, among other things, nevertheless has been foundational to the semiotic study of subcultures, and adding to the understanding of punk as representing working-class whiteness while being inspired in part by black musics such as reggae. With punk, hip-hop, and subculture often discussed in terms of resistance, a study of such cross-pollination of meanings will also help examine the revolutionary potential of such musics.

Punk Aesthetics

British punk has been defined as a style of music, an attitude, a sartorial style, and an economic system (as in, a Do-it-Yourself aesthetic and distribution structure).[5] Acknowledging that this essentializing of genre is by definition reductive,[6] I explore how the "residual culture" of punk (to invoke Raymond Williams's term)[7] hybridizes with newer cultural artifacts. British punk's influence spread internationally, in particular, after the Sex Pistols tours of 1975–1978 (Guerra and Bennett 2015), and elements also carried on into post-punk, Oi!, hardcore, 2-Tone, Riot Grrrl, and other stylistic offshoots of the '80s and '90s.

John Encarnacao discusses punk aesthetics as an attitude over a musical style, pointing to anti-establishment ideals, technological dystopianism, and rhetorics of spontaneity, inclusion, independence, and oppositionality (2013, 2). British punks, as a recognizable subculture, felt alienated from a society that had gone wrong (exactly what was wrong with society was left more ambiguous, as Tremblay and Duncombe have noted [2011, 3]), and, to quote Hebdige, they were "dramatizing

Britain's decline" (Adams 2008, 477). There was an element of shock in the music, using the "rhetoric of crisis" both linguistically and musically. Angry vocal delivery with shouts, profanity, bad singing as oppositional and signifier of rage were aligned with a perceived amateurism (or Do-It-Yourself/DIY aesthetics). Gelbart's musical description seems apt:

> Riffs built on a few powerful chords, or simple drum patterns . . . a rejection of virtuosity and trained skill, bass lines featuring repeated quavers articulating harmonic roots . . . often deliberately careless approach to ensemble playing, a vocal technique that combined shouting and singing or was calculatedly lazy about pitch and rhythm, the prominent use of lower-class London accents and vulgar slang, lyrics designed to shock the establishment, and underlying it all a raw fury that overwhelmed the performance so that in live concerts the playing often deteriorated into violence even mid-song. (Gelbart 2011, 234)

The two bands that represent the canon of British punk most forcefully are the Sex Pistols and (early period) The Clash. Punk became tied up with politics, in the case of the Sex Pistols with "God Save the Queen" and its critique of the monarchy, and the political messages of Clash vocalist Joe Strummer. According to Ruth Adams, the Sex Pistols were "unlikely guardians of English heritage, albeit expressing a history which stressed the popular cultural and the radical dissenting pamphleteering elements of that heritage rather than the more conventional (pro)monarchist and aristocratic aspects" (2008, 471). And although the Sex Pistols created a challenge to conventional Englishness, they "arguably spot lit the very institutions that it normally sought to destroy" (Adams 2008, 470).[8]

Though it has been argued that it is "Punk's refusal to conform to any stylistic formation that gives it its power" (Encarnacao 2013, 18), as Adams (2008), Dunn (2008), and Gelbart (2011) have shown, punk has arguably become codified, in sound, attitude, and gesture. As happens in any cultural field, certain aspects and signifiers become dominant, the source of parody and swift signification such as for use in commercials. (Dunn 2008, 196).

Ruth Adams writes that the Sex Pistols were inheritors of a working-class music hall tradition in Britain (rather than rock and roll), and that their critique of monarchy was in a post-WWII " 'tradition' of dissenting, yet quintessentially English culture, this time from earlier in the 20th century. Both the 'Angry Young Men' of the 1950s and the 'satire boom' of the 1960s set out to attack the 'complacency' of consensus Britain and the 'unthinking attitudes of respect' which still predominated" (2008, 474). Adams continues to discuss the Sex Pistols brand of punk that "could be argued to be a reframing of national identity in the image of (certain elements of) the working classes . . . of the (post-)industrial city rather than the pastoral fantasy of the countryside" (476). If punk was absorbed, and reframed, into nationalistic hegemony, then this appropriation made possible a wider influence on future art and styles, for example the Young British Artist movement in the 1990s and the Sleaford Mods.[9]

The punk era of the 1970s was one of changing demographics for Britain, in particular, the post-WWII immigration from the Commonwealth. Despite the subcultural influence from West Indian music such as ska and reggae that affected Britain in the 1960s and '70s, British punk became associated with whiteness. If we are to use the oft-cited and misinterpreted Clash song "White Riot" as an example, the song was inspired by the 1976 Notting Hill Carnival riots, which were incited in response to mistreatment of black residents by the police. Dick Hebdige's study of subculture theorized the location of a "white ethnicity" in punk,[10] a "translation" of black ethnicity (Hebdige 1979, 62), and soon becomes a dominant narrative in British punk discourse—punk was an attempt for many white youth to locate their own ethnic identity in Britain in response to the country's increasing multiculturalism.[11] Punks did this through nihilism and shock value, and in some respects, it was white protest music inspired by black protest music. To paraphrase The Clash, they wanted a riot of their own.

As the subject of race and genre looms over this chapter, it is important find a balance between critiquing racialized genres, and further essentializing them (to invoke Paul Gilroy's concept of anti-antiessentialism, as utilized effectively by Rollefson 2008).[12] But as Jon Stratton and Nabeel Zuberi have written, though "[r]ace and ethnicity are discursive fictions . . . they function in the world with real consequences . . . ideas about race and ethnicity, for better or worse, continue to inform and organise understandings of music" (Stratton and Zubieri 2014, 5).[13] The fact is that the history of the music industry is tied into a history of race and of genre,[14] two concepts which have been constructed for a number of economic and ideological reasons. To deny the persistence of race in genre and British culture more widely is to proliferate stereotypes further, to deny or ignore the possibilities of critique that might help foster change.

Sleaford Mods

Initially conceived in 2006, the Sleaford Mods currently comprise vocalist/rapper Jason Williamson and beat-maker Andrew Fearne, who joined in 2010. Both originally from outside of Grantham, the two are based in the post-industrial city of Nottingham (in the East Midlands of England). Their latest albums *Divide and*

Exit (2014) and *Key Markets* (2015) have received critical acclaim, and they have toured sold-out shows in the UK and Europe frequently. Media reception has been glowingly positive, placing the group within the frame of punk poets, social realism, the white working class, and post-industrial cities. Writers also claim that they are the authentic representation of disillusionment with a growing inequality gap under Tory Britain. The Red Train Blog wrote of hearing Sleaford Mods for the first time:

> I wanted to jump to my feet and rip down Oasis, Stereophonics and Arctic Monkeys posters. That was the soundtrack of the prosperous, optimistic New Labour era. Sleaford Mods is the soundtrack of NHS privatization, benefit sanctions and Etonian rule. I was instantly a fan.
>
> Sleaford Mods are breathing some much-needed fresh air into popular music. They are different, crude and rude, but also shine a light onto the lives of ordinary people reminiscent of the work of L. S. Lowry. In an age when popular culture is dominated by Dragon's Den and Benefits Street, Sleaford Mods show that we can aspire to more than the hollow worship of capitalism. They have been compared to the Sex Pistols and to the Specials, but I think it is a disservice to give them retro comparisons. We have too many throwbacks right now. Sleaford Mods are an original outfit, a product of 21st century Britain. (The Red Train Blog, 2015)

For many, their style will not resemble conventional rap music; it often avoids the rhythmic rapping associated with the genre (while still rhyming in many cases, especially choruses), and also avoids a number of clichés from Hip Hop Nation Language (e.g., "yo," "you feel me," or other aspects of African American Vernacular English; see Alim 2006) in favor of localisms (a thick East Midlands accent with more references to national everyday culture, and terms like "mate" are as frequent as "fuckin'" and "cunt"). The vocal delivery most resembles white British MCs such as Mike Skinner of The Streets, but Williamson's reception has also drawn comparisons with Mark E. Smith of the Fall, punk-poet John Cooper Clarke, Ian Dury, and Neil Crossley (of Half Man Half Biscuit). Williamson himself has cited Mark E. Smith and The Wu-Tang clan as influences.

The localized Midlands accent, coupled with its angry delivery, can be heard in resistance to Received Pronunciation accents. The midlands pronunciation of the "u̲" sound in words is in opposition to RP and can become a defining characteristic for already-shocking words such as "fuckin'" and "cunt." In RP, the *strut* vowel sound (bus, shirt, gut) represented by the phonetic symbol /ʌ/, in (West) Midlands dialect (e.g., Birmingham) is generally pronounced with the same vowel as f<u>oo</u>t (book, put; phonetic symbol /ʊ/). But in East Midlands dialect, the u̲ sound may place the jaw and tongue in a lower position, such as "goat" /əʊ/ in RP or /o/ in General American (GA), or even "north."[15] The vowel sound in "bastard" which would use the "bath" vowel in RP /ɑː/ becomes a more open vowel sound, /æ/ (as in the "bath" of General American or "trap" in RP). These subtle differences are particularly audible in contrast to RP, and the interpretive communities that can read regional dialect well will recognize the East Midlands-ness in the vocal delivery of Sleaford Mods.

Given the historical associations of the Midlands with industrial cities, Midlands accents signifying working-class identity is an already established link. Of punk, Simon Frith writes that the privately educated Joe Strummer developed an explicitly working-class voice through accent which became a defining feature of punk. Johnny Rotten drew from football supporter chants and stage cockney in the '60s to develop an accent associated with the proletarian (cited in Laing 1985, 58). Similarly, the Sleaford Mods utilize an accent associated with the working class, the local, the everyday, and in resistance to "the establishment."

Musically, though earlier tracks in their career sampled songs from The Who and The Yardbirds, *Divide and Exit* further strips the sound down to short loops of mostly bass and drums in a punk style, the "buzzsaw drone" as Robert Christgau called it (cited in Laing 1985, 66), alongside occasional synth stabs. A musical comparison of the bass and drums of Sex Pistols' "Roadrunner" [16] with "Tied up in Nottz" show a number of stylistic similarities, including a similar drum pattern and bass line melodic shape, something which is not lost on listeners that are familiar with punk.

The Sleaford Mods's lyrical topics range from bad jobs, to bad bosses, hatred of the middle class, capitalism, nationalism, celebrities, the decline of "good" rock music (and rock stars who sold out), posers and trendiness, and toilet humor. The lyrics are at once observational and critical; sarcastic, sneering, and generally disdainful— but also humorous (Williamson says in interview about their music, "If it don't make us laugh, then it's not a very good tune" [Channel 4 News 2015]). They reflect the everyday social realism not dissimilar to lyrics from The Kinks' frontman Ray Davies updated to reflect the Tory-Lib Dem coalition era (2010–2015). Others have compared such realism with the work of Alan Sillitoe (from Nottingham, part of the "angry young men" of the 1950s, famous for novels such as *Saturday Night and Sunday Morning*) and other kitchen sink dramatists of the 1950s and '60s (e.g., John Osborn, who wrote the 1957 play *Look Back in Anger*). Given the Midlands connection, others have also compared their depiction of bleak Midlands life with the film world of Shane Meadows, in particular, the powerful *This is England* (2006), which depicts skinhead teenagers in 1983.

The "stream of consciousness" style of lyrics also could be compared to the "word salad" of Dada artists, a link made by Dave Laing in his groundbreaking book *One Chord Wonders*: "much punk use of language involved both the shock of the new (importation of obscenity, politics, etc. into popular lyrics) and the shock of the real (justification of this importation by the assertion that this is what happens on the street)" (1985, 78). The music video to "Jolly Fucker," filmed by Alan Sillitoe's son David, shows the song being performed live, and demonstrates the frenetic, tick-driven performance style of Williamson. The opening lyrics are as follows:

> Promote yourself
> Look like a cunt
> Vodka parties
> Cushioned walls in a shit club
> I ain't bothered where it goes
> I gotta job
> I rot away in the aisles of the Co-Op mate, no prob,
> French Fancies
> Mr. Kipling Acid dances
> Let's laugh at local record plants
> Elitist hippies
> Arrogant cunts
> Ian Beale
> Tight trunks
> Tight pants
> Grammar wanker
> Walk the plank pirate manky
> Sixty kids where's mine?
> Wasting money on shit coffee all the time
> Fish fingers
> Take the batter off
> I can't believe you had kids
> Fuck off
> Jolly Fucker (x3)
> Mr Jolly Fucker

One may wish to argue that the lyrics are unified and rail against a particular representation of middle-class values, but in its performance, the frenetic pace of delivery and banal references give the impression of a "word salad." The energy of Williamson in live shows also echoes punk, as Laing wrote that "nearly all the bands established an identity and reputation through the live show . . . For punk rock, it seemed vital to maintain a fidelity to the live context within the recorded one" (Laing 1985, 53).

On "A Little Ditty," Williamson alludes to the artists of the Britpop era, and the perils of fame such as drugs:

> No hassle, doing beak like that with a kid at your mums
> Paramedics, you shoulda thought about that one
> Heart stopper, boom clear
> What happened to Richard, all I can see is gear
> Breathless, incinerate, processed cheese
> Become what you hate, become what we are
> A series one with dreams to reach a series four
> Drive, dive, six packs, drive, drive, white teeth, kit-kat
> Take the money and run, join the elite
> You sold yourself to no-one
> Pied piper, whiskey notes, the wonderwall fell down on you

"Beak" is slang for cocaine, and "gear" is also a reference to Richard Gere, and that the posh lifestyle of a "Richard" (associated with middle to upper class in the UK not to mention Gere's role in *Pretty Woman*) has declined through drug use. The "wonderwall" is a reference to the Oasis song from 1995, one of the signature tracks of the Britpop era.

Williamson describes the origins of the group: "I just wanted to rap and it came out like it did. Kinda accidental. You think, 'oh right that's not quite how I wanted to sound' and then thinking, 'Actually, that's quite good'" (Ellis 2014). Fearne writes of the writing process, "He'll probably have two verses and a chorus, and I'll have some loops. It's done really quickly. Once we did three tracks in a night. So it's kind of a super-punk rock essence of making music. When punk was about three chords and ''avin' it'—as it were" (Ellis 2014).

The music video for "Tied up in Nottz" opens with a shot of the city center of Nottingham, the clock of the Council House, which then moves to the protagonists buying cans of beer at a SPAR shop (from their point of view). We then see the two waiting to catch the bus on a damp, grey day. The song itself is first heard through Ferne's mobile phone, reflective of the way many youth cultures in the UK play and listen to popular music (see Bramwell 2015). Once they step on the bus, we get a view from their perspective, terraced houses, football fields, and shop fronts. The video therefore is framed by symbols of "the local," local shops, houses, playing fields, and citizens performing "everyday" banal activities, all of

FIGURE 4.1 Sleaford Mods, "Tied up in Nottz" (2014)

which symbolize English localism. We see the two members of Sleaford Mods at the back of the top deck of the bus, which oscillate with everyday images of the city outside the window (see Figure 4.1). The lyrics of the first verse are as follows:

> The smell of piss is so strong
> It smells like decent bacon
> Kevin's getting footloose on the overspill
> Under the piss-station
> Two pints destroyer on the cobbled floors
> No amount of whatever is gonna chirp the chip up
> It's the final countdown by fuckin' journey
> I woke up with shit in my sock outside the Polish off-licence
> "They don't mind" said the arsehole to the legs
> You got to be cruel to be kind, shit man
> Save it up like Norman Colon
> Release the stench of shit grub like a giant toilet kraken
> The lonely life that is touring
> I got an armful of decent tunes, mate
> But it's all so fuckin' boring

The lyrics reflect an engagement with double entendre and wordplay such as the "tied up in knots/Notts" of the title (Notts is the postal abbreviation for Nottinghamshire as well as slang term for the city), or the "bacon" of the second line being linked to Kevin Bacon and his film *Footloose* (but as metaphor for drunkenness). Though the '80s glam metal anthem "The Final Countdown" is actually by the group Europe, the misrecognition of Journey seems to comment more on the frequency of misrecognition rather than their own lack of knowledge, or perhaps a comment on the banal interchangeability of '80s hair rock bands. In any case, the lyrics and the imagery of the music video show a particular vision of British life, in this case, getting too drunk and waking up outside an "off-licence" (mainly-alcohol-selling) convenience store.

The YouTube comments below the video point to the reception of "Britishness" and to other musical frames of reference such as the Sex Pistols, The Fall, John Cooper Clarke, and Blur (see Table 4.1). Other UK rappers are mentioned such as Mike Skinner and Scroobius Pip as well as the age of the group ("mid-life crisis"), class identification ("new voice of the working class") and potential zeitgeist/demographic of the "austerity generation." Though these identifications will inevitably represent a disparate group of worldwide users, such comments get to the heart of the reception of the group and their representation of "Britishness" for many.

The lack of rhythmic regularity (apart from chorus material) as well as the lack of conventional singing on choruses stylistically add to the sense of anarchism and opposition to more mainstream forms of popular music, arguably "punk-ifying" rap through its irregularity of delivery. Their vocals represent opposition made audible, as punk did.

The song "Tiswas" discusses the "Dinosaurs on Denmark Street" as representative of the decline of rock music, and compares aspects of society to kids shows such as "Tiswas" and "Spit the Dog." On "The Corgi," Williamson laments the fact that the Queen's Corgis are treated better than her subjects. Rebellion is always at the level of the individual, small scale rather than speaking for a collective. It is a personal "fuck off" to individuals rather than a rallying cry for others to join the cause. On "You're Brave," he states, "nicked the biscuits. Wanked in the toilet . . . polish *that* you connoisseur" to his middle-class acquaintance. There is opposition to the middle and upper classes, those who are "poseurs," and to the government ("Like three months of rain, nobody likes a fuckin' Tory reign / The prime minister's face hanging in the clouds like Gary Oldman's Dracula" on "Liveable Shit"; "This is the human race, UKIP and your disgrace" on "Tweet Tweet Tweet"; "Cameron's hairdresser got an MBE / I said to my wife you better shoot me" on "Tiswas"). The right-wing UK Independence Party (or UKIP), is also the subject of Sleaford Mods's 2014 "Alternative Christmas Message," sponsored by the magazine *New Musical Express* (alternative to the Queen's annual Christmas day speech):

This year has seen the people's alternative grow stronger—UKIP. What fucking alternative? It's a message of class pride and guarantees in giving you a white

TABLE 4.1

YouTube Comments for "Tied up in Nottz"
"This is the most British thing ever"
"The best bit of British work I've come across in years"
"Well if the sex pistols were beamed up into a UFO and they went through a wormhole to eventually arrive back in the UK in good old 2015 I'm sure this is what they would sound like!!"
"Says everything about this country . . . sounds like something you would knock up Sat on the bog, pissed up on a really bad crate of stella"
"They made it looked like they are incredible lazy that's their thing they're calling out the bullshit of the world no artist has done that since scroobius pip or had that much anti-establishment passion since the clash . . . punk guitar riffs, hip hop breaks +spoken word=class tunes"
"It's all been done"
"Shane meadows-core"
"Best thing since sliced bread . . . +The Fall"
"This is the piss head that tries to make conversation when you go out for a fag"
"Remnants of the Streets" response: "no it definitely doesn't sound like the streets"
"Only English can provide this kind of music . . ."
"Sleaford mid life crisis"
"Britpop version of rage against the machine"
"Nottingham's gods of punk-hop. The new voice of the working class."
"Anyone else shout PARKLIFE after every line?"
"Charlie Harper meets Liam Gallagher as the Pet Shop Boys for the austerity generation"
"Like John Cooper Clarke vs The Streets."
"Thank you Sleaford Mods for being the realest band of this shitty age"

neighbour if you get these cunts into power. This has been the last straw in our tolerance of anything to do with English identity and its supposed values. Fuck my English identity. My identity is my creation and nobody else's. (Sleaford Mods 2014)

This was particularly important given the run-up to the 2015 General Election, many issues of which are featured on their album *Key Markets* (2015). UKIP's strict stance on immigration and desire to leave the EU have marked them as particularly xenophobic, conflating nationalism with xenophobia. As Williamson states, he sees

English identity as something he would rather eschew in favor of a more individual-istic, un-collective identity, aligned with the individualism found in punk aesthetics.

In addition to his skepticism toward the notion of an "English identity," Williamson also criticizes varying signifiers of Englishness, and by implication, overt flag-waving nationalism altogether ("Sat at the back of the bus with a noisy twat. St. George's flag twat" on "Liveable Shit" and "St. George's flag on white van" on "Tweet Tweet Tweet"; and condemning drunken hooligan violence by stating "Denouncing the value of somebody else's flag whilst viciously believing in theirs / Fuckin useless / This well-trodden street" on "Under the Plastic and NCT").

Class is a large theme in the lyrics in general: "Claiming family tax credits all your fuckin' life" and "The working class rears its ugly fuckin' head once more" on "Wack it up Bruv"; "Culture's for pricks" on "Tramp stamps and trendy bollocks"; "I can't believe the rich still exist, let alone run the country, mate," stated on both "Air condi-tioning" and "Black Monday"; "Shiny inventions, unobtainable for the real, obtain-able for the tits . . . big car, small life, that's just the way it is" on "Black Monday"; "I've got called an anarchist / That's for the middle-class trainspotters" on "Tiswas"; "I won't talk to nice people if they look rich. I know, it's not on, mate. I'm such a fuckin bitch" on "Under the Plastic and NCT."

Lyrics against the middle class have led interviewers to ask them of their own working-class ethos, of which they tend to reply that it wasn't the intention to speak to the working classes, but to simply describe their own personal experiences. Williamson states in one interview: "We're not socialists, we're not fucking com-munists and we're not Billy Bragg-ists. We're just talking about what we've been through. And we're doing it in a way that is just normal to ourselves" (Bychawski 2015). In this sense, they are aligned with hip-hop (and punk's) gravitation toward social commentary and critique, and grime music's lyrics as an ethnography of local conditions (Barron 2013).

Like the Sex Pistols, the Sleaford Mods critique becomes at once dissent and sym-bolic of the quintessentially "English." To cite Rivita (a brand of rye crackers), the wonderwall (representing Oasis and Britpop), Mr. Kiplings (mass-produced cakes), and the St. George's flag also means to draw attention to it. Its references form a bri-colage that existed most overtly in punk fashion, and is found more intra-musically in collage-style hip-hop production (e.g., The Bomb Squad). The everyday refer-ences and imagery of "Tied up in Nottz" creates a different type of nationalism from the flag-waving variety—a more banal nationalism that we saw in this book's first chapter.

To return to the associations of punk with whiteness, while Sleaford Mods are more than vocal about class, comments on race are usually absent, unless it is related to the ethnic nationalist views of political parties such as the English Defense League

(EDL) or the UKIP ("EDL twat. Tommy used to work on the docks. Union went all white. He fuckin' loved it. Take it down there, take it down there" on "Jolly Fucker"). The associations with the tacit whiteness of punk, and the color-blind "othering" of punk subculture, to quote Traber on LA punk:

> unwittingly repeats the ideological patterns of the dominant culture by privileging the importance of the self and self-interest, thus treating the Other as an object to be used for their own desires. Despite the call to be free from external influence, what LA punk shows is that without critically questioning our notions of the individual we take those discourses of the center with us everywhere we go. And this finally weakens punk's transgressive potential, for the individualism at punk's core forecloses the possibility of collective action that could more effectively challenge the problems they are protesting. (Traber 2011, 90)

The Sleaford Mods demonstrate their opposition to seemingly everything, showing their radical individualism on their sleeve through elements of punk aesthetics. Though some of their lyrics attack politics and class division, when asked in an interview if the songs demand change in the world, Sleaford Mods respond with a categorical "no" (Channel 4 News). They risk falling into similar traps as punk did, failing to exist outside the dominant racial culture,[17] and with their individualism masking the revolutionary potential of their message. In other words, while their rhetoric is filled with critique and social realism, it lacks a sense of social responsibility to accompany it.[18]

Lethal Bizzle

Born Maxwell Ansah in Walthamstow (London) to Ghanaian parents, Lethal Bizzle was an MC in the early 2000s grime scene with the More Fire Crew (whose hit "Oi" from 2002 was a top 10 UK single). He had his first hit single as a solo artist in 2004 ("Pow! (Forward)"), and subsequently rose to notoriety in the political spotlight to a certain extent for having a 2006 print media debate with then-leader of the opposition, David Cameron, responding to Cameron's criticisms of rap music as promoting violence (Bizzle 2006). Bizzle argued that rap empowers kids and that Cameron should work with them rather than lay the blame on young rappers. Cameron wrote a response to Bizzle's *Guardian* article in the *Daily Mail*, arguing that references to guns and knives in popular culture do indeed do harm (Cameron 2006; for an account see also Zubieri 2014, 188). It was around this time that Bizzle started to collaborate with groups like punk band The Gallows; such hybrids were being touted as a combination of grime and indie music, or "grindie" (Heawood 2006; see Zubieri 2010).

Grime is a predominantly black British musical form in its origins (Barron 2013; Bramwell 2015). It draws from earlier styles (like UK garage, dancehall, drum and bass, hip hop, and African-Caribbean MC traditions), was born on the estates of London in early 2000s, and initially distributed through mixtapes, pirate radio, and the internet (Jeff Chang called it "black Atlantic Futurism," 2004). Grime, according to Adams, shares punk's DIY ethos (2008, 481), and like punk, many grime artists participate in the successor to Rock against Racism, "Love Music, Hate Racism." Journalist Lloyd Bradley wrote, "it's called grime for the same reason punk was dubbed punk: in order to draw attention to its scuzzy street origins" (quoted in Adams 2008, 482).[19] In other words, grime could have only risen from the convivial multicultural hybrids of the postcolonial cities of the UK, just as hip-hop rose from the specific conditions of the post-"white flight" 1970s Bronx.

In 2007, Lethal Bizzle released "Babylon's Burning the Ghetto" on his second full length album, *Back to Bizznizz*. "Babylon's Burning" was a cover of the 1979 song by punk band The Ruts, released as a B-side to "Bizzle Bizzle," which was followed up by a rap cover of "Police on my Back," a 1968 song by the Equals also covered by The Clash (see Stratton [2013] for an extensive analysis of those three versions). The title itself invokes Rastafarian culture, as Babylon for them represents the Western world that has oppressed the African diaspora (including British imperialism and neocolonialism). It also invokes the materialism, inequality, repression, and sensual pleasures of the Earthly world, as opposed to Zion, the promised land and Heaven on Earth that Africa represents. The Ruts song is representative of punk's appropriation from and appreciation of reggae and Rastafarian cultures, now translated by Bizzle for the rap music context.

The music video invoked imagery of London Council Estates (the UK equivalent of "the projects"), with a young black individual watching television news of rioting and police in the streets. The boy gets angry, puts a hoodie on, and proceeds to throw the television out of the window. Imagery of burning, fights at the estate, and other violent scenes are located alongside Lethal Bizzle's rapping. The council estate, and violence within it, is presented as a symbol of the failings of society (of "Babylon"), and from the tone of the lyrics, the failings of the government to create a secure world for its people. The imagery resembles the tension and violence on the Council Estates depicted in the Franco Rosso 1980 film *Babylon*, which was about a group of Afro-Caribbean youths in London who ran a sound system and dealt with racism and police antagonism on a daily basis.

"Babylon's Burning the Ghetto" mentions reggae tropes of "war" and "emergency," and invokes criticism against both Tony Blair and David Cameron as not being effective leaders, and neglecting the plight of those living in the ghetto. He raps, "Tony said he'd make the world a better place but he lied, and when the war's on, all he does is hide." The single depicts a picture of Tony Blair holding a gun aimed at Bizzle. As one reviewer said, "the song itself is a furious tirade at British politics and society, from railing at both major parties and leaders . . . and their lack of attention to the wild and desperate 'outskirts' of society, propelled by seething beats and sirens" (McAlpine 2007).

Cynically speaking, and mentioned in the press at the time, the gesture of a rap cover of a punk song could be read as a desire to cross-over into the BBC mainstream (Petridis 2007). This criticism relies on the perceived racialized essentialism of the mainstream British pop music industry as white (with Radio 1 promoting British artists who are white), and that engaging with punk is an attempt to broaden grime's listenership to mainstream/whiter audiences (beyond the arguably racial ghettoization of artists on the BBC 1Xtra radio station, something discussed by Asian Network DJ Nihal; see Plunkett 2015 and BBC News 2015).[20] Bizzle's desire for success (and for Radio 1 morning play) can be seen on his video blog: one in particular (February 12, 2012) shows his excitement that his single was played by Fearne Cotton on Radio 1 before midday, something which had not happened for him in five years (bizzlevideos 2012). His desire for mainstream success is echoed by the lyrics on the album stating that he is trying to find a way to get on the cover of indie-focused music magazine *New Musical Express* (Petridis 2007).

But the cross-stylistic collaboration can also be read another way: grime culture was DIY, yet the rappers wanted to share it with the masses. Grime was not an insular subculture, but a generation of black English youth that felt a part of their surroundings. Grime was willing to embrace an expanded audience, to quote Lloyd Bradley, who compared the grime generation with previous first- and second-generation post-Windrush Black Britons: "while partly for pragmatic commercial reasons . . . like Soul II Soul before them, they saw themselves being as much a part of the UK as anybody else" (2013, 385).[21]

Lethal Bizzle's incorporation of punk music to his rap style may have served to expand his listening base, but another reason he did so was to insert himself into traditions of resistance, both traditions of Afro-Caribbean resistance in the '70s and '80s as well as the white punk traditions that responded musically to such events. In comparison to the praise Sleaford Mods received from media reception, Bizzle's experiment with punk had a more cynical reaction. One reviewer writes, " 'Babylon's Burning the Ghetto,' meanwhile, gamely attempts to splice the Ruts' 1979 hit with a hip-hop beat, but loses the original's urgency in the process. The result, alas, sounds like Limp Bizkit, while the lyrics reveal a grasp on current events you might best describe as shaky" (Petridis 2007). Another review states, "Nowadays, on planet Indie, Bizzle is ubiquitous. It seems as if the MC will champion any white boy in drainpipes in order to be accepted into what is now the epicentre of British pop music. This cross-genre pollination is risky" (Miller 2007). While the latter review does cite the album as successful given Bizzle's infiltration of indie clubs, Bizzle largely abandoned the punk and indie rock scene in subsequent albums, choosing to go back to grime roots songs, including the "Pow 2011" re-working of his 2004 hit.[22]

In addition to wanting to return to his grime roots (and fan base), another reason may be due to something observed by Rehan Hyder: "Interestingly, black musicians [e.g., Dub War, Audioweb] working within 'white' genres such as rock and metal have been frowned upon by the cultural essentialists, since they do not conform to a fixed and essential definition of blackness" (2004, 41). In light of this, is Bizzle's re-conformity to his original genre by returning to grime after this album because of such essentialized definitions of race and of genre? With reference to postcolonial melancholia, if Bizzle as Ghanaian-British is a reminder of the imperial past, perhaps "grindie" music is an uncomfortable reminder that these categorizations were always more complex than industry-defined genre systems would allow.

In another act of stylistic appropriation, Bizzle is credited with popularizing the term "Dench" (as from actress Judi Dench) to mean something good in hip-hop parlance. He first used it on record for his single "Dench Stamina" (2010) and now co-owns a Dench clothing line with his cousin, the footballer Emmanuel Frimpong (Bury 2013). One press release has Frimpong sounding the praises of actress Dench:

"What better way to celebrate Judi Dench's astonishing range of performances than with a range of lifestyle clothing made from quality fabrics," said Frimpong. "Myself and Mr Bizzle have been massive Judi Dench fans ever since we saw her moving performance as Lady Catherine de Bourgh, in the 2005 big screen adaptation of *Pride & Prejudice* and we simply had to express our admiration for Britain's best-loved actress . . . Lethal and I love Judi so much that we once spent a whole weekend watching the entire boxset of her tender early '80s sitcom, *A Fine Romance*. She truly is a national treasure. DEEEEENCH!" (quoted in Bloomfield 2011)

The origins of the term, as Bizzle has said elsewhere, may come from him playing videogames, or perhaps it derives from the word's proximity to "hench" (as in a physically imposing guy, i.e., a henchman).

Despite the haziness of etymology and likelihood it was all a joke anyway (from Bizzle or these journalists), the "black" appropriation of (tacit English) "whiteness" (covering punk songs, saying "oi," or invoking "Dench") turns the slave economy of the black Atlantic on its head in ways that complicate notions of Englishness. If we look at this through a Black Atlantic lens, such behavior has long been part of African-derived Signifyin(g) and trickster traditions (Gates Jr. 1988; Floyd 1995). And in the entrepreneurial spirit of grime (White 2018), he is profiting from this. Journalists writing about his clothing line, such as Bloomfield, write, "DISCLAIMER: We don't know if Emmanuel Frimpong or Lethal Bizzle really are fans of Dame Judi Dench, but we do know they have released their own range of 'DENCH' tees" (Bloomfield 2011). If we interpret this with a racialized lens, is Bloomfield essentially asking if young, BAME men could possibly be a fan of Dench's period dramas? (Bizzle and Frimpong will no doubt be aware of these racial assumptions in the humor of their statement.) Such a gesture, and ensuing reception, questions assumptions and engages with postcolonial anxieties in less-than-comfortable ways.

To quote Paul Gilroy, "Culture is conceived along ethnically absolute lines, not as something intrinsically fluid, changing, unstable and dynamic, but as a fixed property of social groups rather than a relational field in which they encounter one another and live out social, historical relationships" (quoted in Hyder 2004, 14). In many ways we need to consider methodologically the distinction between these ethnic cultural fixities (as social constructions with real consequences) alongside the messier complexities of everyday experience. The relationship between ethnicity and the everyday lived experience is an important realm for sociologists, but we also need to balance this with a close interpretation of these musical texts, however much they are essentialized, which also shape subjectivities. The realms of culture and everyday politics are engaged in a complex dance, and the residual culture of punk (and its racial associations), continue to hybridize with more current artistic forms such as hip-hop, transforming each other in the process. Or perhaps this hybridization is still challenged by the "frozen dialectic" between black and white cultures that Hebdige wrote about in '70s punk: "a dialectic which beyond a certain point (i.e. ethnicity) is incapable of renewal, trapped, as it is, within its own history, imprisoned within its own irreducible antimonies" (Hebdige 1979, 70).

Conclusion: The Limits of Genre Hybridity and Symbolic Resistance

The intersections between punk and rap represent a unique niche in pop that reflects issues of class, race, and notions of resistance in neoliberal Britain. While the niche is predominantly a male one, it is worth mentioning that there are some resistant female rap-punk examples such as Lady Sovereign's cover of the Sex Pistol's "Pretty Vacant" on the special edition release of *Public Warning* (2006—released only in the

UK). This is one part of a multitude of other genres outside of punk and rap that demonstrate similar notions of resistance. Although neither Sleaford Mods or Lethal Bizzle mention racial issues lyrically, the "absent presence" of race (Apple 1999; M'charek et al. 2014) is there, not least in the genres chosen to utilize and their racialized (and gendered, and class) associations.

The canonized and historicized elements of punk provide a bridge from the soundtrack to 1970s and '80s Britain under conservative rule and imperial decline, to the twenty-first-century Britain dealing with the aftermath (and continuation) of such political conservatism. Rather than attribute nostalgia to a resurging interest in punk as so many writers on Britpop and other British pop styles have in those contexts (see Bennett and Stratton 2010), punk music can be used to show what has arguably changed little socially and politically since punk's heyday. As the Sleaford Mods state on "The Corgi," "history repeats itself like BBC2."

The use of punk, musically, and in flow, lyrical content, and performance attitude gives it a sense of "roots music" for the Sleaford Mods that can lend ideological weight to their oppositional critiques. Sleaford Mods perform a unified anti-establishment statement in terms of lyrics, delivery, and music. Their reception aligns with frames of working class whiteness (Zubieri 2001, 21),[23] a stereotype which flowered after WWII, but existed long before in genres such as music hall (Peddie 2012).[24] Although music hall audiences tended to be a heterogeneous mixture of classes, members of the middle and upper classes believed it to be a genre authentically expressive of the working class.[25] As Peddie notes, "the staged manipulation of the image of the working class function to ensure that the meanings disseminated actually became part of the social identities of the working classes" (Peddie 2012, 130). In other words, performative depictions of working-class Englanders are indeed showing their working-class audiences how they should be, rather than the other way around.

For Lethal Bizzle, punk as signifier of opposition lends weight to his political and social critiques, while simultaneously placing him into an essentialized "white" resistant tradition partially based on black resistant inspiration from reggae. Bizzle is attempting to reach a wider audience through the syncretism of the "resistance vernaculars" of Multicultural London English dialect, rap style, and punk music. And as Zubieri writes, the English MC is defined by "code combining" rather than "code switching" (in Stratton and Bennett 2014, 191), engaged in a "multilogue" rather than dialogue with other cultures (Blake, quoted in Collinson 2010, 173).[26]

In both examples, we face two unavoidable problems regarding the radical and revolutionary potential of punk appropriations in rap music, similar to those that British punk faced in the 1970s and the early 1980s in Los Angeles. First, the individualism expressed through punk risks promoting a neoliberal interest in the self and reinforces the status quo or dominant ideology. While Sleaford Mods were universally praised and Bizzle's experiment met with skepticism, the outcome is the same: a reinforcement of the status quo rather than resistance to it. Birmingham's Centre for Contemporary Cultural Studies came to the same conclusion almost forty years ago—subcultural resistance was symbolic resistance only.

Second, despite the disruptive potential of such hybridity, cross-genre collaboration can further essentialize the genres used. Joe Strummer of The Clash once said: "This isn't white reggae . . . this is punk and reggae. There's a difference. There's a difference between a ripoff and bringing some of *our* culture to *another* culture" (quoted in Duncombe and Tremblay 2011, 7). But to paraphrase Duncombe and Tremblay, the cross-racial and cross-cultural solidarity explained by Strummer still "reinforces cultural and racial distinction." Even when trying to bridge the worlds, "you create fixed and essentialized categories" (2011, 7).[27] In other words, when you say your music mixes genre x and genre y, you are immediately essentializing x and y, even when one does not intend to. For the Sleaford Mods, a (white) punk identity is reinforced while Lethal Bizzle's cross-racial solidarity places his track in the black Atlantic's tradition of musical syncretism while nevertheless further essentializing such racialized genres.

Notes

1. Underneath the surface, there are of course a number of exceptions to this idea of punk musicians as only white (e.g., Bad Brains, Poly Styrene, Don Letts, Pure Hell, Death, Los Crudos, Fishbone, not to mention the hundreds of punk groups outside the Anglophone world), and *White Riot* (2011) shows both the challenges of being a non-white punk fan or artist as well as how diverse certain aspects of the scene are as does the 2003 documentary *AfroPunk*. From a slightly different angle, Brinkurst-Cuff (2015) argues that true punk rebellion has always existed in black culture, and points to punk elements in Death Grips, Bad Brains, FKA twigs, and that there has been a long history of punk traits like a particular "attitude" and counter-culture in black culture pre-punk.

2. My focus in this chapter is on English punk specifically, which is not to deny the substantial contribution of American proto-punk and punk bands such as The Kingsmen, MC5, The Stooges, New York Dolls, Patti Smith to the development of the genre. There are also important connections between hip-hop and punk in the early 1980s, not least Malcolm McLaren calling hip-hop the black punk rock in the period 1981–1982, but also British punks like Jon Baker who started the hip-hop label Gee Street Records, and Ruza Blue who co-promoted the parties at club Negril which first brought Bambaataa and Rock Steady Crew downtown. She would later run the Roxy with Jon Baker which was crucial for creating the media fad that helped hip-hop spread internationally (see McNally 2015; Lawrence 2016).

3. I am aware that many won't consider Sleaford Mods to be a hip-hop group or resemble hip-hop sonically. I would argue, however, that their influences from the rap world, as well as their

spoken word delivery over looped beats (that use punk sounds) place them at the edges of the hip-hop universe in some respects, while intersecting with a punk universe where they are much more centrally located, and more blatantly utilize punk's sonic signifiers and attitudes.

4. The Centre for Contemporary Cultural Studies was a research center in Birmingham (UK) from 1964 to 2002. Its scholars drew from the Marxist thought of Althusser and Gramsci, feminism, sociology, critical race theory, and provided a number of methods for studying culture. Important works include *Resistance through Rituals*, *The Empire Strikes Back*, *Feminism and Cultural Studies*, and *Policing the Crisis*. Stuart Hall was director from 1969 to 1979 and other important scholars associated with the center include Angela McRobbie, Dick Hebdige, Paul Gilroy, Hazel Carby, Paul Willis, Richard Dyer, and Lawrence Grossberg.

5. Stacy Thompson discusses punk cinema as a "identifiable aesthetic, bolstered with a correlative economics" (Thompson 2004, 64). She notes that punk cinema usually has an aesthetic that mimics punk music's speed, frenetic energy, anger, antiauthoritarian stance, irony, style, anomie, or disillusionment, and economically, a DIY ethic that focuses on modes of production, with punk filmmakers needing to become their own producers (Thompson 2004, 49).

6. As a musical style, punk music is much more diverse than the label implies, but as Gelbart notes, it is possible to isolate elements that were taken at the time "as guiding lights of punk" (Gelbart 2011, 234).

7. Raymond Williams discusses residual culture in relation to dominant and emergent culture. Residual cultural forms are "work made in earlier and often different societies and times, yet still available and significant" (1982, 204).

8. The place of the Sex Pistols and The Clash's brand of punk in the rock canon is well established, and many of punk's defining features can be seen through parody: on a 2013 *Saturday Night Live* sketch framed as an episode of a longer documentary entitled the "History of Punk," Fred Armisen played the character "Ian Rubbish" of fictitious band Ian Rubbish and the Bizzaros, an anti-authoritarian punk rocker who actually liked Margaret Thatcher. Rubbish, clearly a play on the name Johnny Rotten, was replete with Sex Pistols-esque musical and performative gestures (and bassist Steve Jones made a cameo), complete with a rebellious appearance on the Bill Grundy-hosted *Today* show. The punchline is that punks should be anti-everything, so it is shocking to find a controversial conservative leader the subject of songs named "Sweet Iron Lady" alongside side anti-monarchy songs like "Cunt in a Crown." What the parody shows is that the Sex Pistol's anti-authoritarianism toward English/British symbols help define punk to a non-UK, in this case, American (SNL), audience. It also shows the long-standing problematic relationship between punk and success/fame for a genre that so forcefully represents opposition.

9. This is also not to suggest that Sleaford Mods and Lethal Bizzle were the first artists to combine aspects of rock, punk, or metal with rap music. The Beastie Boys, as a former punk band, infused punk and elements of humor to articulate difference among other rap groups in the 1980s (Garrett 2015, 316). The Anthrax version of "Bring the Noise" (1991) with Chuck D is another example, and the genre of "Nu Metal" often included collaborations with rappers, or incorporated rap into their vocal styles (e.g., Korn, Limp Bizkit, Staind, Slipknot). Rap-rock hybrids such as music of Kid Rock could also be said to be exemplary of a fusion of rock and rap, in the spirit of songs like "King of Rock" (1985) by Run-D.M.C (see Kajikawa 2015, 65–71 for a longer discussion of this track). Kajikawa writes, "By engaging rock music directly, Run-D.M.C. did more than bring black music to a white audience. They helped scramble racialized genre codes to transform what rap songs could mean and to whom they could direct their messages" (2015, 65). Newer

bands like Milton Keynes's rap-metal band Hacktivist, active since 2011, have sustained the grime rap-metal hybridity to much success.

10. "This parallel white 'ethnicity' was defined through contradictions. On the one hand it centered, however iconoclastically, on traditional notions of Britishness (the Queen, the Union Jack, etc.). It was 'local.' It emanated from the recognizable locales of Britain's inner cities. It spoke in city accents. And yet, on the other hand, it was predicated upon a denial of place. It issues out of nameless housing estates, anonymous dole queues, slums-in-the-abstract. It was blank, expressionless, rootless. In this the punk subculture can be contrasted against the West Indian styles which had provided the basic models" (Hebdige 1979, 65).

11. What this shows, among other things, is that despite musical linkages between ska from Jamaica as an adaptation of R&B/rock and roll chord changes, and reggae and punk is that history shows how racial meanings associated with these styles shift in ways that do not neatly overlap with their sources.

12. "I would like to propose that Afrofuturism reflects a strategic version of what Gilroy first refers to as "anti-antiessentialism" in his article "Sounds Authentic: Black Music, Ethnicity, and the Challenge of a 'Changing' Same" (1991, 123–28) and later as "anti-anti-essentialism" in his *The Black Atlantic: Modernity and Double Consciousness* (1993, 96–110) (Rollefson 2008, 90–91). "As Gilroy sees it, essentialist arguments are of questionable political efficacy, but because of continued inequality it is not yet time for the free-floating identities of postmodernists. He writes: 'the unashamedly hybrid character of these black Atlantic cultures continually confounds any simplistic (essentialist or anti-essentialist) understanding of the relationship between racial identity and racial non-identity, between folk cultural authenticity and pop cultural betrayal'" (1993, 99)" (Rollefson 2008, 91).

13. Or to echo Banks and Toynbee on jazz, "Our aim, then, has not been to reduce jazz to any essential ethnic qualities or to reinforce spurious racial divisions, but to explore how such qualities and divisions—and the perceptible variations they include—come to occupy such central (and difficult and controversial) roles in the formation of, in this case, national jazz cultures" (Banks and Toynbee 2014, 108).

14. In the rap music context, Kajikawa (2015) has most convincingly explored the relationship between race and recorded rap music, in particular, discussing how artists like Eminem perform a notion of "whiteness" as a strategy for carving a space for himself in the rap industry, and how artists like Public Enemy, N.W.A., and Run-D.M.C. negotiate the idea of "blackness" sonically. In the British context, Toynbee, Tackley, and Doffman (2014) have theorized the complexities of race and music within black British jazz.

15. My thanks to linguist Steven Gilbers for helping me with this linguistic distinction.

16. "Roadrunner" is a song written by Jonathan Richman and recorded by his band the Modern Lovers. A version of "Roadrunner" was recorded by the Sex Pistols as a rough demo in 1976, and then overdubbed for the 1979 album *The Great Rock 'n' Roll Swindle*.

17. "Insisting that punk was more important than race didn't change the sizable degree of privilege Whites derived in mainstream and punk culture as a result of their skin color, language, and so forth" (Duncombe and Tremblay 2011, 11).

18. This is a similar sentiment to a journalist critique of punk by John Roderick in *Seattle Weekly* in an article entitled "Punk Rock Is Bullshit": "To the degree that punk has a governing philosophy, it's a fundamentally negative one. Punk only tells us what it hates. It has never stood for anything; it stands against things. It is not an intention indictment; it is a reactionary

spasm" (Roderick 2013). For Roderick, he notes that punk rock did not defeat Reaganism and Thatcherism or end the Cold War, nor did it prevent the "Imperial Bush dynasty" or prevent the commercialization of culture. While his article has come against opposition, not least those who point out that other subcultures have also not been able to accomplish these tasks, Sleaford Mods very much represent this anti-everything stance without any political solutions.

19. "But comparisons with punk begin and end with the shared DIY ethic because, whatever the cut of its trousers, punk was white men with guitars, looking to distribute their music widely and make money by touring. It made sense to the mainstream music business and was quickly assimilated. By contrast, grime's new underground remains more self-contained than punk ever allowed itself to be. Pirate radio stations are central to this genuine independence. In essence, the scene is a 21st century version of the sound system, the music medium that came to Britain on the Empire Windrush" (Bradley, quoted in Adams 2008, 482).

20. The ghettoization of the BBC's non-white artists onto 1Xtra reflects a wider trend for the promotion of "urban music" artists, and supporting those from ethnic minority backgrounds. To quote Kajikawa in the US context, "Although all kinds of people make and listen to rap music, the industry that produces it has tended to focus almost exclusively on cultivating and promoting black male artists" (Kajikawa 2015, 5). These sentiments were shared just before grime's mainstreaming around 2016 so the idea that grime is marginalized has been less true since Nihal's comments.

21. Lloyd Bradley writes, "What they had to offer—exactly as they wanted to offer it—was relevant to everybody else. This was the breakthrough in self-realisation that so many previous generations of London black music had not quite managed, and did a great deal to bolster grime's spirit of independence" (Bradley 2013, 385). "That kind of enabling self-confidence relied on financial security, which came from success, which brought greater self-confidence and led to increased success . . . Pretty quickly, grime had achieved a self-sustaining upward spiral, rooted in a commercial system that was so incredibly straightforward it was about as close to a meritocracy as is possible in the music business" (Bradley 2013, 385–86). Grime artists "pulled off such a coup not by adapting to the mainstream, but by dragging it along with them, and were able to do so because they virtually ignored it" (Bradley 2013, 377).

22. It is worth noting that the mid-2000s and early 2010s student town club night market was indie driven at a time when grime artists were being policed out of live performance. Form 696 was in effect from 2008 to 2017, a risk assessment form which the London Metropolitan Police requests promoters and licensees of events to complete and submit fourteen days in advance of an event in twenty-one London boroughs. The form asked numerous pieces of information, including the style of music performed (until 2009) and the likely ethnic makeup of the audience. The form was criticized as racist and had a real effect on grime artists being able to perform in London's live venues (Bramwell 2015). My thanks to James McNally for reminding me of this important point.

23. As Zubieri has written, the working class of kitchen sink dramas have been defined in cultural terms rather than explicitly political ones: "This may have been politically disabling but nonetheless has shaped the development of working-class subjects" (Zubieri 2001, 20).

24. Ian Peddie writes on the emergence of the East London costermonger stereotype (Albert Chevalier in the nineteenth century), the cockney and songs like "It's Nice to Be Common Sometimes" (1935) sung by Daisy Hill and written by George Ellis.

25. "The notion that the music hall offered authentic working-class expression was widespread and ensured that as a form of entertainment it was an important site of struggle. After all, as many critics have pointed out, Britain was a nation built upon 'cohesive inequality,' and there were many willing to invest time and effort in ensuring it remained that way" (Peddie 2012, 130). "Behind such sentiments, however, lay the dilemma of the experience of class and, crucially, how it would be represented. Ensuring that the 'common' was interpreted as a shared and palatable affirmation through which the meaning and image of what constitute appropriate notions of working class were contested. Consequently, songs such as 'It's Nice to be Common Sometimes' owed their very existence to the fact that by the time they appeared so much of the entertainment the music halls identified as threatening to the social order, especially anything approximating to class conflict, had either been purged or appropriated and reconfigured to the point where it had been emptied of much of its original potency" (Peddie 2012, 131).

26. "While British pop has developed in dialogue with America, it, 'has been since the 1950s as multilogue, a mixture of musics intersecting in the various urban centres to produce among other things various forms of British reggae; two-tone; Bhangra and Indi-pop; and indeed skiffle, punk and indie-pop; with all these being constantly subject to interactive evolution and reworking" (Blake, quoted in Collinson 2010, 173).

27. "But cross-racial, cross-cultural solidarity brings with it a big problem: it reinforces cultural and racial distinction. In recognizing distinction, even if the goal is to bridge the difference, you inevitably end up creating fixed, contrastable, and partially essentialized categories. In order for Black and White to Unite and Fight, to stand shoulder to shoulder in solidarity, each category has to be discrete and assigned a dissimilar character proper only to itself" (Duncombe and Tremblay 2011, 7).

> *Tommy: "Doesn't it make you proud to be Scottish?"*
> *Mark "Rent-boy" Renton: "It's SHITE being Scottish! We're the lowest of the low.*
> *The scum of the fucking Earth! The most wretched, miserable, servile, pathetic trash*
> *that was ever shat into civilization.*
> *Some hate the English. I don't. They're just wankers. We, on the other hand, are*
> *COLONIZED by wankers. Can't even find a decent culture to be colonized*
> *BY. We're ruled by effete arseholes. It's a SHITE state of affairs to be in, Tommy,*
> *and ALL the fresh air in the world won't make any fucking difference!"*
>
> —*TRAINSPOTTING* (1996)

5

POLITICS

"Colonized by Wankers": Performing the Scottish Independence Debate through Hip-Hop

TO SOME, *TRAINSPOTTING* was a stereotype. Renton's diatribe on national self-hatred, defined in opposition to England as perceived colonizer-oppressor, is presented against the backdrop of the Scottish countryside, as landscape is so often the synecdoche of national symbolism (Edensor 2002, 37). To others, it was an accurate representation of the failings of the Thatcher government, breaking Scottish stereotypes of tartanry and Kailyard romanticism in favor of a more banal, everyday sense of nationalism (Billig 1995; Zumkhawala-Cook 2008). Together with the "Braveheart effect" (Edensor 2002),[1] both *Trainspotting* and *Braveheart* (1995) raised the profile of Scotland internationally while fueling internal debates around Scottish identity and self-government. The successful 1997 referendum for devolution of powers to Edinburgh, and the establishment of a Scottish Parliament, only furthered these debates.

While both films essentialize some of the stereotyped "us" vs. "them" sentiments between Scotland and England, more nuanced debates continued after devolution regarding Scottish political representation and its capacity for self-determination in Britain and the EU (Scotland has been majority pro-EU whereas a slim majority of England's voters in the referendum voted to leave). In 2014, a referendum was held on independence for Scotland, led by the Scottish National Party (SNP). The

Brithop. Justin A. Williams, Oxford University Press (2021). © Oxford University Press.
DOI: 10.1093/oso/9780190656805.001.0001

British media often reduced the "Yes Scotland" campaign as reflective of "Scottish nationalism." In reality, however, it was a campaign that underplayed traditional nationalist symbols in favor of arguing for more political representation, in part, given the difference in politics between left-leaning Scotland and the ever-increasing right-wing Westminster government. The SNP promoted a "civic nationalism," more about citizens' rights and having a political voice than any ethnically defined nationalism or historical claims to Scottishness. Given these complex tensions and homologies between Scotland vs. England, or Scotland vs. Britain, hip-hop becomes a complex site where these identities are negotiated on the level of the individual and community. Murray Pittock has written that, in contrast to the cultural scene in England, "Scotland now marches to a different drum" (2008, 135). Just how that "drum" sounds within Scottish hip-hop is a particularly appropriate place to start.

Scottish hip-hop had a formidable role to play in the 2014 Scottish referendum on independence, and this chapter seeks to unpack some of the debates within while looking at accent, features in the music, and tropes of stereotype and humor. I investigate two case studies in particular: the group Stanley Odd's songs on independence and Loki's dystopian concept album *Government Issue Music Protest* (2014). These artists are only but two of other politically tinged Scottish rappers like Mog, and Louis from Hector Bizerk, part of a thriving scene in the 2000s and 2010s Scotland including Penpushers, Livesciences, bEINg emcees, and many others (Gieben 2018).

This chapter discusses the independence debate as performed in hip-hop which deals with issues of power, economics, stereotypes, and civic nationalism in a postcolonial era. I will show how these artists reinvent and subvert the notion of "Otherness" and minority identity by using humor and wordplay to critique stereotypes of Scottishness, Englishness, (African American) mainstream hip-hop, and most politically, the status quo. Stanley Odd and Loki address the referendum in different ways, but both utilize rapping as a folk protest medium by which to sound out their concerns and relevant debates surrounding independence.

A Brief History of Scottish Politics

The story of Scottish unionism in the modern era, and equally, the story of desire for home rule, begins with the Act of Union in 1707. Since the unification of various northern kingdoms in the ninth century, The Kingdom of Scotland has had periods of tension with their southern neighbor. Battles with the English ensued in the high and late middle ages, perhaps most famously in the thirteenth- and fourteenth-century events dramatized in *Braveheart*, specifically, the 1298 battle of Falkirk and 1314 battle of Bannockburn. In the twentieth century, the Scottish National

Party (founded in 1934) gained prominence in the 1970s, calling for a devolution of powers from Westminster. Devolution went to referendum in 1979 and failed, not because the vote was unsuccessful (it was a majority yes for voters), but the result did not achieve 40% of the total electorate. In other words, not enough people went to the polling booth for it to be effective, and this issue of voter apathy became a key point of contention before the 2014 referendum.

The 1980s under Thatcher was perceived as disastrous for the Scottish, with the closure of steel yards and pits hurting many local industries as but two examples. At the end of the 1980s, the Scots protested against Thatcher's introduction of the poll tax (a.k.a. Community Charge), in particular, that it was to be introduced in Scotland a year earlier than the rest of the UK. This added to a growing movement for Scots to have more power over their affairs. The shift to New Labour leadership in Westminster in 1996 helped to usher in a successful referendum on devolution in 1997. Scottish parliament began in 1999,[2] and the Scottish National Party became a majority government in Scotland in 2011.

Devolution has been interpreted both as an "intimation of necessary internal decolonisation" (Aughey 2013, 30) and part of a long cultural process where the "old imperial form of Britishness decays" (Gardiner in Aughey 2013, 30). The independence referendum in 2014 ultimately voted no 55% to 45%, but the campaign for independence brought a number of eloquent and creative voices together to discuss the benefits and drawbacks of British and Scottish political systems. Since at least the 1990s, when Alex Salmond became leader of the Scottish National Party, nationalism has been drawn on civic lines rather than ethnic ones (unlike the UK Independence Party; see Bhain 2012; Torrance 2014; Daisley 2015).[3]

Scotland can and has played into its "minority" status: after all, Scotland's population of five million people composes only 8% of Great Britain and Northern Ireland's total population (England is 84%). As a "stateless nation" [4] (McCrone 2001; McCrone and Bechhofer 2010, 923) or "nation within nation" (Smith 1986, 2001) it shares characteristics with Brittany, Quebec, Wales, Catalonia, and Cornwall. J. Griffith Rollefson has written on minority identity in Europe, and how the increasing appropriation of African American culture forms to help express such identities:

> In the transactions surrounding minority hip hop in Europe the American example has become something more than just a phase; it has become something iconic and universally assailable to a degree that the dominant modalities in which minority identities are now lived are American ones ... minority identity in Europe today is increasingly heard to be a matter of African-American music. (Rollefson 2008, 485)

It will come as no surprise, then, that hip-hop is used to voice Scottish indepen-dence debates. There are some issues with Scotland's claims to a "minority identity" given its history of unionism, role in British imperial history, and the overwhelm-ingly Caucasian ethnicity of the region performing a style globally associated with (usually African) diasporic peoples.[5] Nevertheless, for the Scottish context, minor-ity has less to do with ethnic-based definitions than in other world regions and more to do with population and representation in British government, bolstered by the shift in focus to civic nationalism (e.g., better services, less social and economic inequality, etc.).

To cite Sarah Hill's invocation of George Lipsitz on postcolonial musics for her study of Welsh hip-hop, the Celtic-ness and "stateless nation" status of Scotland place them in a "family of resemblances," for which marginalized people worldwide use hip-hop as medium. This "family" is defined as "persons located in historically marginalized communities within a dominant culture and they exploit their own marginalization as a means of self-empowerment" (Hill 2007, 183). The Celtic Diaspora could be a useful frame for political strategy, a "strategic essentialism" (Spivak 1996, 214) used to perform strong identities in nations like Wales, Brittany, Ireland, and Scotland.

Often, this family of otherness in hip-hop is defined ethnically—difference becomes a strong defining factor in the rhetoric of hip-hop, as the style was originally conceived as African American music which could be compared to the subaltern states of other ethnic minorities in a given country (e.g., Turkish German, French African, or aboriginal Australian). Race and hip-hop are often intertwined, follow-ing Schloss's quote that "The rules of hip-hop are African-American, but one need not be African-American to understand or follow them" (Schloss 2004, 10), though in light of Rollefson's observation, the use of African American identity often puts global rap in a family of resemblance defined, in part, by minority ethnicity. Given the wide Anglo-Saxon population of Scotland, however, otherness is performed via other means, yet one might argue that othering is a less important feature in the independence debate than the fight for political representation.

It is also possible to frame Scottish hip-hop as part of a wider nexus of "Yes" campaign creativity, and within the long history of Scottish protest song. From the Jacobite songs in the eighteenth century against the Acts of Union to the nationalis-tic poetry of Robert Burns set to music ("Scots wa Hae"), there was often a national-istic stream in Scottish song under union. There also existed mid-nineteenth-century songs supporting home rule, including criticism of Scottish MPs too concerned with London and English issues (Dossena 2013). Worker protest songs in the early twentieth century from the Red Clydesiders were recorded in their *Proletarian Song Book* (1923), similar to the *Little Red Songbook* (Dossena 2013).

In the 1960s, the campaign against Polaris, Britain's first submarine based nuclear weapons system, operated by the Royal Navy and at Clyde Naval Base (which continued until 1996, and was then replaced by Trident), resulted in protests by the Glasgow Song Guild and their most famous "Ding Ding Dollar" (Scots Language Centre). "Both Sides of the Tweed" was a protest song against Union written by Glaswegian folk singer Dick Gaughan after the 1979 devolution referendum. The Proclaimers in 1988 questioned Scotland's lack of political autonomy in "Cap in Hand" ("I can't understand why you let someone else rule this land, cap in hand"), a song that became the number one download in Scotland in September 2014, and in "Letter to America" (1987) they lamented the loss of a number of industrial factories and jobs, part of a long tradition of Scottish emigration songs.[6]

There were musical demonstrations against poll tax in the late 1980s (including early hip-hop songs against the tax—"Demonstrate in Mass" by Sugar Bullet and "The Frontal Attack" by Dope Inc, both from 1991, see Hook 2018, 97), and older musicians in pro-independence concerts in 2014 reminded audiences that they had also performed in those earlier demonstrations (English 2014). In finding and using a previous generation's political discontentment (Zamora's [1997] idea of the "usable past") we have the possibility to eschew a longer history of unionist sentiment (Marsden 2014). As Ian Peddie reminds us, music does not protest by itself in a vacuum—music is made to be protest music via the meanings that audiences and performers give them. Peddie writes, "Always socially produced, music is *made* political or revolutionary. Contextually defined, often tactical in its immediacy, and antithetical in its challenge to the status quo, music obtains its meaning and effect from the social milieu in which it is produced, disseminated and interpreted. In short, music never 'is,' rather it becomes" (2012, xiii).

For the 2014 independence debate, music was often used to supplement humor-based perspectives in both mainstream media and independent video sharing. Zara Gladman, under the name "Lady Alba" performs a parody of Lady Gaga's "Bad Romance," sarcastically taking the position of a no voter, and the reasons why they want to stay in a bad romance ("I want your weapons, I want student fees, I want a country run by Tory MPs, I'm voting no" . . . "I like being told what to do" "gonnae no [don't]"). The user "Yew Choob" ("choob" as the phonetic spelling of "tube" in Scots dialect and as Scottish vernacular for idiot) created parody videos including "We didn't start the Union," to the tune of Billy Joel's "We didn't Start the Fire," in a similar historical narrative as the Joel original, but recounting the history of Scotland, ending with a prediction of a yes vote in for Independence in 2014. In the mainstream, Sky News created a video of Scottish National Party Leader Alex Salmond edited to sing "I Want to Break Free" by Queen; "Better Together" campaign leader Alistair Darling singing Rick Astley's "Never Gonna Give You Up";

and Prime Minister David Cameron singing Taylor Swift's "We are Never Ever Getting Back Together." This independent video sharing fad to "songify" the news and other speeches with auto-tune had clearly now crossed over into more formal news programming.

There is a risk that using humor to frame what is a serious political situation will undermine or make light of the independence referendum, but this is in a longer tradition of irony, sarcasm, and parody used for political message in Scotland and wider Britain. "Satire in general, whether on talk shows, in cartoons, or songs, has become more politically effective than editorials or speeches in changing mass political opinion" (Rodinsky in Peddie 2006, 26–27). As we will see in more detail in the next chapter, humor is both a distancing mechanism and a powerful weapon to assert and question identities. The Sky News examples use the long-running trope of England and Scotland as lovers in a relationship (as we will also see with Stanley Odd), citing classic songs which allude to such relationships. Gladman, on the other hand, decides to play the persona of the oppressor in parody, the colonizer or unionist supporter, to mimic and mock the assumptions of staying in such an unbalanced relationship. The use of John Williams's "The Imperial March" (from *Star Wars*), which was played from bicycle in Glasgow to accompany Scottish Labour MPs meeting in Glasgow, shows a use of pre-existing music in protest. The YouTube user "Empire Biscuit"[7] shouted "Welcome Imperial masters" repeatedly to the soundtrack (posted September 11, 2014) to the annoyance of the MPs. Both Empire Biscuit and Zara Gladman use pre-existing song, with attached associations, but provide new meaning, an idea of "creative adaptation" which is crucial to a number of protest movements (including the student protests in Tiananmen Square; see Samson in Peddie 2012, 540).[8]

Both humor and other cultural responses of protest and social movements powerfully shape and redefine cultural action itself, providing collective identity with new meaning. Eyerman and Jamison most effectively set out this position vis-à-vis the relationship between social movements and culture:

> Our claim is that, by combining culture and politics, social movements serve to reconstitute both, providing a broader political and historical context for cultural expression, and offering, in turn the resources of culture—traditions, music, artistic expression—to the action repertoires of political struggle. Cultural traditions are mobilized and reformulated in social movements, and this mobilization and reconstruction of tradition is central, we contend, to what social movements are, and to what they signify for social and cultural change. (Eyerman and Jamison 1998, 7)

To translate this into the context at hand, the "Yes Scotland" campaign, and groups like National Collective[9] were reshaped and formed by culture while they also were active agents in creating and shaping the cultural responses to the Scottish Independence referendum debates. The two intertwined arenas flexibly and fluidly shape each other, and despite the fact that the referendum upheld the status quo politically, the cultural and political spheres are forever changed by the social movement and the art that inspired and was a byproduct of it.

Stanley Odd

Formed in 2009, Stanley Odd is a musical group based in Edinburgh. Led by the frontman rapper Dave "Solareye" Hook, they are most often categorized as "alternative hip-hop." Their sonic palate is highly varied, with female vocal hooks, sampling, and an emphasis on live performance. Hook completed a PhD (2018), which was an autoethnography of his work, and his work points out the themes of marginality and outsiderdom in their music (2018, 70–85), as well as a chapter on their Scottish independence songs (2018, 95–120). Issues covered in the songs, written between 2011 and 2014, include "sovereignty, the legacy of colonialism, social justice and equality, to economic structures, community and democratic models" (96).

The track "Antiheroics" from the 2012 album *Reject* directly addresses the Scottish independence debate (Hook 2018, 100–102):

> All these questions about government
> Do we show a first foot or a stiff upper lip?
> Are we Antiheroic or frantically stoic?
> Got emotion but can't seem to show it?
> On the breadline or standing below it?
> I'd rather dance with the poets than bank on a bonus
> Government centre: is it London or Edinburgh?
> Leaving the franchise or emptying the register?
> Fighting the power or shooting the messenger?
> Is it Saxons, Romans or Viking oppressing us?
> I mean how far back do you go historically?
> Hunting and gathering, farming and foraging?
> Rule Britannia, cool Britannia, cruel Britannia
> Do you want to stay the full Britannia?

The chorus immediately follows:

> This is pure. Anti. Hero. Material.
> Most of the people that I know don't really vote

From homeland agents to home invasions
It's all changing at the polling stations.
It's Pure. Anti. Hero. Material
Sing it on the terraces like "here we go. Here we go"
If you do nothing you can't say change is overdue
so let yir feet do the talking at the voting booth

Solareye's comments about "how far do you go back historically" acknowledges the moving target of historiography, and the flexibility of the subaltern role depending on the perspective of the oppressed or oppressor. Though the CD liner notes place his lyric as "full Britannia," his accent also would suggest a double meaning as to some listeners it will sound like "fool" Britannia. The chorus points to voter apathy and aims to rally the community around voting, and emphasize the everyday nature of voters singing from the "football terraces," as "here we go, here we go" is a chant sung at matches. In other words, if such enthusiasm can be expressed in sporting fandom, then Scots should encourage voting with a similar enthusiasm.[10] "Fighting the power" is itself an intertextual reference to US rap group Public Enemy's famous 1989 song, used in Spike Lee's *Do the Right Thing*, one of the most powerful and most recognized protest songs in an era where US rap was at a peak of black nationalist protest.

The list of questions provides a sense of ambivalence while pointing out two sides of the debate. About Scottish National Party leader Alex Salmond, he asks of the "big fish in small pond": "Is it King Alex the Enslaver or Alex the Emancipator?" Solareye raps about the national stereotypes that the Scottish have had to suffer, and balances it with the English ones:

Of course we're all junkies and alkies
With Victorian maladies kept in smack by Southern Salaries
Using rudimentary tools and making cave drawings
Days spent in crack dens train spotting
Parasitic, cancerous, sponging off philanthropists
That's why the NHS needs Lansley to dismantle it.[11]
Well if that's what you'd call truthfulness
Then the South is all skinheads and football hooligans
Waving St. Georges flags, towie-types,[12] and wags[13]
Lock stock and cockney rhyming slang
Thugs and privately educated tory toffs[14]
With a shared affinity for tea and xenophobic thought.
All these assumptions lack any insight
I'm in surround sound and they're the stereotype

The lyrics reference a number of features associated with England: tea, the National Health Service, St. George's flag, cockney rhyming slang, and the long-held stereotype of the cockney East London costermonger which was developed as far back as music hall in the nineteenth century (see Peddie in Peddie 2012). The idea of the Scot as alcoholic or junkie, intellectually backwards, and sponging off the financial resources of its Southern neighbor is also presented alongside the English stereotypes. *Trainspotting* is alluded to, in contrast with the reality tv show *The Only Way Is Essex* and the Guy Richie film *Lock, Stock and Two Smoking Barrels*. There is also an element of humor as well as wordplay ("bank on a bonus" or "I'm in surround sound and they're the stereotype"), as Solareye criticizes those who don't wish to vote for fear their data will be used elsewhere, yet blindly use websites like Amazon and Facebook:

> They say if you register to vote yi get trapped in the database
> better stockpile identities, cutting passports with razorblades
> And the census was just another way to appear on the radar, caught
>   in the big brother state.
> Let me get this straight,
> you won't vote to conserve personal data management[15]
> But still have a facebook page and buy stuff on Amazon?
> Of course we're being watched. It's a modern fact.
> Putting an X in the box says yir watching back

Wordplay,[16] irony, and humor questions those aforementioned essentialisms and simultaneously create a separate yet overlapping sphere of culture—creating a unique stylized space which intersects with hip-hop culture quite forcefully, but translates it into its own. Finland may be a particularly interesting parallel, as the first wave of Finnish hip-hop involved a lot of humor, essentially "comedifying" rap.[17] A key characteristic of Finnish discourse being to treat things not so seriously as compared to US models: "Here once more the point is not whether or not this is so, but that in this way Finnish-ness becomes constructed in a certain way—and this Finnish way, so to speak, is based on essentialized and canonized notions of the nation and its people as being somehow more humorous than the 'original' representatives of rap" (Kärjä 2011, 85–86). Scottishness in Scottish rap was not constructed in the same way as Finnishness was for first generation "Suomirap," but humor did become a distancing element for Stanley Odd and other Scottish rap groups who felt less related to the American mainstream rap scenes.

"Antiheroics" ends with a descending harmonic minor progression reminiscent of lament, with a double-tracked string quartet—two violins, viola, cello—playing over the chord sequence. The verse material consists of C minor and G minor, oscillating every two measures. Given that the two minor polarities do not create a strong pull to the C minor tonic (as a G major dominant V chord would), perhaps this is representative of the ambivalence or difficulty weighing up two sides of the argument. But at the end of the track the "lament" plays eight full times for over two minutes, changing the emotional tone of the song. The chords cm cm/B♭| cm/ A♭ cm/G| fm cm/E♭| G7/D cm essentially create a natural minor descending scale in the bass. The G7 also adds weight to the dominant pull back to C minor in ways that we did not hear on the verse and chorus. On the one hand, the gesture of lament could be read as drumming up emotion for the cause. After the referendum result, the lament could be heard as a lament for the "Yes Scotland" campaign itself and its values. "Antiheroics" demonstrates the complexity of the debate depending on one's perspective, while advocating for a more toned-down, less stereotypical discussion of national values. In the end, perhaps the lament is for those who do not vote, and the negative effects of the consequences of voter apathy.

The track "Marriage Counselling" from the same album decides to use the trope of Britannia and Caledonia as personified and in a relationship (see Figure 5.1).[18] They write letters back and forth to each other, in the style of Eminem's "Stan" (2000). Lines such as "PS Half of me doesn't want to leave you," "I don't need you to fight ma battles for me, So tell yir mates in Faslane they need a new address,"[19] and "I've got the same group of friends as you, so stop implying that if you were to get shot of me France, Germany and Spain wouldn't talk to me," personify the relationship in a clever and tongue-in-cheek manner. Britannia responds, and includes the line, "Since Culloden, it's been like a constant battle," referring to the final Jacobite uprising in the years 1745–1746.

FIGURE 5.1 Stanley Odd, "Marriage Counselling" (2012)

Britannia alludes to the Scottish stereotypes:

> Bitch bitch moan moan. Give me a break,
> All you ever seem do it complain.
> Maybe it's all that booze in your brain
> Or your woozy again from the smack running through your veins
> You're nothing but a drain on me and it's plain to see
> You've developed more unhealthy habits that I need to pay to keep.
> Basically you need stop your foolish ways
> Stop pulling away and start pulling your weight.

Caledonia responds:

> Pulling ma weight? Who do you think yir talking tae?
> This is exactly what's making me want to walk away.
> I'm tired of stating all ma reservations.
> I think we should maybe try a trial separation.
> You're blatantly economic with the facts.
> Arrogant, self-centred, living in the past.
> Reliving your former glory most days now.
> Back when you were the biggest bully in the playground.
> A shadow of your former self and it's plain to see.
> You're falling apart and trying to put the blame on me.
> I used to make things, inventions, you curbed my creativity.
> You held me back, injured me by ending ma industry.
> All I'm saying is the balance in the relationship isn't right.
> Either change or I'm leaving, it's decision time.

The lines "Arrogant, Self-centered living in the past, / reliving your former glory most days now, / back when you were the biggest bully in the playground" echo Gilroy's critique of postcolonial melancholia (Gilroy 2004). Reducing political tensions to the metaphor of a relationship perhaps additionally helps to emphasize the "everydayness" of the debate.

One crucial element to the track is that the sonic landscape changes between Caledonia and Britannia. Both beats have a similar drum figure and harmonic underpinning, but Caledonia's verses have a lighter synth texture in a higher register, which also accompanies Solareye's more optimistic verbal delivery (he can be seen smiling in the music video, whereas Britannia does not). Britannia's sonic world has a low pitch, minor-mode descending figure, which could be interpreted as more villainous, and Solareye's delivery as Britannia is a calmer, but more patronizing delivery. The video shows the two on either side of a black line, with Caledonia wearing a Diadora-made Scotland t-shirt and Britannia on the other side wearing a white t-shirt with the Union Jack Flag and a baseball cap with "OBEY" on it.[20] Through multi-accentual, theatrical vocal delivery and soundscape (similar to Akala's "The Thieves Banquet" in Chapter 3), it is clear that Caledonia's is painted in a more optimistic light, while lyrically both sides of the argument are again represented, perhaps more overtly so than "Antiheroics."

After *Reject*, their album *A Thing Brand New* (2014), featured the track "Son I Voted Yes," which is a letter to Hook's son explaining why he voted yes in the referendum. Harmonically simple with sparse piano chords and a vocal hook, the quasi-lullaby stays out of the way of the lyrical message, which discusses when he was young and Scots were protesting against Thatcher and notes a wider history of pro-devolution protest. The lyrics suggest a brighter future ("Cause a yes vote provided hope"), and tries to point to the values and reasons for voting for independence:

> This isn't about the colour of skin
> Or where you were born, or who you call kin
> It's about pure and simple geography
> And caring for everyone responsibly
> It's about people facing poverty with immunity
> And building and supporting our communities
> Too many people want off the path we're following
> It's time to change how we "do" politics
> Responsibility and independence
> Leading by example of the messages we're sendin'
> Character traits we hope for our kids one day
> So why wouldn't we want it for our country?

The first lines suggest the civic nationalism over ethnic nationalism espoused by the Scottish National Party, and fetishize place over "blood" claims to citizenship. In Hook's words, it was a "counterargument to the nationalism of ethnicity and land ownership" (Hook 2018, 109). The song states the importance of localizing power, and the responsibility nations should have for caring for its citizens. The comparison with having traits for children and for country help to frame the generational arguments (and an earlier verse explains when Solareye was his son's age they had a "wicked witch of Westminster" and saw graffiti that read "no poll tax"). He acknowledges some of this ambivalence again by stating that "the older you get the less you see things in black and white," and that a yes vote wouldn't solve everything, but that he didn't want another lost generation of youths angry with their parents for the decisions they made. The video of the song, which shows Solareye writing the lyrics in pencil in a notepad (see Figure 5.2), went viral and has seen 231,000 views on YouTube as of this writing (Rimmer 2015), a large number for independent regional UK rap.

Musically, the eight-measure chord progression is repeated throughout the song, each chord lasting one measure, and falls squarely on beat one of each bar: D–D/F#–G–D–G–D–A–D (I–I$_6$–IV–I–IV–I–V–I). The song opens with an opening chorus and piano chords no more complex than major triads and in the upper half range of the piano (giving the accompaniment a childlike quality), and the vocals add syncopation to the otherwise one-a-measure downbeat harmonic rhythm. The melody of the chorus covers the range of a sixth, but it focuses mostly on first, second, and third scale degrees of D major, which also adds to the quasi-simplistic quality. While the subject of Solareye's address is his own son, the song was released on September 3, around two weeks before the referendum took place, and thus became a political message which could be targeted to still-undecided voters.

Stanley Odd's lyrics represent a complex engagement with both sides of the independence debate. Solareye addresses stereotypes with an element of humor to highlight their absurdity. Using the past history of Scottish protest for home rule, as well as personification and metaphor are also techniques to critique the status quo. For "Son I Voted Yes" the tropes of melodic and harmonic simplicity, with an emphasis on vocals, help give it an honest and confessional feel, and the primacy of the lyrics help to get the message across (seemingly) unmediated. The vocal delivery of the song was more spoken than rapped. Hook describes the song as "A subtle manifesto,

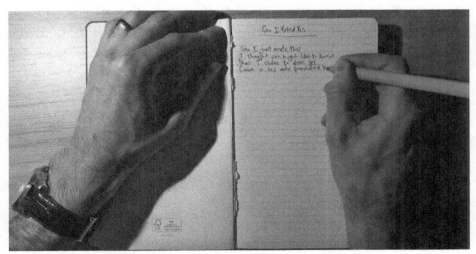

FIGURE 5.2 Stanley Odd, "Son I Voted Yes" (2014)

(w)rapped up in a poem; a protest song masquerading as a nursery rhyme; a case for change and an honest letter to my son. My rap persona is different, more gentle, addressing a child, explaining complex issues in simple terms using child-like imagery related to fairytales and children's stores. This is all intentional" (Hook 2018, 110).

Scottish accents (Hook 2018, 45–50), local and national, could be heard as a resistance vernacular in contrast to "toned-down" Scottish accents often used by Scots working in England and pro-union Scots such as Gordon Brown and Alistair Darling. The resistance vernacular is potentially bolstered by hints of Multicultural Youth English (which incorporate elements of Jamaican, American, and other dialect; Kerswill 2013, 2014), such as the way Solareye says "rrregister" or "aggrrression." It's the language of postcoloniality and can be a powerful cohesion and distancing mechanism.

Referring to historic battles and Scottish slang ("Choob," "gonnae no") is another intertextual element which emphasizes Scottish identity. Given the tone of Solareye's critique, it is a form of banal nationalism (Billig 1995) which may seem at first glance to not take itself too seriously. If overt nationalism is partly defined by its national heroes, then banal nationalism is filled with the "antiheroes" of social realism and everyday life.[21] National identity as it plays out in the everyday, less flag-waving, version becomes a careful balance between reinforcing those aspects which define the nation, and performing a sense of identity that dismisses or denies the existence of national traits. (See Chapter 2 for a wider discussion of British nationalism in rap.) "Antiheroics" and "Marriage Counselling," in particular, reflect on the national misrepresentations and stereotypes between Scotland and England, with "Son I Voted Yes" providing the more clear-cut argument in favor of independence. While Stanley Odd do not use the colonial critique of *Trainspotting*, for example, ("we're the scum of the Earth," could be compared to Franz Fanon's *Wretched of the Earth*, the 1961 study of the dehumanizing effects of colonization),[22] Stanley Odd's lyrics do have a postcolonial awareness of inequality in terms of national representation, and espouse the civic duty to vote. Related to the latter, the desire for self-government is where Scottish civic nationalism and "Son I Voted Yes" are in alignment.

Loki's Dystopia: Government Issue Music Protest (G.I.M.P.)

In his book on science fiction, utopia, and dystopia, Tom Moylan writes that "Dystopian Narrative is largely the product of the terrors of the twentieth century. A hundred years of exploitation, repression, state violence, war, genocide, disease, famine, ecocide, depression, debt and the steady depletion of humanity through the buying and selling of everyday life provided more than enough fertile ground for this fictive underside of the utopian imagination" (Moylan 2000, xi). As Laura Miller has noted, dystopian fiction is for the purpose of warning us about dangers of some current trend. She writes, "This is what will happen if we don't turn back now, they scold" (Miller 2010). Writing about the features of the dystopian young adult novel, April Spisak sees "a vivid and well-described setting" as well as "a strong protagonist who has been shaped by his or her current situation" and "a dismal conclusion that leaves the reader feeling slightly uneasy" (Spisak 2012). These features not only fit the young adult dystopian novel (e.g., Collins's *Hunger Games*, Roth's *Divergent*), but appropriately fits the features of Loki's Scottish dystopian hip-hop concept album, *Government Issue Music Protest* (2014).

Government Issue Music Protest (or *G.I.M.P.*) by rapper / journalist / blogger / activist Loki (Darren McGarvey) was crowdfunded on Indiegogo, and released on 5 November (Guy Fawkes Day[23]) 2014, and was a concept hip-hop album depicting Scotland's future in 2034 if the majority voted no in the independence referendum. Loki has been part of the Glasgow hip-hop scene for a number of years. In the mid-to-late 1990s, while a teenager, he developed his rap style under the mentorship of the first wave of Scottish hip-hop acts such as Big Div, Sace, Defy from 2-Tone Committee (Gieben 2013). He has been extremely active on the Scottish hip-hop battle scene (e.g., Don't Flop Scotland), and at the time of this writing, has written seventeen albums since 2003 (selling all of them on Bandcamp). In the mid-2000s he wrote and presented eight programs for BBC Radio Scotland that examined the root causes of anti-social behavior and social deprivation. In 2012 he co-wrote the National Theatre Scotland production *Jump*, and has appeared as a commentator on STV's *Newsnight*, *Question Time*, and other programs. He is also a community leader, as founder of programs that enable young people in charge of the services they use. He has reached national visibility after rehabilitation from alcohol addiction, re-emerging onto a thriving Scottish hip-hop scene in the early 2010s. His 2018 book *Poverty Safari*, an account of systemic poverty and what it does to communities, was the recipient of the Orwell Prize for political writing in the same year.

More than the extensive album art that is included with the album, the lyrics of *G.I.M.P.* paint a picture of "New Glasgow" in 2034, "the world's first mega city" dominated by a giant tower for the professional classes, surrounded by slums. Retirement has been outlawed, creativity must be approved by government license, and genetically engineered wasps have been spreading "paganda virus," which destroys human beliefs and values. The National Health Service has gone private, missing children have become an epidemic, people are over-medicated, and like Orwell's vision of the future, the media constructs truths that serve specific political purpose. Loki plays a journalist in the story, and by the end of the album, discovers the missing children in a huge factory sweatshop alongside other disturbing imagery. Moylan had also pointed out that the twentieth century began as capital "entered a new phase with the onset of monopolized production and as the modern imperialist state extended its internal and external reach" (Moylan 2000, xi). In other words, one could say that dystopia is also a product of postcoloniality while having the potential for urgent contemporary political critique. This can also be heard in the news report that Palestinians are continuing to wander the globe to find a home, while the Israeli executive is given the Nobel Prize (see Appendix for all news reports on the album). Palestine, for many British rappers, becomes both real and symbolic representation of postcolonial inequality (and Mandatory Palestine was created by the British after WWI until 1948). The focus on labor here is an important theme, and he points out current inequalities and exploitation in a powerful way, similar to Banksy's famous critique of working conditions for Korean animators in his commission of the opening to The Simpson's "Money Bart" episode in October 2010.

The album opens with "The End" when Loki decides to hijack a government drone in order to destroy the New Glasgow tower, set to a sample from Philip Glass's soundtrack to *Koyannasquatsi* (dir. Geffrey Reggio 1982). Loki raps, "This is someone who is prepared to die for a democracy." Therein we have the morally ambiguous line between "terrorist" and "hero." Musically the album includes a variety of soundscapes, multiple genres including softer acoustic guitar tracks, classical string soundscapes, and samples of speeches from Alan Watts and comedian Bill Hicks.[24] The collage of styles and sound sources used, as well as the album's framing with numerous news reports which help paint the picture of dystopia, give it the atmosphere of a post-hip-hop album, eschewing both the sonic and linguistic tropes of Hip-hop Nation Language. The identifiable Glaswegian accent of Loki adds to the album's localism while the polystylistic soundscapes add to the "concept album" categorization.

On track 7, "The Unimportance of Being Idle" (produced by Sace from II Tone Committee), the listener receives the most overt debate over Scotland and Scottish independence between Loki and a dinner party guest who represents a more right-leaning member of society. There is additionally a tension when the guest calls Loki "working class." Equally, the dinner party guest espouses stereotypes of the middle-class or upper-class who have little concern over social problems like homelessness:

DINNER GUEST: My life partner has finally forgiven my smarmy past.
    Put the cords down I'm sick of wearing Aldi bags.
    She untied me from the cooker I'm like "Yaldi, Yas,"
    then she fucked my ass in a black Peter Capaldi mask.
    I'm a modern man who indulges razzmatazz.
    Acid jazz takes the edge off of Alcatraz.

I am free to purchase hats and pajama pants
and I have a right to assemble simple cabinet packs.
I'm meetin ya at half three for a chai tea after my tai chi
I have a social media degree and I buy brie.
A homeless man collapsed and died on my way to high tea, why me?
I take pride in how I look now I'm tanning good.
Trying to do my bit by purchasing organic food.
So sick of my dad going on about Ayn Rand,
I just wanna jam with my live band.

LOKI: So wicked and devilishly false is that common objection:
they are poor because they are idle, interjection.

DINNER GUEST: I'm all for welfare helping the vulnerable, but alcoholics and junkies,
single mothers with big families, pensioners that didn't save and young people that
never stayed in school, I don't think much of them.
On their leather couches smoking fags watching wide screen televisions with central
heating and seven children.

LOKI: Aren't you just a feat of conventional wisdom.
How intellectual of you.
I can't tell you how relieved I am that people like you form the regrettable prism
through which politicians view our electoral system.

DINNER GUEST: Sorry not following, please elaborate.

LOKI: Well how many poor people do you meet on an average day?

DINNER GUEST: I don't have to witness that. I read the broad sheets.

LOKI: . . . This is fabulous, not only are you misappropriating blame based on your
dipstick analysis,
but you're spreading unsubstantiated myths concerning underclass families' multiple disadvantages.
I'm not absolving the apathetic masses, they're the ones who are happy to get treated
like a bunch of fannies.
That's why the rich feel safe when they're flaunting the wealth the poor have given
up so they take the world all for themselves.

DINNER GUEST: But you can't deny there is a problem.

LOKI: No shit, the problem is the economic model.

DINNER GUEST: But you and I did ok out the economy.

LOKI: Yes but we owe more than we own obviously.

DINNER GUEST: But the market is the root of all our personal autonomy.

LOKI: Maybe so but tell me what's autonomy?
In a boom and bust economy that produces global inequality,
and causes damage ecologically.

Listen smarmy, dinnae start me [i.e., don't start a fight with me].

This is my fuckin dinner party, so be quiet and sip your fizzy chardonnay Sorry if you feel disparaged,

my class prejudice is a front like your marriage.

DINNER GUEST: But they're lazy and they don't wanna work.

LOKI: Is that right next you'll be telling me that there all on drugs.

DINNER PARTY: Well it's true.

LOKI: No it isn't, what a lot of gough.

Most people on benefits work, you can look it up.

DINNER PARTY HOST: Maybe so, but I'm not being funny, they wouldn't be poor if they knew how to manage their money.

LOKI: I'm sorry here if I'm insulting your cleverness but you're lack of wit is clearly masked by your eloquence,

you're the contestant of smug irreverent mob, I expected mare [more] of your intelligence.

Can you see the inherent prejudice of your sentiments can be refuted with some basic evidence.

DINNER GUEST: Somebody's has had too much wine as for benefits well we need to pay down the deficit.

LOKI: The only deficit issue is the attention span of so-called citizens who really need to get with the plan.

You incredible snob, some folk could be doing with getting a job . . . You're off your nut [you're mad] if you think the deficit is actually caused by benefit fraud.

DINNER GUEST: No need to be vulgar. After a few drinks, you working-class folk really show your true colours.

As we all know resorting to vulgarity is a substitute for a lack of vocabulary.

LOKI: I don't mean to be rude, I'm just sayin, shut the fuck up you're a disgrace to higher education.

Your unconscious philosophy indirectly oppresses the majority through tolerance of poverty.

In reality, they're struggling, but you'd rather tell yourself they sit about waiting for your money to trickle down.

It's easy to take a very rigid position, make moral judgement about life fae [from] your fitted kitchen, can't you see it plain mate?

I'm not being funny.

Tolerating poverty is costing you and me money.

So if you're all about fiscal responsibility then drop the fuckin' act fae yir armchair citizenry.

I don't mean to be rude, I'm getting sick of it.

Somebody's gotta call time on these idiots.

People think it's unfair and so I concur the country is run by millionaires that
I never voted for.

Loki plays both characters, himself in his own voice, and the dinner guest in a more flattened accent (like Solareye in "Marriage Counselling"). The accent is still Scottish, but it is more nasal and breathier. The debate critiques the "armchair citizenry" of the middle class, accusing them of uncritically digesting information written about the lower class from media outlets. Clever wordplay such as the double meaning of "assemble" is shown through statements about the guest's "right to assemble simple cabinet packs," subverting the listeners' expectation of the political "right to assemble" by using the metaphor of IKEA-style furniture to also paint the blandness of the man's political views (and perhaps an association of IKEA's capitalist uniformity as a feature of the middle class). Western middle-class exotic comforts such as tai chi and chai tea are juxtaposed against poverty and homelessness. Stereotypes of the lower class are presented, as they are in the media, against the idea that those on benefits are often those who do part-time work who still cannot find enough employment to cover the basic cost of living. The line, "The problem is the economic model" reflect the leftist aspects of the "Yes Scotland" campaign, in that the yes vote was seen as a rejection of neoliberalism rather than a rejection of English or British nationalism in favor of Scottish nationalism. The debate alludes to wider structural issues, and the apathy of those who cannot see such issues. It is a rallying cry as much as a critique, almost Socratic in its didacticism for the listener.

What is particularly fascinating about the dystopian world that Loki paints is its commentary on current society. Essentially it is a "this is what happens if you vote no for independence," and points out the triviality of some news reports ("weighing up the pros and cons of refrigerated coleslaw"), the deep class divide as represented by the tower and the slums, and the eradication of symbols of civic nationalism such as the Scottish Parliament. In the dystopia, "Parliament Ruin" will become a tourist attraction for the next Olympic games.[25] As Tim Edensor has written of nationalism in everyday life, the nation has "sacred centres" which can be unique to a country's "moral geography" (Smith 1991, in Edensor 2002, 45). They may point to past cultures (Stonehenge, Pyramids) or national history (Statue of Liberty, Nelson's Column) or to a nation's modernity (Empire State Building, Sydney Opera House). Again, the banal aspects of nation come to the fore, and when confronted with the possibility that they may be taken away, it becomes a powerful reminder of what defines individuals, communities, and nations.

One reviewer of *G.I.M.P.* writes, "The finished article expresses the beginnings of a realisation of what it means to many Scots to belong to a devolved state without the security of genuine sovereignty and self-determination. This perspective is expressed through a starkly dystopian vision of future Scotland which continues to be ruled by "billionaires I never voted for" and containing the derelict ruins of the Scottish parliament building repurposed as a tourist attraction" (Bone 2014).

To quote Moylan again, "Since 1909, with 'The Machine Stops,' dystopian writing has consistently confronted the historical contradictions and conflicts of the century. Some dystopias explore the oppression of fascist or bureaucratically deformed social states, others delve into the controlled chaos of capitalist society, and a few linger over the horrendous details of everyday life" (Moylan 2000, 180). The Scottish parliament has become a symbolic site of Scottish nationalist power, and the invocation of "Parliament Ruin" in the media broadcasts would be one of the more powerful images of the concept album.

G.I.M.P. looks at everydayness through the lens of the media, which inevitably touches on Scottish politics. The media reports discuss the slum population and their management by the police, the professional class in New Glasgow Tower, NHS privatization, and Palestinian exile. It is through these news reports that Loki's dystopia is framed. The first report is as follows:

This is an emergency government issue broadcast, live from Parliament Ruin in the heart of New Glasgow. You join us as we witness bizarre scenes here at New Glasgow Tower, home to the country's professional class. The view from the slums is dramatic as we have learned a hijacker manning a government drone is encircling the massive, free-standing structure. Security personnel have been scrambling all around us, including the Royal Air Force, who, as we understand are concerned about attacking a craft in such a densely populated area. You can feel the fear on the ground here among the slum population, most of whom have never lived to witness an attack on British home soil. It really is like something out of a movie. Wait, we are seeing some activity on the craft, a door on the vessel seems to be opening yet we cannot get a glimpse of the pilot. People down here are gripped by panic as officials and security forces appeal to the people of New Glasgow to keep calm and carry on.

The synthesized arpeggios are slow and ominous as the anchor reads her report and creates a prologue to Loki's rap. After this, we get another broadcast from the same anchor, which lends more insight into the type of world we have entered:

NHS stock has soared to the top of the FTSE 1000 after announcing it's working on a possible cure for a mysterious strain of dementia which attacks human beliefs.

It is not a coincidence, that the accent of the news reports are flattened Scottish accents which more closely resemble "BBC English"/RP, juxtaposed against Loki's much stronger Glaswegian accent. The album was targeted in particular to working-class youth, a desire to create something entertaining that also has a political message. On a blogpost discussing his own motivations for the album Loki writes:

> So why did I decide to take on a project like this? There are lots of reasons. The main one is that the referendum is looming and I feel working class people, especially the youth, are not being engaged in the debate. To me this makes no sense as, collectively, they have the most potential power. I want to do my bit to re-dress the balance and make politics entertaining and relevant to those who would normally dismiss it.
>
> To do this, I need to offer more than just my opinions. To do this I need to present more than one perspective. What *G.I.M.P.* will offer the listener, is a rollercoaster ride that puts Scottish society front and centre. The good, the bad and the downright ridiculous. Due to the nature of the referendum and its high profile, then it means I can truly focus solely on being true to what I per-ceive as 'Scottishness.' I don't have to worry about radio, or blogs not under-standing my accent. (Loki 2014a)

His sentiments reveal that, for him, rap is too easy to get into, creating a lower-quality product in the process. For him, there are many who think they can rap, that there is a lot of low-quality rapping going on. In another blogpost for the *National Collective*, Loki wrote that hip-hop has become far too politically apathetic, almost as a signifier of coolness for some. Seeing hip-hop as an art, he writes, "I feel a lot of art, generally, is a wee bit too cosy. Too much emphasis on technical prowess and presentation. Real art should come with a hint of menace. Alan Moore describes art as 'an explosive substance.' I think we're too caught up in being accepted and liked by our fellow artists that we have subtly assumed a lesser role for ourselves in society" (Loki 2014b).

Like Stanley Odd, the focus is not about discussing or eradicating overt displays of nationalism (stereotypes are addressed in order to be debunked), but showing Scottish voters a sense of the lived reality, and that their quality of life is a result of political consequences. Loki enacts this through dystopian fiction to shed light on the current situation, and Stanley Odd performs this by discussing the multiple sides of the independence argument. It is clear that both artists are directly addressing the Scottish people and any apathy they may have, but the two rappers do so in contrast-ing ways. As Loki wrote on his Blog before the album was released, "It's not a time for sitting on the fence. It's a time to make a stand . . . and back up your assertions. I'll be voting yes . . . and this album is my attempt to explain why" (Loki 2014a).

Conclusion: Post-Referendum Scotland

The result of the referendum on September 18 was ultimately a rejection of independence. An even more impressive statistic was the 84.6% voter turnout by Scottish residents, the highest percentage in any UK election or referendum.[26] Reasons cited for the "no" majority vote include a shared history and identity of Britishness, wanting to keep the status quo in a time of economic instability, prestige of the UK, more devolutionary powers promised by political parties, defense fears, and support for parties other than the Scottish National Party (RT 2014).

Perhaps the silent majority also echoed the "tacit majoritarianism" (Modood and Salt 2011, 3) of Britishness, and that even the more subtle forms of unionism experienced daily (as part of banal nationalism) kept the idea of Britain as a positive, stable desire. In reality, however, this was not a monolithic us versus them, but a nuanced interweaving of Scottish and British identity, if indeed it was ever about identity. And as some stated, the referendum result was due to class and political priority rather than simply expressing a sense of national identity (Myers 2014).

What the Yes ("Yes Scotland") and No ("Better Together") campaigns did was to invigorate debate about political representation in the UK, consciously or subconsciously grappling with issues of national identity and the "nation within nation" status of Scotland. Hip-hop, Loki believes, "has been given a bit of space to exist because it was beneficial to Yes. And I think hip-hop kicked everybody's arse in this debate. A lot of young people who live on housing schemes were directly engaged in the independence debate as a result of the hip-hop artists who chose to speak about it" (Eaton-Lewis 2014).

To quote again from Eyerman and Jamison, "Social movements are processes in formation; they do not spring already formed to take their place on the stage of history. Rather, they can be conceived of as contingent and emergent spaces which are carved out of existent contexts; they are creative, or experimental, arenas for the practicing of new forms of social and cognitive action" (Eyerman and Jamison 1998, 21). Scotland's debates over independence became such a space—where creativity, parody, humor, and a variety of cultural forms were presented, appropriated, and experimented with.

The language and medium of hip-hop as a folk music and as a form of protest song has provided a way for Scottish youth cultures to debate and spread issues around

Scottish independence. By no means was hip-hop the only artistic method that took part in the debate,[27] but as "the people's music," its use was intended to speak to demographics who feel unrepresented, oppressed, and perhaps "colonized." While Stanley Odd or Loki do not use the overtly colonial critique of *Trainspotting*, for example, their music does fit into similar hip-hop traditions of social commentary and critique.

Stanley Odd's songs that discuss Scottish independence set forth the main arguments, refute national stereotypes, and do so with verbal skill and humor. Loki's post-hip-hop concept album, part of a long history of dystopia as protest, highlights key themes that represent values Scottish people purportedly hold dear, hybridizing the dystopian with polystylistic hip-hop to critique the media, class inequality, Tory government policy, and labor exploitation.

The Scottish case, however, problematizes hip-hop as the voice of the subaltern often defined in ethnic terms: hip-hop could be said to represent postcolonial resistance here, but it is being used for a people that were arguably very much part of and reaped the benefits of the imperialism of the British Empire (lest we not forget capitalist proponent Adam Smith was Scottish). These rappers are aware of this and do engage in those discourses, but for the independence debate, the cultural amnesia of Scotland's role in Empire is replaced by a performance of Scottish national identity defined largely through civic nationalism.[28] The goal is sovereignty, self-reliance, and political representation but in a neo-colonial world where, to quote Tim Edensor, "the nation-state seems to be threatened by large, supra-national federations which organise around trade, social legislation and law (for instance, as with the European Community) . . . it seems as if the spatial container of power here is expanding to transcend the national" (Edensor 2002, 38). Although many European countries are in fact reinforcing the nation-state in some cases, the SNP's campaign for independence has persistently argued support for membership in the European Union, currently a divisive issue in Britain.

As Lipsitz has noted, families of resemblance in the African diaspora have a "shared skepticism about the nation state, an identification with the lived experiences of ordinary people, and an imaginative, supple, and strategic reworking of identities and cultures" (Lipsitz 1997, 33). This also applies to Scottish hip-hop. The "Otherness," or outsiderdom (Hook 2018, 70–85), that is performed here has to fall under other parameters (class, nation, creed, the "Celtic fringe") than ethnic ones. Humor is often used, for example, as a distancing mechanism, and as we will see in the next chapter, can be used to signify difference. Humor in both Stanley Odd and Loki's lyrics use humor as a method to entertain and engage, and to create a debate that acknowledges the complexities of national identity and points out absurdities of stereotypes and assumptions regarding class and national symbols. Depiction of the everyday adds to the idea of the performance of Scottish civic nationalism, and the performance of a Scottish identity based on citizenry and its "ordinary-ness."

These examples demonstrate a syncretism between Scottish political song, protest folk music, and hip-hop. The format of the concept album, for Loki, may help distance himself from the singles-orientated nature of the mainstream rap market. They could almost be categorized as post-hip-hop soundscapes, with a musical polystylism that resists pigeonholing (as sonic complement to quick speech-like flow in a thick Scottish accent), though very much indebted to hip-hop influence. Given that Loki's album was crowdfunded on Indiegogo, and Stanley Odd's music is for purchase on Bandcamp, they are perhaps under less pressure to adhere to traditional genre frames of the music industry.

To echo Dai Griffiths and Sarah Hill's sentiments on Welsh hip-hop (e.g., Y Tystion), Stanley Odd and Loki's brand of Scottish hip-hop only seems possible in a post-devolution Scotland (Griffiths and Hill 2005, 221). Hip-hop music, along with other styles, helped successfully to mobilize high voter turnout in the referendum.

Despite the results of the referendum, Scottish nationalism had strong voter support less than a year later in the 2015 general election. On May 7, 2015, the Scottish National Party had a historic landslide victory, winning 56 out of 59 seats in Parliament (BBC News 2015). Labour lost 40 of their seats and 10 liberal democrat seats in Scotland. It seems that the "Yes Scotland" campaign and the role of hip-hop within it, helped to stir support for debating these important issues, and bolstered support for the Scottish National Party. Even if another referendum on independence does not happen in the next generation or more, the fact is that hip-hop was an important voice protesting the status quo and continues to be a political tool across the globe. Many feel that the SNP landslide in the 2015 General Election as well as Scotland's support of the EU suggest that another Independence Referendum may be likely. If so, it is clear that hip-hop will be at the forefront of the debate. Hip-hop is no longer only "CNN for Black People" (to quote Chuck D of Public Enemy's famous comment), it is also CNN for youth-driven political movements around the globe.

Notes

1. "Many commentators cite what they call the 'Braveheart effect' in contributing to this renewed national awareness. Yet popular responses to the film highlight many of the ambivalences and conflicts about the constitution of Scottish identity and the representation of Scotland, and these themes are far from recent. The reactions of Scots partly indicate the difficulties of sustaining narratives of national identity in a globalising world" (Edensor 2002, 145). The Scottish National

Party used the iconography of the film to hand out leaflets in support of the part and in independence, part of a 'head and heart' campaign ('TODAY IT'S NOT JUST BRAVEHEARTS WHO CHOOSE INDEPENDENCE [IT'S ALSO WISE-HEADS] AND THEY USE THE BALLOT BOX.' On the other side is the slogan "YOU'VE SEEN THE MOVIE . . . NOW FACE THE REALITY") (Edensor 2002, 151).

2. "With the creation of the Scottish Parliament and the Welsh Assembly in 1998, the UK has been transformed from a centralised state to a distinctly asymmetric devolved system . . . In recent decades regional pressures for stronger autonomy have induced central and federal governments around the world to devolve powers and resources downwards to the meso level" (Tijmstra 2009, 732).

3. Salmond was leader of the SNP from 1990 to 2000 and then again from 2004 to 2014. One writer points out that Salmond has created a modern civic nationalism: "There is a distinct lack of any ethnicity to the contemporary SNP's politics. The almost total absence of cultural nationalism from the Salmond project is indeed striking . . . The argument for independence from Salmond and the SNP remains one of improved services and a more equitable society. There is no blood and soil, no faith or fatherland" (Bhain 2012). The lack of history (and cultural nationalism) in the idea of Salmond's brand of nationalism is also, according to historian Richard Marsden, because Victorian Scotland's evocation of the past was firmly unionist (Marsden 2014). This focus on "bigotry of place" over "bigotry of race" (Daisley 2015) is echoed in who was able to vote in the Scottish referendum: Scottish nationals (including non-citizens) over Scottish citizens who are resident in other countries. While these are the ideas promoted by the SNP, to state that these were the only reasons that citizens voted yes would be an over-generalization: some will have voted for economic reasons, or ethnic, civic, or non-nationalist reasons, or indeed a mix of factors.

4. Technically speaking, since devolution, a reclaimed Parliament, according to McCrone, means that it is no longer a stateless nation (2001, 1), though technically it is still indirectly controlled through Westminster Parliament. McCrone continues, "All societies, of course, tend to reach for the culturally and historically exotic when trying to justify what makes theirs essentially different, but Scotland is more problematic than most. Put simply, it is not a state, and the conventional wisdom is that in modern times sovereign, independent states are the political actors of our stage" (2001, 6).

5. That is not to say that there are no ethnic-minority Scottish hip-hop artists. One of the most well-known rap groups in Scotland are Young Fathers, a trio from Edinburgh, and rap groups Hector Bizerk and the LaFontaines have received critical acclaim within and outside Scotland. The Scottish hip-hop duo Silibil N' Brains (Gavin Bain and Billy Boyd) pretended to be American rappers from California to secure a record deal, outlined in Bain's 2010 memoir *California Schemin'* and was adapted into the documentary film *The Great Hip Hop Hoax* (2013). Some groups, like Young Fathers, are more party orientated and their politics are less overt comparatively, and others, such as Wee D, were publicly opposed to independence, so I do not wish paint the entire Scottish rap landscape as pro-independence political hip-hop.

6. Scottish protest songs also include lamenting the loss of industry (steel, cotton, shipbuilding, coal and cars at various stages in history), and with it jobs and opportunities. Edensor wrote, "In their hit single, 'Letter to America,' the avowedly nationalist band the Proclaimers sing. 'Bathgate no more, Linwood no more, Methil no more, Irvine no more,' highlighting popular Scottish resentment about the disappearance of these symbolic sites of industrial production, the

first two of which hosted car factories" (Edensor 2002, 126). The Proclaimers were important to national identity as they were pro-SNP since the 1980s and sang in very distinctive style with a Scottish accent.

7. Empire biscuits (or imperial biscuits) are particularly popular in Scotland; therefore, the use of the username questions the notion of Scottish identity.

8. "Creative adaptation in performance is an essential ingredient of successful political protest. Contextual factors such as the location and timing of performances were as important as the selection of songs and texts. The call-and-response format of chanting involving large numbers of people might appear to demand little creativity, and yet the interaction between leaders, followers, and audience allowed for considerable creative adaptation" (Samson 2012, 540).

9. National Collective is a nonpartisan group of artists who wished to discuss and promote Scottish independence.

10. My sincere thanks to Jo Collinson Scott for this observation, and for numerous comments and help with lyric transcription for this chapter.

11. Andrew Lansley was a Conservative Member of Parliament (1997–2015) and was Secretary of State for Health from 2010–2012. He enacted the Health and Social Care Act in 2012 which removed responsibility for the health of citizens from the Secretary of State for Health to a new body, Public Health England. Primary care trusts and strategic health authorities were abolished and funding transferred to "clinical commissioning groups." Critics see the act it as a step toward the privatization of the National Health Service (NHS).

12. TOWIE is a reality show which stands for The Only Way is Essex, the county east of London, known for its depiction of young superficial well-to-do socialites.

13. WAGs stand for Wives and Girlfriends, first associated with the women associated with male footballers, traveling abroad with them and photographed by paparazzi shopping, drinking, and socializing in clubs.

14. The term "toff" is a reference to the upper classes. Some say it originates with the term "tuft," a tassel worn by Oxford and Cambridge graduates; or a reference to "toffee-nosed" given that the upper-class men used a large amount of snuff.

15. The behavior also has a precedent in the Poll Tax era, when people kept their names off the polling register to avoid the Poll Tax.

16. Hook writes about the wordplay in his music (2018, 20), and points to one example from "Let ma Brain Breathe": "If hip hop's been dumbed down, here's the upshot / Shining over this lot is like robbin babies at the tuck shop / I heard you were sick son . . . / Mmm . . . seems there's been a 10p mix up."

17. Finland was part of the Kingdom of Sweden until the nineteenth century, then was part of Russia.

18. A longer analysis of the track can be found in Hook 2018, 102–6.

19. Faslane is one of three operating bases for the Royal Navy in the UK, and main Royal Navy base in Scotland. It is controversially known for the submarines armed with Trident missiles. In other words, it is the home of Britain's nuclear weapons, a source of contention in both the independence referendum and in post-referendum politics.

20. The OBEY clothing line began in 2001 by artist Shepard Fairey, the street artist who famously led a campaign in the late 1980s putting stickers of "Andre the Giant Has a Posse" all over the US, followed by the design of the OBEY giant.

21. While Solareye uses the term "anti-hero" as against heroism, I am also invoking the literary concept of the "anti-hero," a literary protagonist who lacks the traditional qualities of a hero. They may abide by a more ambiguous moral code, are more human than superhuman and are flawed characters in some way. Examples include Jay Gatsby, Walter White, Holden Caulfield, and Don Quixote.

22. My thanks to J. Griffith Rollefson for pointing out this important connection.

23. Guy Fawkes Night, or Bonfire Night, commemorates the events of November 5, 1605, when Guy Fawkes was arrested while guarding explosives those involved in the "Gunpowder Plot" had placed beneath the House of Lords. The event annually celebrates the fact that King James I had survived the plot, with Britons lighting bonfires on the night (originally an effigy of Fawkes), often accompanied by fireworks.

24. Watts, on the philosophy of "carpe diem" states: "Now I am not saying that, you know, 'Let us drink today, for tomorrow we die' and not make any plans. What I am saying is that making plans for the future is of use only to people who are capable of living completely in the present" ("Playing the Game of Life").

25. This may be a reference to the suggestion by Glasgow City Council to blow up the Red Road Tower blocks to create a tourist attraction for the opening of the Commonwealth Games in Glasgow in 2014. The suggestion was met with strong opposition among the working class and marginalized communities who used to live in the flats, arguing this was yet another way that economic growth would be achieved at the expense of the working classes. Thanks to Jo Collinson Scott for making this link.

26. While some polls placed an even higher voter turnout among younger demographics (the Ashcroft Poll had only asked 14 people in the 16–17 year old demographic, so the 71% that voted "yes" may be slightly skewed [Leach 2014]), perhaps more than age was social class and earnings, in that poorer areas voted "yes" for independence more than rich ones. "Yes" voters lived in poorer areas (Leach 2014). In terms of Scottish cities, Glasgow did vote for independence and Edinburgh did not. This may point to economic stability versus instability as a root of the need for sovereignty.

27. Space does not permit me to discuss all the artistic movements and examples involved in the independence debate, but I will point to the rap battle scene as another venue for Scotland independence debates. One rapper, Wee D, was publicly a "no" campaign supporter, a fact that was not lost on other rappers. After the referendum, Andrew MacKenzie battled Wee D in the finals of the "Breaking the Barrier" rap battle final (hosted by Crownsound) on March 6, 2015. Round two saw Mackenzie take off his jacket to review a "no thanks" campaign t-shirt, to boos in the crowd ("We should be proud together Danny, this is who we are" . . . "I knew these plebs wouldn't listen. They're just jealous we made a better decision. I mean, see, the yes coalition wanted us to all this stressin and thinkin, it's a terrible mission . . . face it, it's amazing being a male in your 20s in Britain. Why the fuck would we care about things like public spending revision, welfare division, . . . with benefits facing social derision, guys who say we getting held up in prison by the elite sit at the head of a system that connects a network of perverts . . . molesting our children . . . that sounds like some bad shit, but why are we gonna fuck about that we don't have kids. [Wee D, in fact, does have kids] . . . We the real hip-hop, 55%"). By round three, however, MacKenzie rips his no thanks shirt up to reveal a "still yes and proud" t-shirt, showing he fooled Wee D, and indeed was for independence ("How could you fall for that shit?" . . . "I thought you were wiser and older,

dude, and that shit I said in the first round, well, I think you know is true, and changing that corrupt system is only something a yes vote would do. That means I was looking out for your children more than you . . . On the night of what should have been our victory day, you stood still on stage and said 'a no vote is still a vote for change, just change in a different way.' Mate, that shit is fuckin gay. But I sincerely hope you believed it . . . You can't bear change. You don't even have spare change to show for your achievements [then physically throws pocket change at him]. Because you couldn't make a decision well, the state of the nation's a living hell, Dreams thrown down the wishing well, sacrifice the politicians wealth, You said a yes vote was like suicide, Mate, that's just as well because I hope Scotland gets independence and I hope you fucking kill yourself . . . you're a fucking todger, but at least you're not fuckin English") (crownsoundvids 2015). Thanks to Frank Thomas for making me aware of this battle.

28. Raymond Williams: "It can be said that the Welsh people have been oppressed by the English for some seven centuries. Yet it can then also be said that the English people have been oppressed by the English state for even longer. In any such general statements all the real complications of history are temporarily overridden" (quoted in Williams 2005, 10).

6

HUMOR

The Hyperlocal and the Outsider: Humor and Stereotypes in the Parody Videos of Goldie Lookin Chain and Bricka Bricka

GIVEN MAINSTREAM HIP-HOP'S focus on "hardness" and fixed, stereotypical notions of black masculinity, more humorous forms of hip-hop have been less visible in the mainstream, and most certainly less discussed in scholarship.[1] But despite these wider perceptions, humor has existed in all subgenres of hip-hop since its inception. This includes humor in lyrical content, music videos, and comedy skits that appear between tracks on rap albums (e.g., Dr. Dre's *The Chronic*, De La Soul's *3 Feet High and Rising*, Kendrick Lamar's *Good Kid, m.A.A.d. City*, Kanye West *College Dropout*).

While different forms of humor have been deployed to different ends and purposes in hip-hop culture, this chapter focuses on humor in hip-hop parody songs by two groups / artists in particular, the Welsh hip-hop parody group Goldie Lookin Chain (GLC) and the "Eastern European immigrant" character of Bricka Bricka (played by David Vujanic). By comparing these two case studies of "Othering," I will shed light on themes from opposite sides of the insider / outsider coin, raising issues of hyper-localism, race, and regional and national identity. Their music videos perform a notion of "backwardness" (socially, ideologically, and temporally), which highlights and critiques those who suffer from postcolonial melancholia in post-Empire Britain. Through Welsh provincial and Eastern European stereotypes,

Brithop. Justin A. Williams, Oxford University Press (2021). © Oxford University Press.
DOI: 10.1093/oso/9780190656805.001.0001

and through widely mediatized associations of hip-hop with "blackness," the groups spotlight the absurdity of such stereotypes.

Such a study complicates the narrative around hip-hop's ability to represent ethnic difference and marginality, while also complicating what is normally considered "UK hip-hop" by looking at parodies of hip-hop and related genres. But to quote Palmer's book *Taking Humor Seriously*, "what people laugh at, how and when they laugh is absolutely central to their culture" (1993, 89). These texts reveal deeper issues about British attitudes toward themselves and bring othered, less-visible, figures of the everyday at the forefront of British society. What we do get is a celebration of "marginality" and the everyday from normally voiceless UK residents, complicated by the fact that such a performance involves mockery of an arguably reinforced stereotype.

Theories of Parody

Given the cultural-groundedness of humor, it may be particularly productive to investigate specific types of humor *in situ* with their socio-cultural contexts, even when they may overlap temporally and culturally with other forms.[2] To cite studies of the parody-music based television comedy *Flight of the Conchords*, humor is achieved when genres invert expectations (Zemke in Giuffre and Hayward 2017, 120; Braae 2019).[3] More generally, studies have shown that "incongruity is a necessary condition of humor" (Brøvig-Hanssen 2020).[4] This is the case for parody even more so than other types of humor because it deals with imitations of arguably more fixed ideas such as the relationship between music genre, race, and stereotypical notions of gender. Echoing this, the philosopher Simon Critchley wrote, "we might say that humor is produced by a disjunction between the way things are and the way they are represented in the joke, between expectation and actuality" (Critchley 2002, 1). For hip-hop parody, this is between what an audience *expects* to see/hear in a hip-hop video and what we *actually* see/hear.[5]

With Goldie Lookin Chain and Bricka Bricka, we are dealing with the "ironic inversion" (Hutcheon 2000, 6) of parody through the use of stereotypes based on nationalism and ethnicity vis-à-vis what viewers expect hip-hop performers' identities to be (normally non-white and American). The parody employs a dual target—in addition to parodying the stereotyped personae through rap (e.g., the Welsh, the Eastern European), they also provide a parody of hip-hop's mainstream stereotypes (i.e., the original hip-hop artist). These parodies can express prejudgments which are normally repressed by some, and thus the humor can rationalize the prejudices felt toward such groups (Howitt and Owusu-Bempah in Lockyer and Pickering 2009,

50). Similarly, "superiority theories" of humor state that the function of humor is to make one feel superior to another (Hobbes, Critchley, Aristotle), thus affirming and enhancing one's own social membership (Lockyer and Pickering 2009, 51). Gillota writes in the context of ethnic humor, "We joke about race and ethnicity because it is often socially unacceptable to talk about these issues openly. Humor provides a socially sanctioned release valve" (Gillota 2013, 5). This is, of course, heavily dependent on context for what ethnic humor is socially acceptable—such ethnic humor now would be sanctioned acceptable only if the comedian belonged to that particular ethnic group (e.g., Dave Chapelle, Margaret Cho). Considering these theories of repression/relief, superiority, and incongruity, following Covach (1995), it seems most productive to utilize and extend on theories of incongruity or inversion when looking at elements such as musical (or visual) style in these texts.

Intertextuality becomes a useful frame to discuss the mechanics of parody, given that parody involves a clear relationship between two texts. Hutcheon points out that parody is "overtly hybrid and double-voiced" (200,: 28), and that irony participates in parody discourse as a strategy (31). In this sense, it has a more bitextual orientation than quotation or even allusion (i.e., some clear relationship between the parody and the "original" text it is parodying). If we assume that the interpretive community is vaguely aware of mainstream hip-hop, or more, then we can discuss elements of expectation and subversion in these examples. Lastly, the humor in these videos works on multiple levels depending on the knowledge of the viewer, and we should allow for such overlapping perspectives. This chapter attempts to broaden the cultural landscape of what is considered "hip-hop in the UK" (including YouTube as important media outlet)—while the mode of delivery is humorous rather than "serious," their targets are symptomatic of wider issues regarding twenty-first-century Britain and mainstream hip-hop.[6] I will focus on these artists' deployment and translation of hip-hop stereotypes, musically, lyrically, and visually to create a complex critique of their cultures and of hip-hop itself.

When we discuss the term "musical parody" in this context, it means that a song will likely involve a little-transformed musical track (almost like karaoke), or re-performed track that attempts to emulate the original. This can also be echoed in a music video as well as a solely-audio track. We can follow Serge Lacasse's definition of parody (from Genette): it maintains "the stylistic properties of the original text [the music and performance style] while diverting its subject [lyrical content]" (Lacasse 2000, 41). For example, Polish-American parody artist Weird Al Yankovic has a band re-perform material to sound the same as the original, though sometimes replacing guitar solos with accordion solos, alongside some hand-made percussive squelching and farting sounds. The lyrics will have changed, and in terms of music video, we will have the figure of Yankovic though often in a similar situation as the original video (and this is where the disjuncture provides humor). We often have the same characters, such as the same janitor from the "Smells Like Teen Spirit Video" for the "Smells like Nirvana" video in addition to the same high school gym and Yankovic wearing a similar outfit to Cobain. As the music stays the same, and often the performance approach, the difference lies in the artist, his vocal delivery, and the lyrical content. For both case studies in this chapter ("Fresh Prince of Cwmbran" and "Hard in Da Paint"), the original musical elements are retained while the ethnicity and nationality of the performers, and their lyrical context, have changed. Mimicry is a key element in performance style. In the case of Yankovic this occurs in the vocal performance, and his *attempt* to sound like the original is also a way to highlight the incongruity while the band performance provides a more constant variable, as well as elements of the music video's lexicon (setting, characters, costumes), syntax, and style.[7]

As Hutcheon and Harries point out, the reading of any ironic discourse "requires a triple competence: first linguistic competence, understanding the doubly-coded signifiers, and understanding their juxtaposition. Second, the reader must possess a generic competence in order to understand the logonimic system is being parodied. Finally, the spectator must also exhibit an ideological competence in understanding that norm violation is occurring and its implications" (Harries 2000, 109). In other words, we need to know at least some of the connotations of the original norms so that we know they are being transgressed. This will vary between people, but I believe we can talk safely of some norms in the interpretative community which will hear hip-hop and rap as a black popular phenomenon. Additionally, some of the Welsh and Eastern European references will be more nuanced for those with competence of those languages and cultures.

Charles Hiroshi Garrett discusses the use of humor in hip-hop as a strategy for articulating difference, and is careful to point out that just because something is funny, it does not eradicate the seriousness of a given message. He notes that early rap parodies like Rodney Dangerfield's "Rappin Rodney" (1984) and Mel Brooks "It's Good to Be the King" (1981) "typically upset (and also upheld) common expectations surrounding hip hop and its (young African American male) performers with respect to race, class, generation, and gender" (Garrett 2015, 332). Garrett also discusses Weird Al's parodies of "Gangster's Paradise" (Amish Paradise) and "Ridin" by Chamillionaire (called "White & Nerdy"), and how "exaggerating comic difference" allows Weird Al to rely "on a common technique used by Parodists" (332–33). Garrett concludes, "Joking about hip-hop genre expectations not only helps to reinforce them, but also enables outsiders to mock, embrace or comment on hip hop. In each case, musical humor serves to mark difference at the same time as it offers the potential to connect, negotiate, and engage" (Garrett 2015, 334).

Discussing humor as articulating white ethnicity in hip-hop in another context, Antti-Ville Kärjä writes on the use of humor in Finnish hip-hop as a strategy for articulating both whiteness and Finnish identity, what he notes as a "construction of Finnish identity vis-à-vis blackness" (2011, 83). Suomirap and its "comedifying," Kärjä argues, is "part of a broader cultural logic whereby somehow too different, disturbing or even threatening identities are distanced, and one's own identity kept safe" (2011, 88). White Finnish-ness is therefore kept intact rather than black African American affiliations which go othered. In the case of Goldie Lookin Chain and Bricka Bricka, the use of humor to articulate difference as otherness *and* whiteness is played out in these characters almost as a defense mechanism as it is with the Finnish case, in relation to hip-hop as articulation of blackness. These parodies comment on the parodied hip-hop text, hip-hop more generally, hip-hop's affiliation with a particular African American stereotype, as well as the commentary on stereotypes of white otherness such as "Welshness" and "Eastern European"-ness.

Goldie Lookin Chain

Goldie Lookin Chain (GLC) was founded in 2000 and hail from Newport, Wales.[8] The group boasts a large membership: 2Hats, Billy Webb, Eggsy, Mystikal, Mike Balls, Adam Hussain, Rhys, Graham the Bear, and former member Maggot. Their work often references pre-existing rap cultures of an earlier era. For example, the use of track suits can suggest an earlier (now backward) 1980s Run-D.M.C.-era fashion, but could also represent the "chav" stereotype depicting Britain's (particularly white) lower classes (Jones 2011), or the current penchant for track suits in grime music. The album titles *Straight Outta Newport* (2005) and *Fear of a Welsh Planet* (2017) also point to this referencing of mainstream rap culture ten to twenty years earlier.

The group's parodies often play on a particular stereotypical notion of "Welshness" as provincial and backward, whose status has a subaltern quality compared to England, but derives national identity through local signifiers and the Welsh language. Although Wales became part of the UK in the 1536 and 1543 Acts of Union, Welsh residents have, in many ways, considered themselves a distinct entity, particularly in relation to the English, who have London (via Parliament) as the site of central power and authority. More so than Scots Gaelic or Irish Gaelic, the Welsh language has maintained a strong and visible presence with the rapid development of *Cymdeithas yr Laith Gymreg* ("The Welsh Language Society," established 1962), students learning the language in school, and dedicated Welsh-language radio and television programming.[9] Approximately five hundred thousand people speak Welsh in an overall population of around three million. Sarah Hill writes, "Since the Second World War, Wales has undergone an extended period of self-examination, community formation, and political activism, and over the part fifty years, Welsh musicians have appropriated a variety of Anglo-American musical styles to expedite the Welsh quest for national self-definition" (Hill 2007, 3). Such momentum reached new heights with the 1997 devolution of powers and the protests in 2001 against "Welsh" not listed as a separate ethnicity on the British census, demonstrating how the Welsh consider themselves separate in certain respects. This is complicated by the relationship with its English neighbor as they share citizenship within the UK and other shared elements of banal nationalism (some newspapers, grocery stores, currency, etc.), not to mention the relationship with wider global factors such as international fast food chains. I realize that such language treats "Wales" as a monolithic entity which in reality it is not (north vs. south, towns vs. cities). For this this study, however, we are dealing with a performance of Welshness, which for GLC, does not attempt to get to the heart of the wider complexities of Welsh identity and reality.

While Wales was never a colony of Britain, we still may be able to apply some logic of a "postcolonial Wales" as written by Aaron and Williams (2005). They will have been subject to colonial thinking as part of Empire in addition to the uneven power relationships within the nation-state, creating some level of ambivalence in this relationship. Despite this, Welshness is perceived as a subaltern cultural identity in relation to Englishness in Britain. The Welsh have been viewed from the center as culturally backward, flattened into stereotypes in many cases to reflect this power relation. GLC performs these stereotypes knowledgeably and ironically while demonstrating hip-hop aesthetics and values through content that can appear at a disjuncture with how those hip-hop aesthetics are portrayed in the mainstream. What we see here is a performance of the uneasy relationship between the global and the local mediated by an unequal power relationship between Britain's nations. Additionally, Blanford argues that Wales needs continually to perform its identity partly to compensate for its not being a nation-state (in Aaron and Williams 2005, 178).

Wales's popular music industry has had to deal with the wider cultural choices of local versus wider appeal, and some of this has to do with the choice to perform in Welsh, English, or a combination of the two. Since the 1990s there has been a resurgence of Welsh popular music partly based on a rise in popularity from the British mainstream and internationally, journalistically dubbed the "Cool Cymru" boom.[10] In addition to Welsh-language hip-hop, there are also numerous artists performing Anglophone Welsh hip-hop, including Fleapit in the early 2000s and their producer Leon who ran the Cardiff label SFDB. Important precursors to GLC were

The Headcase Ladz, who were more idiosyncratically Welsh than later rap artists such as Mudmouth and Ruffstylz (Anonymous 2009). There are also Welsh grime artists as well, Astroid Boys and Antizzle as but two examples (McLaren 2012).

In terms of humor more generally, the Welsh have been the target of jokes from the English as an Othering as a prime examples of Hobbes superiority theory. The topics of such jokes involve rural life and a sense of mental and lifestyle backwardness:

> A prominent Welsh minister travelling home one night was greatly annoyed when a young man much the worse for drink came and sat next to him on the bus.
>
> "Young man," he declared, "do you not realise you are on the road to perdition?"
>
> "Oh, hell," replied the drunkard. "I could have sworn this was the bus to Llanelli." (Rhys 2015)

Jokes like this often hinge on the local, the constructed Otherness of Welsh people and place names, in particular the "dd" and "ff" and "ll" double consonants. One jokes states, "I used to go out with a Welsh girl who had 36DDs. It was a ridiculously long name" (Rhys 2015).

A majority of Welsh jokes found online and elsewhere allude strongly to (male) farmers having sex with sheep.[11] These jokes often share a similar form, with little variations which often have puns involving "ewe" and "u" or some other double meaning. It also presents the vulgar and horrific prospect of a sexual act with an animal, painting the Welsh farmer as a stereotypical Other who engages in bestiality. Although GLC do not joke explicitly about sex with sheep, their humor does come from a similar view of Wales as provincial, less exciting than perhaps other urban styles and communities that normally engage in hip-hop culture in the mainstream. It is worth pointing out that we are dealing with a masculine humor (Braae 2019),[12] engaging primarily with male stereotypes, as they also intersect with notions of masculinity from mainstream hip-hop culture.

Returning to GLC's parodic music videos, their song "Eastenders Rap" (2011) pastiches the grime genre while parodying the long-running London-based soap *EastEnders* (broadcast since 1985). The track and music video plays on the idea that this would be the dominant representation of London for such a naïve and provincial group of people. To choose a long-running soap opera fits the frame of parody, and much of the lyrical content parodies the over-dramatized plot elements of the show. The rappers point out that "fruit and veg make you terminally ill" in London, which points to character Mark Fowler who worked at his family fruit and vegetable market stall and contracted HIV ("Look at Mark Fowler, he got the AIDS, from working on a barrow the simplest of trades"). The lyric comments seem to fit the sentiments of a "Remember the episode when . . ." line of thinking, and when the plot details of character deaths are strung together, one can see the absurdity in how this wouldn't accurately represent London life. Attention to detail waxes and wanes, and seems to echo vague remembrances from certain episodes: "Yo, like, I saw this one episode when a man jumped off the top of a building and he had blood coming out of his face and that." GLC perform a naïve Welsh reception of London-based dramatized depictions of the "everyday."

In a clever conflation of the East End locality of the television show and the East End origins of grime music, GLC use a quasi-grime soundtrack for the song featuring similar sounding instrumentation and rhythms. Unlike Weird Al Parodies or the other parodies discussed, pre-existing material is used ("EastEnders theme") but is transformed into a grime track. Grime music, which originated in areas such as Bow in the East End of London with artists such as Dizzee Rascal and Wiley, is characterized by quick rapping to minimal, electronic-sounding beats. GLC speed up a sample of the "EastEnders Theme" (sped-up samples as a technique found in the early work of Kanye West), fusing sample-based hip-hop with English popular culture. Without wishing to make too direct a link between the sounds of grime and "Eastenders Rap," comparing a grime classic "Pow" by Lethal Bizzle (re-orchestrated and re-issued in 2011 but originally from 2004),[13] will show the similarities sonically with the "Eastenders Rap."[14] Most similarly to grime is the kick drum and snare drum sounds which form the basic beat of the "Eastenders Rap"—a similarity that will not be lost on an audience familiar with grime. GLC with their large lineup of rappers are also similar to grime videos like "Pow" (2004) which feature short verses of rapping by multiple members of the group.

The music video to "Eastenders Rap" includes the title screen (a map of the Thames river and East End of London) alongside the title theme. Rhys and other rappers in the group adopt a distinctively lower register for their rapping on the track as well as attempting an accent from the East End of London. The lower vocal register could be used to signify a heightened notion of masculinity located in grime music (Boakye 2017). The chorus is as follows: "I wouldn't want to live in London / if it's anything like *EastEnders* / it's full of murderers and rapists, weirdos and sex offenders."

The video incorporates a "pop up video" style of providing information about London and the series as text with the iconic *EastEnders* backdrop, adding to the comedic effect of further commentary on the show and of London from this naïve perspective. Three of these are: "In its short history *EastEnders* has amassed a higher child mortality rate than all of the worlds developing countries combined, multiplied by two"; "Drinking in the Queen Vic can result in teenage pregnancy, coronary failure, bankruptcy and death"; and "Over 423 million people watch *EastEnders* worldwide. Most people think London is just like *EastEnders*." One line states, "This shit doesn't happen in my own town," again dividing the fictitious world of soap opera London and Wales.

One of the biggest "punchlines" to the music video, however, is based on London's geography. Referencing the East End of London (the then-fictional E20 postcode when the show was founded), as well as grime (many say the genre was founded in Bow in E3, but E3–E14 have been a hotbed of grime activity), one would expect that the location of the music video would be in some E postcode. This is not the case. The music video is shot outside Camden Town tube station, firmly NW1 and a hotspot for tourists to London (see Figure 6.1).[15] Like other visitors to London, Camden would be a safe and touristy locality, whereas the East End of London has far fewer tourist attractions while also solidifying its "of-the-street" reputation (a signifier of hip-hop authenticity). In other words, E3 represents "real London" whereas Camden would represent some sort of synthetic or façade geared toward those who do not reside there. In genres like hip-hop and grime, postcodes are extremely important and for GLC to get this "wrong" is a "misreading" symptomatic of their wider misreading of the soap opera as journalistic reality. The song and video poke fun at the soap opera, London tourism, and the chasm between London and non-London inhabitants and assumptions about each other. Ultimately, the hyperlocal Welsh outsiders conclude, "I wouldn't want to live in London," thus reaffirming their belonging and identity as Welshmen rather than anything else.

The song "The Fresh Prince of Cwmbran" is a parody of the television show theme to *The Fresh Prince of Bel Air* (1990–1996), the sitcom starring Will Smith about a

FIGURE 6.1 Goldie Lookin Chain, "EastEnders Rap" (2011)

kid who leaves the "hood" in Philadelphia to live with his aunt and uncle's family in upper class Bel Air, California. The lyrics and video sing the praises of Cwmbran, a post-WWII town close to Newport in South Wales. The rappers, sunburned as they are on "holiday," point out the town has pubs, a leisure center, a biscuit factory, and a farm that tourists can visit. The song brags of both places entirely unique to Cwmbran (Greenmeadow Farm, Llantaram local Church hall, Llandegfedd reservoir) and of chain establishments like the JD Weatherspoons (pub), Iceland (frozen foods), Matalan (clothing and home goods store), Premier Inn (hotel), and McDonalds (fast food). The variety of locations discussed in the video demonstrate the complexity of Welsh identity.[16] Rapping about the uniqueness of a location defined in part by international and national chain stores is an irony not lost on the group and its international audience. Bragging that you can come look at "tits in the pool" at the leisure center or get arrested hanging around a secondary school perhaps suggests that such lack of excitement could lead people to questionable activities, or it could simply be a nod to mainstream rap's penchant for misogyny and oversexualization.

A recurring point in the song is that the town has free parking ("With fantastic free parking you can park any days"; "if you take your car you'll always find a place"; "I never found a place with parking quite like Cwmbran"). As names of highways are often referenced in certain forms of US rap, GLC tell people to travel on the "A0451 to Cwmbran." Despite seeing world localities (including the convenient rhyme of Japan), they are still impressed with the song's title town ("I went around the world from LA to Japan, I never found a place with parking quite like Cwmbran"). Lyrically, the global is ironically Othered alongside the local.

Cwmbran was a "new town" created in 1949 to provide post-war employment in proximity to the South Wales coalfield. Given the decline of the coal industry, like the fate of many British seaside towns, in has a "stuck in time" feel. Given that the rappers are bragging about fairly "adequate" features standard to most British towns (cinemas, hotels, pubs, leisure centers, secondary schools are all features of most British towns and cities), the song paints an "everyday" rather than special destination:

> Now, this is a story about a standard Welsh town
> With adequate facilities come on down
> They got a cinema, biscuit factory built to plan
> I wanna tell you all about a place I know called Cwmbran

This celebration of mundanity might be a British penchant for being understated in contrast to the exaggerations in mainstream US rap, but it is also aligned with celebrating one's locality in hip-hop. They give the sense that little has changed in Cwmbran for decades, and perhaps fears of demographic changes brought about by EU migration is one reason that Wales voted to leave the EU in the 2016 referendum. Torfaen (Cwmbran's county) voted leave 59% to 40% with 70% turnout and perhaps this manifestation of postcolonial melancholia, and GLC's critique of it, are somehow interlinked. This is where one thread of humor lies: a direct response to those who might find little change desirable, GLC remind us of how boring and uninteresting such a predicament can be. "So if you come from far away like Essex or Vietnam, just remember it's the place where indoor shopping began." Conflating Essex and Vietnam is telling, using the parodic techniques misdirection or exaggeration, essentially stating that Essex (in the east of England) might as well be Vietnam for the stereotypical Welsh provincialism represented. To state that in Cwmbran you can "reach your goals: from drainage to locksmith to pest control" suggests that its inhabitants' ambitions are far from lofty.

GLC's celebration of averageness also feels like an ironic celebration of "backwardness," parochialism, and provincialism, traits not normally celebrated in rap unless it is a nostalgic celebration for "back in the day." While nostalgia and localism are elements celebrated in mainstream rap, "Cwmbran" does not perform nostalgia so much as an unchanging Cwmbran, though such simplicity made be providing the "escape" that tourists may look for. But the joke is that Cwmbran is not an ideal tourist destination by most people's definition. I would argue that the backwardness is part of the group's humor aesthetics and that there is an overall sense that these artists are not quite up to speed with the world in a pop music culture that fetishizes the new or the "next big thing."[17]

The choice to use *Fresh Prince of Bel Air* is worth further interrogation. The show aired from 1990 to 1996, and ran in syndication in the UK on Channel 4. In Wales, SC4 broadcasts the Welsh-language programming as well as Channel 4 (UK-wide) material including the *Fresh Prince of Bel Air*. Similarly, the choice to parody *EastEnders* (broadcast on BBC One in Wales) is another comment on how Wales is subjected to London-based television and culture as well as American products distributed globally. The genre of rap used for the theme song was tame even for the time, pop rap as opposed to gangsta rap or other styles. Not only does it then reference an out-of-date rap style, but one which could be heard as "uncool" or not edgy enough.

Using these texts through a Welsh parodic lens goes to highlight the hybrid nature of Welsh identity, part Welsh, part English, American, and global. To quote Hill and Griffiths, "That the vast majority of the media in Wales—press, television and radio—is owned, controlled and accountable to bodies beyond its border is indisputable" (Barlow, in Aaron and Williams 2005, 208). Like *EastEnders*, one might argue that people in Wales are subject to foreign imports that do not necessarily represent their inhabitants, and the use of rap as yet another import also helps to highlight these notions of difference (if Wales is known as the "land of song" then what does rapping do to disrupt this?). Additionally, the song and music video also go to highlight how the global and national can be inscribed *into* the local in complex ways. Lastly, GLC encouraging their listeners to spend a day trip there or come stay the night to Cwmbran assumes an imagined audience that travels modestly and infrequently. In other words, the GLC audience (not the real audience, but the imagined addressee of GLCs persona) could not afford a more lavish holiday. In postindustrial Wales, this speaks both socially and economically to the limited mobility of its perceived inhabitants.

GLC makes fun of assumptions about Wales while at the same time parodying the mundanity of a Welsh town with a sense of hip-hop's proclivity toward aspirationalism. This represents some of the complexities of Welsh (artistic) identity: the centrifugal global force which intersects with the centripetal local force which Paul Carr sees as a creative balance and dialogic tension between the commercial imperatives of the global and the Welsh identity of the local (Carr 2010, 281). Therefore, while humor has the potential to disrupt and question social conditions, GLC's music is also very much a product of these wider tensions and may perform a "conservative transgression" (Harries 2000, 130) of them.[18] These tensions are enacted on a daily basis, and even if they are spotlighted and mocked, they seem somewhat stuck between the push and pull between global and local in relation to English hegemony.

Bricka Bricka

In 1998, when he was five years old, David Vujanic moved from a predominantly Croatian part of Serbia to London (in an interview he states, "my dad came over in 1998 and we did what we had to do to get here"). He was an asylum seeker from war-torn former-Yugoslavia who found citizenship in Britain. He has since become a YouTube personality, creating popular parody music videos as well as being one of the "filthy fellas," a group that hosts one of the most watched football fanzine channels on the internet.

Influenced by characters such as Borat and groups like the Lonely Island, Vujanic began to make parody videos in 2011 with a group he named the "Tea Towel Gang" but subsequently parodied Waka Flocka's "Hard in da Paint" through a character called Bricka Bricka on April 14, 2011.

Bricka Bricka is a self-described "Eastern European man," a construction-working immigrant who will do numerous jobs for low wages. His character espouses a number of stereotypical qualities of this Othered stereotype: a day laborer who will do any job for a low wage, is uneducated, sexist, and enjoys drinking on the job and fighting.[19] He is potentially threatening to native males as he raps, "I like your girlfriend very much," eats raw chickens, wears tracksuits, and brags that he can break bricks with his head. "Hard in da Paint," a basketball term, now becomes a comment on migrant labor and the stereotypical jobs many Eastern Europeans in the UK currently adopt. Unlike Flocka's original track and video, Bricka Bricka is hosted exclusively through the third-party video site YouTube and not part of the commercial recording industry in the same sense. The inclusion of this example may not seem emblematic of what we think of as "UK hip-hop" at first glance for a number of reasons. However, its circulation and consumption in an increasingly changing music world suggests that musical "products" such as this should be considered in a wider study of popular music culture.[20] Whether or not one wants to consider it part of the UK hip-hop sphere, it works on one level as a parody of US hip-hop and thus relies on some knowledge of Waka Flocka's style of hip-hop to resonate as parody. It plays on the racial (and other) differences between the two versions, and the braggadocio of Flocka's style is adapted to Bricka's ability to live cheaply and work hard.

Bricka Bricka reflects anxieties and critiques of Eastern European immigrant stereotypes that have become increasingly prevalent over the past fifteen years or so. In the single largest expansion of the European Union, in 2004, a number of countries from the former Eastern Bloc were included: the Czech Republic, Estonia, Hungary, Latvia, Lithuania, Poland, and Slovakia (the other countries were Cyprus, Malta, and Slovenia). Britain was one of the few EU countries that decided to open its labor market immediately, unlike others that imposed restrictions on employment for up

FIGURE 6.2 Bricka Bricka, "Hard in Da Paint" (2011)

to seven years. This contributed to substantial migration to the UK from compara-tively poorer countries. Many of these migrants helped to provide cheap labor in menial positions. The right-wing media helped to fuel a moral panic against such migrations (almost as an "invasion"), depicting many immigrants from countries such as Poland as benefit scroungers, mentally and socially backward, heavy drink-ers who contribute to crime and anti-social behavior.[21] Representative headlines include: "Migrants DO take our jobs: Britons losing out to foreign workers, says official study" (Express 2014); "The truth about East European migration: One in 30 Latvians are living in Britain, one in 60 Poles are also over here—and statistics don't even show latest influx" (MailOnline 2014); "Britain must say 'no' to European workers" (The Telegraph 2013, quoted in Pompova 2015, 7); "EU says UK must dole out MORE benefits: Brussels takes legal action to force Britain to lift restrictions on migrants claiming handouts" (MailOnline November 2014); "Britons 'less likely to have a job than East European migrants': Finding contrast with other countries with high immigration" (MailOnline April 2013). Though evidence suggests that such claims are misrepresenting the figures,[22] these migrants are depicted as invaders who are straining the country's resources.

While the notion of a "Eastern Europe" was arguably constructed in the Enlightenment rather than being a newer product of the Cold War (Wolff 1994), Buchowski (2006) argues that after the 1989 revolutions, Orientalizing the Eastern Bloc went beyond simply a geographical "iron curtain" issue. This restructuring was largely based on new capitalist frameworks, divided by those who adapted to new systems versus those who did not. Buchowski's study argued that Said's notion of orientalism shifted and transformed in the context of the "new order" that emerged in 1990s post-socialist Eastern Europe (Buchowski 2006, 465). The 2004 expan-sion of the EU has arguably reframed the geopolitics of a constructed "Central" and Othered "Eastern Europe" (Kuus 2007), associating central EU countries as more "Western," with more "European" qualities in contrast to their Eastern neigh-bors. Melegh (2006) argues that it established a new second tier around the West European core states (194), a two-tier system that could be adapted and applied to the divisions we find in the West's (and the UK's) opinion of Eastern Europe (its reputational geography, we could say, see Slater and Anderson 2011), and of UK migrants from the region.

Returning to the parody, the original "Hard in da Paint" (2010) is an example of mainstream Southern US hip-hop of its era. Originally from Atlanta, Waka Flocka (full rap name Waka Flocka Flame) was signed to 1017 Brick Squad Records (led by Gucci Mane). From his 2009 debut album *Flockaveli*, the single "Hard in Da Paint"[23] is simplistic in its beat and lyrical message: primarily, that Flocka is tough and should not be crossed. The music video depicts the rapper among the "Jungles" of Los Angeles, the Baldwin Village area of Los Angeles and home to the Black Peace Stones gang's California branch (a.k.a. the Jungle Stone Bloods).[24] Members of this community surround him rapping, and by the end of the video he meets with one of the senior members of the gang, and is almost symbolically initiated into the community via the "O.G." (original gangsta). The lyrics include:

> I go hard in the mu'fuckin' paint nigga
> Leave you stankin' nigga
> What the fuck you thinkin' nigga
> I won't die for this shit
> Or what the fuck I say (Brick Squad)
> Front yard broad day wit da S.K. (ba ba ba ba ba ba bow)
> See Gucci, that's my mothafuckin' nigga
> I hang in the Dale wit' dem hit squad killers
> Waka Flocka Flame one hood ass nigga
> Ridin' real slow bendin' corners my nigga

The lyrics espouse a number of stereotypes of southern US hip-hop of this era: the braggadocio which involves gun violence (S.K. is a reference to a particular type of automatic rifle) and threats ("what the fuck you thinkin'"), as well as shouting out label owners and others. Bragging about sexual prowess and describing women as property are features when he says "Gotta main bitch (And) gotta mistress (what else) / A couple girlfriends, I'm so hood rich." We also have profanity and use of the "n" word, common in gangsta rap.

The original version of "Hard in Da Paint" is problematic in its glorification of violence, misogyny, and criminality, but for our purposes, this track and accompanying video become the frame by which Vujanic translates the original into Bricka Bricka's version. As Flocka is part of "Brick Squad," we can see how the character translates into a construction worker who brags about how he can "break bricks with his head," and is so poor that he bought his daughter a brick for her birthday. The music video takes place in (presumably) Vujanic's backyard with an amateur, low-production quality to it. The same musical track from Waka Flocka is utilized but Bricka Bricka raps over it using intentionally parodic broken English (and being less rhythmically integrated with the music). Instead of the "ni**a" word ending every line in the original, Bricka uses "motherfucker" (pronounced in bad English as "motherfakir") instead for the opening lines:

> Eastern European in the house motherfucker
> Do loft cheap price motherfucker

> I like to drink motherfucker
> Break bricks with head motherfucker . . .
> Homebase motherfucker
> Paint, brick brick sweat sweat
> . . . On back of truck we used to come to UK ([shouts in
>   background:] Eastern Europe)
> Minimum wage, build loft, do garden, cheap labor, 13 hour

In the opening, we have an acknowledgment of origins (however geographically general), as many rappers shout out their home towns and wider localities (e.g., "South Side," "West Coast"), acknowledging commercial brands ("Homebase") as well as echoing conservative worries that these immigrants are coming in stealing jobs. Bricka goes on to say, "20 pound a day / tax evading / pay no rent / sleep on floor in house save money on rent" and brags, "I so hard / I sometimes eat cement." After work, he drinks "Irish ale" and has a kebab for two pounds ("kebab, 2 pound, is my diet"). In short, Bricka Bricka plays to the stereotypes and worries of conservative Britain, and in using hip-hop creates a frame to celebrate and brag about such "worrying" characteristics. With its status as creating a voice for marginalized peoples, and lyrical topics that include self-identification and associations with local alliances, hip-hop becomes the ideal soundtrack for this character. Particularly due to the amateurism of the video, we do not have a rapper flanked by his community. He is largely by himself in the video apart from brief scenes depicting his daughter. While Flocka's video provides a sense of the urban and community, we could argue that Bricka's video domesticates the immigrant. All of his bragging seems to have an impotent quality to it without a community or an appropriate setting for such activities.[25]

In terms of material used for the character, he no doubt draws from the anxiety and moral panic represented in headlines and stereotypes from right-wing newspapers, though interestingly his portrayal does not consider the group an entire drain on the nation's resources. Though he does mention "tax evade[ing]," Bricka contributes to the economy through his labor, though arguably undercutting other laborers who want to work for a legal wage. In an interview, he has also stated that a large basis for the character is his own father, whom he no longer speaks to, but he even used his father's van for the video ("Straight no Chaser" 2016). There are also no doubt intersections with the misogyny of "yob" and football culture, also prevalent in Serbia and Eastern Europe, and perhaps more specifically comparative to the "gopnik" stereotype (Yegorov 2016)—Eastern European youths who wear Adidas tracksuits, and squat drinking beer and eating sunflower seeds. Proliferated on internet memes, videos, etc., the gopnik translates loosely into some of the "chav" or "white trash" stereotypes in Britain and the US respectively, and perhaps Vujanic's doubleness (and/or his "in betweenness") as Slavic and British intersect through some of these tropes. He can be very much viewed as a trickster figure, as Weaver and Ozieranski (2016) have written of Polish jokes in the context of European Union labor migration: "the humour of the Polish migrant is a trickster discourse and thus assertive, outward looking and sometimes directed toward the impositions of the centre" (588). They see the trickster as a traveler and a liminal figure, able to mobilize humor "to resist cultural reductionisms and forced representations" (582). To exaggerate such stereotypes is to call them into question, and at once shows a character who is becoming part of the multicultural fabric of Britain.

The Bricka Bricka character in some ways is reminiscent of the minstrelsy stereotype (Lott 1993; Lhamon Jr. 2000; Pickering 2008) of African Americans as uneducated, oversexualized, and enjoy eating chicken and watermelon (though here we get a diet of kebab and beer). While the minstrelsy stereotype also included lazy in its categorization, Bricka Bricka brags how many hours a day he works, and how low the wage is that he receives. In fact, he starts to brag about his sexual prowess before he realizes he needs to go back to work ("I have very big dick, but, I must [tone of voice changes from confident to dejected], go back to work now I go eat my sandwich and I earn money, bye everyone"). Bricka Bricka employs a number of problematic stereotypes, but his assertion of how hard he works can be read as a sly dig at English natives who may be more work averse than his migrant worker compatriots.

Bricka Bricka also represents a tradition of "ethnic humor," including Jewish and African American humor in post-WWII America (Gillota 2013), and such immigrant stereotypes could be traced to nineteenth-century vaudeville and earlier (but with different figures in the "Other" position, such as Irish immigrants to the US). Gillota writes that the insider/outsider or center/margins binary drives most ethnic humor throughout the twentieth century, and "It underlies the ways in which we often talk about race and ethnicity" (Gillota 2013, 2).[26] These figures who have been painted as threatening by various groups are brought to the forefront through parody. Vujanic's "ethno-drag" performs these controversial stereotypes in an exaggerated manner, and the level of humor or offensiveness interpreted will be dependent on the socially situated contexts of individual YouTube viewers.[27]

The use of a hip-hop song as parody also suggests associations with a stereotypical notion of mainstream hip-hop "blackness," as well as the braggadocio, oversexualization, and the importance of calling out of important commercial brands (in this case, Homebase and Sports Direct). While US hip-hop's embrace of capitalism tends to point toward luxury items (Gucci, Rolex, and other high end brands), this parody points to both the poverty of the immigrant stereotype, and tropes of the "chav" wearing cheaply made tracksuits from Sports Direct and TK

Maxx.[28] The simplicity of the beat and lyrics could also add to the "simplicity" of the character portrayed, both in the case of Bricka Bricka and Waka Flocka's style of hip-hop.

The characterization found in Bricka Bricka, to paraphrase Musa Okwonga, would fall under the category of the "bad immigrant" in the UK, as he recounted to Nikesh Shukla, editor of the collection *The Good Immigrant*:

> The biggest burden facing people of colour in this country is that society deems us bad immigrants—job-stealers, benefit scroungers, girlfriend-thieves, refugees—until we cross over in their consciousness, through popular culture, winning races, baking good cakes, being conscientious doctors, to become good immigrants. (Shukla 2016, "Editor's Note")

Although Bricka Bricka does not represent the BAME community in Britain, the stereotype is firmly "Othered" in multiple ways (and Vujanic is arguably "in between" cultures in ways we will see from rapper Lowkey in the next chapter). While race is a primary factor in minority difference, that in an ever-changing Europe, white ethnicity becomes an ever-complicated affair. As Shukla points out, it is often through popular culture that these "folk devils" can become integrated into mainstream or official British "culture" (e.g., Sir Mo[hammad] Farah and *Bake-Off* winner Nadiya Hussein).[29] The popular culture in the case of Bricka Bricka is the use of hip-hop culture, and while it is the incongruity of black Southern US gangsta rap alongside an Eastern European white immigrant stereotype that gives "Hard in Da Paint" much of its humor context, it is also a *lingua franca* for youth cultures to integrate and share "cultural citizenship" in ways that other forms of citizenship feel unavailable.

Over the years, Vujanic's character has evolved (as has the production quality of the videos) though many of the same stereotypes are performed. After "Hard in Da Paint," he continued to create videos with the Bricka Bricka character. He raps on the parody of Drake's "Hotline Bling," "Immigrant Bling": "You used to call me on my brick phone, late night when you need cheap job . . . Of course I came illegally, doing jobs for any fee." His response to Beyoncé's feminist anthem "Run the World (Girls)" is "Run the World (Not Girls)" and proceeds to tell us why men are in charge rather than women, while his wife (presumably) does cleaning and other chores around the house in the video. Such misogyny is reminiscent of Sasha Baron Cohen's "Borat" character from the eponymous 2006 film, which depicts a journalist from Kazakhstan who interviews real-life Americans while traveling West to meet the object of his desire, *Baywatch* actress Pamela Anderson.

Psy's "Gangnam Style" becomes "Eastern Europe Style," with lyrics that include, "Eastern Europeans we are very very poor, go to USA and Western Europe to get passport / Work very hard then send money back home . . . Clean house, fix doors . . . we have very nice women . . ." The chorus ends "work, work, work drink fight, eastern Europe style"; it continues, "We drink alcohol from the day we are born . . . eastern Europeans we like to wear track suits, Nike, Adidas, Reebok, Lonsdale, Fila tracksuit." He shouts out Eastern European dictators and countries during the song. "Eastern European Style" has since had over four million views, the most popular of his Bricka Bricka videos (see Table 6.1 for a full discography).[30]

With his friend Original K he formed the duo 4N Boyz—their track "Slav Squat" is a "diss" of UKIP and then-leader Nigel Farage in 2015: "Do the Slavic Squat, you know we ain't standin up, we gonna squat on your block, we gonna take your job, UKIP try to send us off, but we keep runnin off." The squatting while wearing track suits is another reference to the Gopnik stereotype, but they are also in Ferrari hats, drinking Fosters beer and wearing a Sports Direct employee uniform. They rap on top of a building, a trope for mainstream UK hip-hop videos at the time (like Lethal Bizzle's 2011 version of "Pow"), alongside a fancy car. The two address Farage directly: "Now back to Nigel. UKIP you're the vermin. I swear your wife is German. Send her back to Berlin. You want to send us back that' a no no. My cousins still coming by the truckloads." The reference to vermin alludes to journalist Katie Hopkins's comments about the refugee crisis in 2015 when she referred to the migrants as "vermin" and "cockroaches." The video gives the sense of sense of response to those events, perhaps showing that what once was a parody on stereotypes in the spirit of Borat can become a force for political commentary and response.

While portraying characters in an unfavorable light is indeed problematic, the act of vocal utterance demands a listener, a viewer—these hidden figures can no longer be unseen or unheard. Humor, perhaps, makes the "Other" figure less threatening, and opens a space through the shared language of popular culture. Jerry Palmer notes that one recurring function of humor is that it provides "relief from tension anxiety or fear" (1993, 88). Thus, these parodies could be relieving the tensions brought about by postcolonial melancholia in a unique manner. In addition to intending viewing pleasure, there exists a "clickbait" element of Vujanic's brand (YouTube Channel entitled "Vuj") which extends beyond these videos into arenas such as Copa 90 YouTube channel. Sharing these videos also encourage user participation and help make them go "viral" (Vernallis 2011, 89). But there is a political element here despite its humorous style, and makes a case for hip-hop parody (and YouTube) to be considered a part of the wider UK hip-hop landscape.

TABLE 6.1

Bricka Bricka Discography (2010–2017)

Original Song	Artist	Date Released	Parody Title	Date Released (YouTube)
"Hard in Da Paint"	Waka Flocka	July 21, 2010	"Hard in Da Paint (Eastern European Re-Mix)"	April 14, 2011
"Run the World (Girls)"	Beyoncé	May 11, 2011	"Run the World (NOT GIRLS)"	May 23, 2011
"Otis"	Jay-Z and Kanye West	Aug 11, 2011	"Otis (Eastern European Re-Mix)" (feat. Kanyowski West)	Sept 11, 2011
"Gangnam Style"	Psy	July 15, 2012	"Eastern Europe Style"	Oct 9, 2012
"Drunk in Love"	Beyoncé	Dec 16, 2013	"Drunk at Work!"	April 2, 2014
"Hotline Bling"	Drake	Oct 26, 2015	"Immigrant Bling"	Nov 2, 2015

Other Tracks

"Immigration"	Don't Jealous Me (feat. Bricka Bricka)	July 24, 2011		
"Slav Squat"	4N Boyz	May 4, 2015		
"Fuck Brexit"	4N Boyz	March 30, 2017		

Looking at these parodies through a postcolonial lens questions any fixed binary divisions between "native" and "Other," or "parody" and "original," and shows GLC and Vujanic rapping back against power relations that they have experience from the subaltern perspective while questioning the revolutionary nature of their message. Pickering writes that, "Postcolonial theory dwells upon ambivalences of meaning and dissonances of identification as key points to be prised open in articulating resistance to relations of power, authority and control" (Pickering 2001, 169).

The most pressing questions that remain, however, are: Does the parody further ingrain these stereotypes within the British cultural fabric? Or do they point a spotlight on their absurdity? Does Vujanic's own ethnic affinity to his subject matter complicate his performance, perhaps even deeming it possible? As Pickering asks regarding stereotypes, "Who speaks for whom and with what consequences?" (2001, xiv). One can see links with African-based trickster figures, and of Signifyin(g) on whiteness and his own heritage. Are we to view these videos with the same postcolonial lens as we would for, say, Riz MC let alone GLC, or do we look at the postsocialist "Othering" of these immigrant communities and their original nations? For Akala, Riz MC, GLC, and Bricka, we are all dealing with some form of minority difference and subalterity, but should we place them in the same postcolonial "family of resemblances"?

Globally, hip-hop music and culture often acts as a mouthpiece for disenfranchised and marginalized groups. It engages in politics and culture in multifaceted and powerful ways, often responding to conditions of difference and is a powerful space for critique, commentary, and celebration. One of the critiques that UK hip-hop offers is a response to the postcolonial melancholia involved in Britain's mainstream (white) narratives. To quote J. Griffith Rollefson, "European hip-hop gives voice to the ideal of equality through anti-assimilationist expressions of minority difference, a set of essentializing and paradox-laden creative strategies that expose the national conflations of race and citizenship in European national imaginaries" (Rollefson 2017, 3). Bricka Bricka and GLC complicate those conflations of race and citizenship further, but such is the paradox-laden nature of postcoloniality. Former Yugoslav and Eastern Bloc nations that were once under Soviet (or at least socialist) control may also share colonial or subaltern anxieties while becoming Othered by Western perceptions. Rap parody provides one outlet to express both pride and critique of any backward-looking sentiments within the context of forward-looking British youth well versed in popular culture and humor.

Conclusion: From the East End to Eastern Europe:
Hip-Hop Parody and Stereotypes

These two case studies of parody hinge on exaggerations of stereotypes and the inversion of a viewer/listener's expectations with regards to hip-hop culture. Instead of a mainstream urban US (African American) environment, we see a "standard Welsh town" and the boastings of an Eastern European immigrant laborer in a suburban backyard. "Fresh Prince of Cwmbran" focuses on leisure while "Hard in Da Paint" deals with labor, two interrelated concepts which are at the heart of postindustrial Britain and its labor force. It is important to remember that the rise of gangsta rap in postindustrial Los Angeles and celebration of gangs depicted in Flocka's "Hard in Da Paint," or Will Smith's fleeing the dangers of Philadelphia for Bel Air, are products of a wider global shift in economic circumstances.

While the performance of Otherness through the white ethnicities of Welsh-ness and Eastern European-ness are at the forefront of these case studies, there is also a class issue underlying them: while Bricka Bricka overtly brags about his poverty and how much he works, GLC's provincial outlook for "Fresh Prince of Cwmbran" suggests a group of people with fewer financial opportunities for mobility (social or geographical). For Bricka, there is a double consciousness at work: at once British and foreign, expressed through the medium of hip-hop as black culture.

Humor and stereotype, as well as hip-hop, often links us to a locality. These case studies deal with two cases of "East"-ness, as Other, misrepresenting or stereotyping due to media representation, in one case a television soap opera and in the other a response to the stereotypes proliferated in the right-wing media about Eastern Europeans. Gillota reminds us that humor is a form of boundary construction, and that the "community of laughter" helps construct a "we-ness" therein (Gillota 2013, 6). And if humor is community building, one line of thought sees GLC aligning itself with a global audience (rapping in English), putting itself firmly in a global citizenship that is "in" on the joke. For Vujanic, he is putting himself in the dominant "Western" community by poking fun at the Othered and demonized immigrant figure, though it is worth noting that a number of YouTube comments point to Eastern Europeans inside and outside Britain enjoying the videos for various reasons.

There is a sense of self-deprecation in both case studies, and they also plays on a notion of inadequacy or failure—neither GLC or Bricka Bricka are living up to being particularly good rappers (or what we expect rappers to be), and some of the humor of discomfort lies in a "they shouldn't be rapping" as well as a "they shouldn't be rapping about THAT" sense. To quote Carlo Nardi on the "comedy of discomfort" for fake realism television like *The Office*: "Discomfort has the effect of internalising social issues, forcing us to deal with the pervasiveness of ideology: morality is not something that concerns the fictional world, but it is summoned up by our complicity in the discrimination process" (Nardi in Giuffre and Hayward 2017, 75). Perhaps these targets of parody, through the performance of them, do help us rethink our complicity toward their discrimination.

Michael Pickering sees stereotyping as a process and practice, endemic of modernity. Europe's modern ambitions gave rise to nationalism and pseudoscientific rationalizations of racial difference, and we can see these developments as having continued influence in current contexts and cultural outputs (2001, xii). To quote Pickering, "This is the dilemma which stereotyping faces: to resort to one-sided representations in the interests of order, security and dominance, or to allow for more complex vision, a more open attitude, a more flexible way of thinking. Stereotyping functions precisely in order to forget this dilemma," (2001, 3–4). Visibility, however, is a double-edged sword, and through the language of hip-hop may help us to remember the aforementioned dilemma in all its layers.

Both stereotypes and the Other "involved attempts to combine and contain contrary themes, but in so doing keep those contrary themes in active view" (Pickering 2001, xi). In other words, we look at Bricka Bricka to humorously point out the absurdity of Eastern European stereotypes (almost as if to say, "they aren't *that* bad") but you are giving those stereotypes a platform, to quote Pickering, to keep those themes in "active view." Such are the paradoxes of postcolonial, postmodern, and hip-hop's aesthetics in particular. Bricka Bricka is a gendered other in the sense that he borrows from a stereotypical exaggerated black masculinity of hip-hop aligned with "backward" gender-relation thinking associated with Soviet cultures. But ask Pickering writes, "For stereotyping to be effective, it needs not to be seen and acknowledged for what it does. To see a stereotype in this way is to start stepping back from it, to begin unravelling its appearance of being natural, absolute, given, the truth and nothing but the truth of what is represented" (Pickering 2001, 71).

One reaction to Vujanic's videos could be against the political incorrectness of the portrayal: "You can't do that! You can't stereotype Eastern Europeans like that!" But what British society through the media outlets have shown is exactly that— they have been stereotyped frequently in some of the most widely read newspapers in the country. As Owusu-Bempah and Howitt remind us, ethnic jokes and humor are not the product of an individual pathology or even a particular group of people, but they are the product of society (in Lockyer and Pickering 2009, 48). Perhaps in all of Bricka Bricka's performed vulgarity, he helps us to ask ourselves "*should* we be stereotyping these individuals?" Should anyone be stereotyping them? This discomfort may have a more important social purpose, as Carlo Nardi writes on mocumentaries: "Discomfort has the effect of internalising social issues, forcing us to deal with the pervasiveness of ideology: morality is not something that concerns the fictional world, but it is summoned up by our complicity in the discrimination process" (Nardi in Giuffre and Hayward 2017, 75). For some, we may see humor as a way of reinforcing the social order and keeping people "in their place," but there is another strand that attempts to transgress those orders, allowing us to question them, and perhaps question the culture originally parodied, in this case, hip-hop culture.

To parody parochialism while critiquing manifestations of Gilroy's "postcolonial melancholia" show how humor can be deployed to resist prejudice and xenophobic strands of the political economy. It also questions the narrow assumptions of who hip-hop music can represent, performing a wide variety of identities and a complex and nuanced set of critiques. These uses of humor may reveal deeper meanings about local rap, social critique, and the notion of one's place in "Britain," whether that be via constructions of "Welshness," the Eastern European "Other," or the next group of "Others" to migrate to Britain.

Notes

1. Exceptions of those who engage with hip-hop and humor include Kaijikawa 2015, Garrett 2015, and Kärjä 2011. More generally, other studies of music and humor include Dalmonte 1995, Covach 1995, Mera 2002, and Kay 2006.

2. While jokes and humor have existed since time immemorial, various thinkers have had different ideas on the function of humor on both individual and wider cultural levels. For example, Plato, Aristotle, Quintillian, and Hobbes have stated that we laugh from feelings of superiority over other people (Critchley 2002, 2). Many writers in the nineteenth century noted that laughter is a relief of pent-up nervous energy, and Freud in the early twentieth century wrote that energy released in laughter would have been used to contain or repress psychic activity (Critchley 2002, 3). Covach breaks down these perspectives into the superiority theory (Plato, Hobbes), relief theory (Freud), and incongruity theory (Kant, Schopenhauer), and he utilizes incongruity theory as applied to musical style in the film *This Is Spinal Tap* (Covach 1995, 400).

3. Nick Braae cites Roger Scruton's theories of humor: at once, laughter serves to make light of our differences as well as cutting down to size individuals or institutions as a safety valve against cultural and societal hierarchies (Scruton in Braae 2019).

4. For a more thorough survey of (particularly psychological) theories of humor, see Brøvig-Hanssen 2020. She writes on mashups and remixes, of which the incongruities which contribute to their humor are one important factor that contributes to their virality online.

5. Parody is a derivative of the Greek term *paroidia* which means burlesque or "counter-song" (Harries 2000, 5). Hutcheon points out that *para* also means "besides" in addition to "counter" so that there may also be a suggestion of "intimacy instead of contrast" (Hutcheon 2000, 32). A number of those who have theorized parody point out the role of inversion, and the fact that what one sees and/or hears subverts audience expectation. Linda Hutcheon wrote that parody "is a form of imitation but imitation characterized by ironic inversion, not always at the expense of the parodied text" (6).

6. Parody and other forms of satire are not foreign to British culture. One could point to graphic satire in early modern England, making fun of figures such as King James, monopolists, and Catholics (Pierce 2008). Beyond seventeenth-century print culture, other forms of political satire existed in publications like *Punch* (established 1841), and depicting figures such as immigrants to Victorian London (such as Italian street musicians) as the target of ridicule (Picker 2003, 42–80). While the type of outsider may have changed over time, the existence of humor and satire targeting foreigners did not. The 1960s, particularly in television, initiated a "satire boom" with news programs like *That Was the Week that Was* (1962–1963) and magazines like *Private Eye* (founded 1961) meant to parody wider politics and culture (Carpenter 2009). Examples of musical humor in the 1970s include groups like Monty Python's *Flying Circus* (1969–1974) ("The Lumberjack Song," "The Spam Song," and "Always Look on the Bright Side of Life" from *Monty Python's Life of Brian*), and the figure of the "Other" was parodied as seen in the "Goodness Gracious Me" 1960 comedy song between Peter Sellers, who plays an Indian doctor, and Sophia Loren, who plays the wealthy Italian patient who falls in love with him. One could look at earlier vaudeville and minstrelsy to also find the performance of racial and ethnic stereotypes for comedy purposes, part of a long history of Othering in Anglo-American entertainment. More recently, Pickering and Lockyer write about the stereotypical characters of Mrs. Merton (played by Caroline Aherne) and Borat (played by Sasha Baron Cohen) in UK humor: "Ali G and Mrs Merton play upon two existing stereotypes, the wannabe gangsta rapper from the South East of England, and the prim but saucy nosey-parker from the North West" (Lockyer and Pickering 2009, 199). Cohen's character can be read as part of a history of "blacking up" by white people, but the Lockyer and Pickering ask was he a white man pretending to be an Asian pretending to be black? For Mrs. Merton they argue that Mrs Merton "invited a nostalgic celebration of a part Northernness in English regional culture—all cobbled streets, flying ducks and homemade jam" (199). The fact that both Ali G and Mrs. Merton were believed to be real people by some audience members and interviewees goes to show that they played into existing stereotypes well, and that the joke was on both the stereotype itself and those who believed in it. While the aim of this chapter is not to find an inherent "Britishness" in these examples, we can point to a long tradition of wordplay, puns, satire, and self-deprecation in British parody and other forms of humor.

7. For a parody group like The Lonely Island, the general style of the music is mimicked rather than a track that already exists. Songs like "I'm on a Boat" (featuring T-Pain) and "I just Had Sex" draw from '90s R&B, sounds from similar technologies, singing styles, and music video imagery (though to more exaggerated effect). The song "Lazy Sunday," rapping about mundane aspects of living in Muncie, Indiana (eating cupcakes, buying snacks from the local convenience store, and watching *The Chronicles of Narnia*), mimics "harder" rap videos that celebrate the everyday ("Nuthin But a G Thang") and plays on the title of the Dre album *The Chronic* (slang for marijuana), by delaying third syllable in the "Chronic . . . les of Narnia" punchline. Penny Spirou has written of the Lonely Island's trademark: "a blend of hip-hop beats and rhymes articulating the absurd/mundane." With "hip-hop as a mode of comedic address" (Spirou in Giuffre and Hayward 2017, 129), she continues, "whiteness is made strange, made different, but also made to be awkward and somewhat mundane" (138). Songs like "Dick in a Box" (2006) parody RnB boy bands including New Edition, 112, Boyz II Men, and Next, questioning hypermasculine identity in these songs—and that their overall function is dual: to make fun of music culture and to make fun of themselves (138). In interviews, Vujanic states that the parodies of The Lonely Island were influences on his Bricka Bricka character.

8. GLC depicted their hometown in the songs "Newport Bouncers" and "Newport State of Mind" (based on Jay-Z and Alicia Keys's "New York State of Mind"), the latter being GLC's answer song to another artist's parody of the song. The music videos to "Newport State of Mind" celebrate the local imagery of the town which is in stark contrast to the metropolis imagery of New York City (an example of the incongruity theory of humor).

9. Examples that feature Welsh musical talent include BBC radio Cymru, *Gwyliwch Y Gofod* (*Watch this Space* youth music show), *Bandit* (on S4C, Welsh-language television channel), *Sioe Gelf* (Welsh language arts show on S4C), and *Gofod* (on S4C). See Carr 2010, 266.

10. Welsh popular music has had a long history, with groups that fall into Welsh language, Anglophone, and bilingual categories (Hill 2007 and Carr 2010, 267). From rock to reggae to hip-hop, and the 1990s groups associated with "Cool Cymru" (Manic Street Preachers, Stereophonics, Catatonia, Gorkys Zygotic Mynci), Hill argues that there have been flowerings of Welsh popular music at moments of crisis in the process of Welsh identity. Hill looks at Welsh hip-hop such as Y Tystion ("the witnesses," feat MC Sleifar and MC Gruff in Aberystwyth) and Pep le Pew who are "at once reverential and ironic" (Griffiths and Hill, in Aaron and Williams 2005, 222). These groups symbolize resistance while also dealing with national self-identity and a marginalized status, like earlier groups such as Datblygu and Llwybr Llaethog, in which hip-hop forms a "family of resemblances" with other marginalized groups, ethnicities, and nations (Hill 2007, 9). I would argue that the parody groups do similar complex performances of marginalization while critiquing both home and outsider perspectives. GLC's Anglophone Welsh categorization in the pop landscape also assumes a wider audience than Welsh-language pop, listened to by some Welsh but geared toward a wider UK and global audience that may see Welshness as Other (and their tour schedule also connotes this engagement with non-Welsh audiences).

11. A plethora of sheep jokes are found online and in books in tourist shops in Wales (Phillips 2002; Jeffreys 2004). Examples include:

Q. How do sheep herders practice safe sex?

A. Marking the sheep with a big X of the ones that kick!

Q. What do you call a sheep in Wales?

A. Fucked ("Sheepjokes")

Q How does a Welshman make a u-turn?

A By winking at her. (Welshjokes)

Q: What do you call a sheep tied to a fence in Wales?

A: A leisure center.

Q. What do you call a Welshman with many girlfriends?

A. A Shepherd. (Welsh Sheep Jokes, Message Board, December 12, 2007, user "Hammer")

Q. What do you call a Welsh prostitute?

A. Baaaaaabara. (user "Sandy_Boots" Aug 10, 2007, "Best Welsh Jokes" Message Board, Army Rumour Service, available at: https://www.arrse.co.uk/community/threads/best-welsh-jokes.65286/)

12. Braae's study (2019) deals with the stereotype of the "kiwi bloke" and its iterations of masculine humor in the music of New Zealanders Don McGlashan, John Clarke (aka Fred Dagg), and Flight of the Conchords (Bret McKenzie and Jermaine Clement).

13. The popularity of the song "Pow" in clubs especially has been recounted in Bramwell 2015.

14. The GLC song was not the first rap song about *EastEnders*—"Eastenders Rap" was also a rap song by Micron a.k.a. Rebel MC and Jungle legend DJ Ron in 1987 (which also used the theme song, but as scratched vinyl characteristic of '80s rap.

15. A number of YouTube comments also point this out, in addition to general quoting of lines viewers found funny. While pointing out the "wrong" postcode has an element of pedantry rather than finding it humorous, I would argue that such disjunctures between what one expects and what one is presented is at the heart of why parody is funny.

16. Carr notes that the GLC song "You Knows I Loves You" includes both a mix of "quintessentially British" references (Felicity Kendall, Argos, Walkers Crisps) alongside more global objects such as McDonalds and hip-hop (2010, 272).

17. YouTube comments point out funny lines from the video, but also comment from viewers from Cwmbran or from other English localities that they argue are worse that Cwmbran.

18. Dan Harries argues that film parody as a genre has become so codified that it demonstrates a "conservative transgression" as it becomes more canonized and less radical, echoing Baudrillard's sentiments that parody makes obedience and transgression equivalent (Harries 2000, 109).

19. In the Netherlands, there is a rapper from Poland (Mr. Polska) who plays similarly with these Eastern European immigrant stereotypes (Dynarowicz 2018).

20. YouTube and other social media were extremely important for the rise and mainstreaming of grime music. For various scholarly studies of YouTube see Burgess and Green 2009; Lovink and Niederer 2008; Snickars and Vonderau 2009; Duncum 2014; and Vernallis 2011.

21. Migrants from Poland have been the largest group from Eastern Europe to come to the UK and have been the biggest target of media demonization (Pompova 2015).

22. For example, Pompova 2015 cites evidence that post-2000 migrants have contributed considerably more in taxes than they have received in state benefits.

23. Going "hard in the paint" is a basketball term which refers to the painted area just around the basketball hoop, and usually defended by the center position on the opposition team. To go hard in the paint means to confidently and aggressively jump toward the rim, regardless of defenders or anything else in your way. This becomes a metaphor for Flocka's aggressive behavior toward any opponents.

24. The Black Peace Stones gang which originated in Chicago first appeared in California in 1969 and from the '60s to the '90s the Black P. Stones operated in the "bity" mid-city area (The City Stone Bloods) and the area known as the Jungles (Jungle Stone Bloods). While being subject to raids by the LAPD, the gang has a few hundred members in operation.

25. In terms of reception for Bricka Bricka's "Hard in Da Paint," the lengthy list of YouTube comments over the past six years fall under a few general categories. By far the most part include those who find particular lines in the video to be funny, and repeat them in the comments. Second, a number of viewers pointing out they knew that the Sports Direct in the video was the one in Brent Cross. There are also a number of viewers who ask which European country Bricka is from, and some have answered with Serbia. Others who are Eastern Europe themselves seem to agree with the humorous representation ("I'm half Polish and this was fucking hilarious" from user IDONTHAVEASMARTNAME), pointing out where they are from and how they can relate, or comment on Eastern Europeans in their own vicinity, for example user "Nathan huxtable" who writes "I first say this video years ago yet I still crap myself laughing from 11 seconds onwards haha I do love eastern europe though . . . the polish and czechs are the only people who work in my

town . . . the rest do fuck all except go to the pub . . ." "sam3333" writes, "They said that about the Irish 50 years ago the english didn't want to work weekends and all the Irish jumped at the chance, they were not used to good money." "Murat Tezgel": "So Fellow Easterns where are we all from?" Some comments are in Russian, some comment on Poland. "Soumaya" writes, "He aint Serbian that's his fake accent he is from essex!!!!" "RushyOnDaStix" writes "good but rasist [*sic*] kinda." Generally, comments are positive, with someone commenting that the video should have more views (some pointing out it is better than the Waka Flocka original).

26. A much longer history of immigrant stereotypes in performance from minstrelsy to vaudeville, radio, and television would be invaluable but is beyond the scope of this chapter and book.

27. The fact that post-conflict Yugoslavia is a place where music including rap has been used to intensify inter-ethnic hostility gives additional meaning to his performances (Balandina 2017). See also Music and Vukcevic in Miszczynski and Adriana Helbig 2017 for a history of Serbian hip-hop.

28. Adidas tracksuits were popular in the 1980s hip-hop scene pioneered by mainstream groups like Run-D.M.C. In addition to the stereotypes of the chav, there maybe also be a comment about the backwardness of using an outmoded hip-hop fashion in the same vein as GLC. For Bricka Bricka, there is the tracksuit-wearing Gopnik stereotype, of which their penchant for Adidas tracksuits dates back to the 1980s Moscow Olympics when Adidas was the official supplier for the Russian team. The track suits had associations with more high-class tastes but now have these similar lower-class associations within the UK ("Why is Adidas" 2015).

29. Sir Mohammad "Mo" Farah is Britain's most decorated track and field athlete and was a refugee from Somaliland. Hijab-wearing Bangladeshi-British (b. Luton) Nadiya Hussain was the winner in the sixth series of the nationally treasured television program *The Great British Bake-Off* in 2015, and has since hosted a number of programs for the BBC and elsewhere. In post-9/11 and 7/7 society, and in addition to the under-representation of Muslim and South Asian communities on British television, Hussain becomes a symbolic representative of her "Othered" characteristics while also portraying an ideal of British multiculturalism and a "fully integrated" Other whose talents and interests match what (white) mainstream Britain engages in.

30. YouTube comments like "Hard in Da Paint" are generally positive: "I will always be proud to be an eastern European no matter what. I'm Romanian and I prefer to get along with: moldovians, serbians, Russians, ukranians, belarusians, Croatians, macedonias, Montenegro, Latvia, Estonians . . . even Hungarians, yes. These are our brothers no matter how hard things are around here" (user blaaaaaaaaahify). Tom Barge writes, "This is why I love Eastern Europeans, always so fun." Another user (tristanauspride) writes, "why? Lol . . . slavs are white niggers." Maya Howard writes, "I'm Polish and I can verify this as 100% true hahah . . . jk but still it's pretty funny." CrashBangAdam writes, "The best part is that white 50 year old men will find this and take it literally."

7

POLITICS, IDENTITY, AND BELONGING

British Rappers of the Middle Eastern Diaspora

GIVEN HIP-HOP'S AFRICAN AMERICAN origins and wider associations with "blackness," it is unsurprising that hip-hop studies in the UK and Europe has focused on the "Black Atlantic" to frame its subjects (Gilroy 1993; Rollefson 2017). And yet, several minority ethnic youth cultures employ the language of hip-hop to express their diasporic hybrid identities in the UK. Rollefson notes the relative absence of writings about South Asian rappers and pop artists, for example, and his work on M.I.A. in particular helps redress this imbalance. But even more absent in the literature on British rappers are those with Arab heritage:[1] either those who are currently based in London (Lowkey, mic righteous, Jaz Kahina, Stylah),[2] or British-born rappers who have moved elsewhere (in the case of Shadia Mansour, to Palestine). Rappers with heritage of the Middle Eastern and North African region (MENA)[3] more generally may feel an affinity with one another (including Iranian-British rappers Reveal and Shay D), and as part of both the Black, Asian and Minority Ethnic (BAME) population. Many of these rappers are based in London, and this shared multicultural locality often helps promote self-identified "urban" communities that go beyond simple denotations of ethnicity or heritage.[4]

Many British rappers with heritage from the Arab-majority world offer a unique perspective on cultural identity, prejudice, and global and social inequalities. They are quick to acknowledge, for example, the role of Britain in carving and exploiting

Brithop. Justin A. Williams, Oxford University Press (2021). © Oxford University Press.
DOI: 10.1093/oso/9780190656805.001.0001

the Middle East under British Empire (including Mandatory Palestine),[5] and point to what they see as current UK-supported injustices: including Israel's settler colonialism, the Second Gulf War, Syrian airstrikes, and racial profiling in a post-9/11, post-7/7 UK. Their voices are uniquely placed to discuss past and present inequality and have been a powerful political presence toward such causes. As we will see, these rappers are often outspoken about the Israeli occupation of Palestine, the US and UK meddling in Middle Eastern countries, neoliberalism, and hyper-capitalism. Echoing Said, many of these rappers feel aspects of their heritage are in exile, and while these rappers are British-born rather than migrants, both their heritage and their exclusion from white mainstream Britain makes them aware of at least two homes.

In discussing Akala in Chapter 2, I pointed to what Paul Gilroy sees as the "diasporic intimacy" between African-based people who feel marginalized and displaced. Though arguably the most theorized on both sides of the pond, the African diaspora is not the only one existent in hip-hop. And while one could argue that it is the African American art form of hip-hop that became the voice of minority groups of multiple ethnicities and identities, a study of the particular diasporic identities involved will reveal an even more diverse palette of postcolonial hybridity. While it would be geographically inaccurate to speak of an "Arab Atlantic," there is however a formidable Arab diaspora around the world, especially in Brazil (6 million), France (6 million), Indonesia (15 million), and the US (3.7 million), compared to the UK's roughly half million. Given the selective memory around the British Empire in cultural consciousness, the Empire's role in Arab nations is often overlooked or ignored. But it should be remembered that the Arab nationalist movement was solidified in the modern era in part through resistance to British rule, through incidents such as the Iraqi revolt of 1920 (against British rule), the 1939 Arab revolt in Palestine, and under Nasser's leadership of Egypt in the '50s and '60s. After the defeat of the Arab coalition by Israel in the 1967 Six-Day War, politically active Arab nationalism began to decline, but its residue remains for later generations who grew up hearing about these histories and perspectives.

This chapter focuses on Iraqi-British rapper Lowkey, the Palestinian-British "First Lady of Arabic Hip-hop" Shadia Mansour, and Iranian-British rapper Shay D.[6] I discuss the ways in which their multi-layered and heterogeneous identities provide a context for wider political critiques, with lyrics frequently discussing war, terrorism, and post-Imperial power relations in the Middle East. Given Britain's role in creating "mandatory Palestine," Iran, Iraq, and other MENA nation-states after the fall of the Ottoman Empire, Arab-British and other rappers of Middle Eastern heritage also engage forcefully with the UK's colonial and neocolonial politics, intersecting with and co-creating Multicultural London Youth cultures in striking ways.

The chapter is divided into three main themes: Palestine, terrorism, and identity politics/belonging. This work helps to highlight an important, diverse, and often academically neglected demographic of UK rappers, adding to existing literature on MENA rappers by addressing British rappers with this heritage. Rappers of the Middle Eastern diaspora in multicultural London and elsewhere form a "family of resemblances" based on a sense of ethnic marginalization as well as by being a product of the lived consequences of (British) Empire.

Palestine

During World War I, the region of Palestine was part of the Ottoman Empire (allied with Germany). The British occupied the region in the period 1917–1918, and during this time British foreign minister Arthur Balfour issued the Balfour Declaration in 1917, promising a Jewish national home in Palestine. After WWI, the League of Nations approved a mandate that Great Britain administered Palestine with the goal of carrying out the 1917 declaration. Mandatory Palestine was then created after the break-up of the Ottoman Empire, led from 1920 by high commissioner Herbert Samuel, who was a Zionist and then-recent British cabinet minister.

From 1936 to 1939, there was an Arab revolt against British rule and open-ended mass Jewish immigration. The revolt was suppressed, ending in weakened military strength of Palestinian Arabs as Britain began to put its attention toward WWII. By 1947, the UN drafted resolutions for the end of the British mandate and for Israeli and Palestinian states which began a Civil War where Israel was victorious and established a state in 1948. The 1948 Palestinian exodus, also known as the Nakba (Arabic: النكبة, al-Nakbah, literally "disaster," "catastrophe," or "cataclysm"), occurred when more than seven hundred thousand Palestinian Arabs fled or were expelled from their homes, during the 1948 Palestine war (Kanaah and Nusair 2010).

In 1967, during the Six-Day War (Hebrew: מלחמת ששת הימים, Milhemet Sheshet Ha Yamim; Arabic: النكسة, an-Naksah, "The Setback" or حرب ١٩٦٧, Ḥarb 1967 "War of 1967"), also known as the June War, 1967 Arab–Israeli War, or Third Arab–Israeli War), Israel took control of the West Bank and Gaza. Arab Palestinians and Israelis were in constant conflict, but it was the first "intifada" (or uprising) from 1987 to 1991 (or 1993) that is seen as a moment of Palestinian resistance against the occupation of the West Bank and Gaza. In 1993, the Oslo accords brought some relative stability and peace in what some see as a "Honeymoon period" followed by a second intifada (2000–2005). This was first sparked when on September 28, 2000, Ariel Sharon forcibly entered Temple Mount/Haram al-Sharif, which led to Palestinian protests. These protests became known as Black October, when thirteen

Palestinians were killed, and two hundred were wounded, leading to further uprising. It is around this time when Palestinian hip-hop groups originate and rise in
prominence.

Much has been written about Palestinian rap groups emerging in the late '90s
and early 2000s, especially the group D.A.M. from Lod (Kahf 2007; Eqeiq 2010;
McDonald 2013a, 2013b; Maira and Shihada 2012; Swedenberg in Hamamsy and
Soliman 2013). The group consists of Tamer Nafar, Suheil Nafar, and Mahmoud
Jrere. These scholars who have studied D.A.M. often cite lyrics from some of their
most popular early songs from 2001 such as "Min Irhabi?" (Who's the Terrorist?)
and "Mali Huriye" (I Don't Have Freedom). Their lyrics express the rigid ethnic
hierarchy of the region, and government policy that creates a two-tier system. Early
in their career, D.A.M. rapped in both Hebrew and Arabic and had two versions
of the song "Born Here." Nafar says, "To describe the problem, I write in Hebrew
to inform those in power, so they could hear me. But to solve it, I write in Arabic"
(Equieq 2010, 61). D.A.M. has been written about as using discourses of exile and
emergence, and that hip-hop created the discursive space in which people were
making choices about style that could reconceptualize themselves and their relations to each other (McDonald 2013a, 72). Though D.A.M. has received by far the
most academic attention, other groups and rappers exist such as Arepeyat (Maira
and Shihade 2012), MC Gaza (Ibrahim Ghunaim), G-Town (Greenberg 2009),
Palestinian Rapperz, and MWR. Ramallah Underground is a musical collective of
rappers and DJs that have collaborated with Kronos Quartet and others, and circulate their music primarily on the internet.[7] Other groups in the MENA region rap
for Palestine, including Tunisian rapper "Weld El 15," Moroccan hip-hop group H-
Kayne, and Al Imbrator who wrote a song "For Palestine" in 2009.[8]

In the US, there are rappers with Palestinian heritage who feel close to the cause
(Iron Sheik, Free to P Project, Patriarch) as well as African American rappers like
M-1 of Dead Prez and Peruvian-American rapper Immortal Technique who rap
against the Israeli occupation. M-1 (and British rapper Lowkey) accompanied the
first convoy of Viva Palestina (a British-based organization) in 2009 which went
to deliver food, medicine, and other humanitarian aid to the Gaza Strip.[9] The Gaza
War of 2008 (also known as Operation Cast Lead, a.k.a. Gaza massacre, and Battle
of al-Furquan) lasted three weeks in the period 2008–2009 and resulted in over
one thousand Palestinian deaths and thirteen Israeli deaths. After this, rapper Lupe
Fiasco, on the track "Words I Never Said" (2011) responded: "Gaza strip was getting
bombed, Obama didn't say shit."

Scholars have placed Palestinian hip-hop within longer traditions of Arab dissenting music (McDonald 2013a, 2013b; George and Piva 2016), and artists have
pointed to US figures such as 2Pac and Public Enemy as original inspiration. For

many scholars, the Palestinian creation of culture (film, music, poetry, or otherwise, regardless of content) in general is in itself an act of resistance (Tawil-Souri 2011). More specifically, those who rap about Palestine not only provide a "voice for the voiceless" (a prominent trope in discussing hip-hop and the title of a song by Lowkey featuring Immortal Technique), but it helps to act as memory and as history, especially in light of active suppression of memory by the Israeli government (who included a parliamentary bill to ban any commemorations of the Nakba; Kanaanah and Nusair 2010, 9). "Talking back" (hooks 1989) to Israeli "negation of exile" and other erasures of Palestinian history (Piterberg 2001), rappers have an important role to play in addressing the cultural amnesia and dehumanization of British-Middle Eastern relations.

"Long Live Palestine" and "Long Live Palestine Part 2"

Rapper Lowkey (Karim Dennis, b. 1986) is one of the most outspoken political voices in British rap. His mother is a middle-class Arab jewelry designer from a politically active family that left Iraq in the 1970s, and his white father from Dover was active in the Socialist Workers Party.[10] He has rapped about several issues, especially wars in Palestine and his mother's homeland of Iraq. He attended the now-famous open mic sessions at Deal Real records in London and received notoriety for his *Key to the Game* mixtapes in the early 2000s. He was also a member of the Poisonous Poets[11] and of the supergroup Mongrel, founded by Arctic Monkeys drummer Matt Helders. He returned to the industry in 2008 with the album *Dear Listener* and in 2011 with *Soundtrack to the Struggle*, in addition to various singles over the years. He has been an outspoken opponent of the Iraq war, as part of the Stop the War Coalition, and has spoken out against the poor government response to the Grenfell tower fire ("Ghosts of Grenfell," 2017) and the US and UK governments bowing to (wartime and otherwise) corporate interests ("McDonald Trump," 2018, "The Death of Neoliberalism," 2017, "Terrorist," 2011). He is part of the Palestine Solidarity Campaign, and traveled to Palestine in 2009 to perform fundraisers for the refugee camps. His EP "Long Live Palestine Parts 1 and 2" released in 2009 (and on *Soundtrack to the Struggle*) speak out against the Israeli occupation of Palestine. He sees hip-hop as a "form of standing up and saying I am here and I demand to be recognized" (quoted in Lee 2010).

"Long Live Palestine" opens with the chant "This is for Palestine, Ramallah, West Bank, Gaza / This is for the child that is searching for an answer / I wish I could take your tears and replace them with laughter / Long live Palestine, Long live Gaza," chanted twice. He raps about how Israel blocked the UN from delivering food, and their bombing of schools, mosques, and hospitals. He pleads to "Imagine how you'd feel if it was your family" and "I'm not related to the strangers on the TV / But I relate because those strangers could have been me." There is an element of "survivor's guilt" in his work, in that a sentiment of "it could have been me" and that the faces he sees in the Middle East resembles his own.

Critiques of capitalism and neoliberalism are also a common theme in his work. He argues against corporations who support Israel and labels the country a "terror state": "This is not a war, it is systematic genocide." For example, in "Long Live Palestine," he raps, "You say you know about the Zionist lobby / But you put money in their pocket when you're buying their coffee / Talking about revolution, sitting in Starbucks / The fact is that's the type of thinking I can't trust." He states, "forget Nestle," referencing the largest food company that has a strong presence in Israel and whose factories are built on Palestinian lands. He states that "Obama promised Israel 30 billion over the next decade / They're trigger happy and they're crazy / Think about that when you're putting Huggies nappies on your baby." Many of the companies mentioned support the Israeli government, or are part funded by them, and movements to boycott such companies exist.[12] He mentions that Israel "drop bombs on innocent girls while they sleep in their beds" and that he views it "from a truly human perspective." The chorus chants "free free Palestine" which could easily be chanted at rallies and resembles a football game style chant (call: "free free" response: "Palestine").

"Long Live Palestine Part 2" expands the number of voices to include a diverse group of rappers who are against occupation. It opens with Lowkey's original chant of "This is for Palestine, Ramallah, West Bank, Gaza" but then states, "It's about time we globalized the intifada." Having multiple rappers on the track creates a "global cipher" which include raps in English, Arabic, and Farsi. They discuss the topic from different angles, alleging Zionism's incompatibility with Judaism, and that Israel's illegal use of white phosphorus should be considered a war crime. Furthermore, the presence of two members of D.A.M. also give a local and perhaps more perceivably authentic perspective to the injustices in the region.

In verse 1, Lowkey aggressively opposes the Zionist project, and alludes to when he was stopped and detained at Ben-Gurion airport in Israel: "I know I'm on a list for being more verbal / curse every Zionist since Theodor Herzl / Balfour was not a wise man / Shame on Rothschild." Herzl is associated with the modern Zionist movement and Balfour had written the Balfour Declaration to Baron Rothschild who was a Jewish banker and leader of the British Jewish community. His verse enables history to be remembered, the British role in the origins of Mandatory Palestine and then Israel, and the founding of the Jewish state on already-inhabited land.

Verse 2 belongs to Tamer Nafar of the Palestinian group D.A.M. His verse is in Arabic and discusses the "Withdrawal from Iraq, like a locust invasion, left only destruction"). Verse 3 is from the Narcicyst (now known as the Narcy, original name Yassin Alsalman) who is an Iraqi-Canadian rapper based in Montreal. Verse 4 is from Eslam Jawwad, a Lebanese-Syrian rapper who raps in Arabic. Verse 5 is in Farsi by Iranian rapper Hichkas. Verse 6 is the London-Irani rapper Reveal (of the Poisonous Poets), in English stating "Israel is a terrorist state . . . War criminals using lethal weapons like white phosphorous / Burns your flesh to the bone / And if you happen to live / You'll be left infected with cancer." Verse 7, in Arabic, is from Mahmoud Jreiri of D.A.M., and verse 8, in English, is by Hasan Salaam an African American rapper based in New York City. The final verse is by Shadia Mansour (whom I will discuss further in the next section), London-born but now residing in Palestine. The start of her verse is striking as she sings, "We should know how" in Arabic and then proceeds to tells us that "Arabic people, our unity is our skeleton / We should learn how to think / We should learn how to deliver a message without shutting doors in our faces." The use of multilingualism creates a sense of global importance while showing solidarity with the Palestinians.

"Long Live Palestine Part 2" is the sonic performance by a community who support the Palestinian cause. This is important considering the relative silence in mainstream British media at the time regarding Israel and Palestine. To cite one intersection of media and political rap on this topic, the BBC caused a censorship controversy in 2011 when it used sound effects to mask the lyric "Free Palestine" from mic righteous's performance on Radio 1Xtra (his first "Fire in the Booth" on December 4, 2010; see Garside 2011).[13] In light of such censorship, it shows the importance of getting these political views across. As Lowkey rapped in "Obama Nation," "I have the heart to say what all the other rappers aren't. Words like Iraq, Palestine, Afghanistan." These rappers are encouraging British (and other) listeners to pay attention to these occupations, bombings, and wars happening in the Middle East.

"The Kuffiyeh is Arab" (عربية الكوفية; "Al ʒarabeyyeh")

Shadia Mansour was born in London in 1985 to Christian Palestinian parents, spending summers in Haifa and Nazareth. Extremely active in London's free Palestine protest movements, she began to MC in 2003 and is now known as the "First Lady of Arabic hip-hop." Many of her lyrics are against the Israeli occupation in the West Bank and the 2008 Gaza offensive. She raps in Arabic, and considers "Arabic hip hop as an uprising in music" (quoted in Lee 2010; see also Isherwood 2014).[14] One of her most well-known music videos is the product of her finding a blue and white Israeli "kuffiyeh" with stars of David (made by an American company; Drury 2017, 4). The kuffiyeh (or kufiyeh) is Syrian in origin, and began being used as a political symbol in the 1930s Arab revolt against the British Mandate and Zionists in Palestine (Shabi 2008). It has since become a resistance symbol and nationalist emblem, but has been appropriated by clothing stores such as Topshop, American Apparel, Oasis, and Urban Outfitters—being labeled "activist chic" or even "Jihadi chic" (Shabi 2008). Urban Outfitters went as far generically to advertise the clothing item as "anti-war woven scarves" (Shabi 2008).

In response to this appropriation, Mansour wrote, "The Kuffiyeh Is Arab" and featured rapper M-1 of Dead Prez who also accompanied the Viva Palestina convoy to provide aid to Gaza. The music video opens with a kuffiyeh over Palestinian lands followed by a graffiti wall that says "resistance." She raps alongside images of local children and adults, including some who are b-boying set against the backdrop of DJ scratching sounds. Sonically, there is a countermelody deeper in the mix, played by a plucked instrument which may suggest more traditional instruments of the region. The chorus, which Mansour sings, uses ornamentation more associated with Middle Eastern music, while the vocals and string lines outline an E♭-minor mode (bass line looped as E♭–A♭–G♭–F). Mixed with a "boom-bap" style hip-hop beat, the music does not hit the listener over the head with tropes of Orientalism, but feels more like a hybrid endeavor, the "four elements" are audible and visible in the music video, as are the specific localities of Palestine and various sonic signifiers of Middle Eastern music. The links with hip-hop and resistance, and the kuffiyeh as a sign of resistance, are overt and Mansour lets us know her anger over the appropriation of the scarf:

صباح الخير يا ولاد عمومنا
Good morning, cousins.

تفضّلو و شرّفونا
Come and honor us with your presence.

شو بتحبّو منضيّفكن؟ دم عربي ولا دموع من عيونا؟
What would you like us to offer you,
Arab blood or tears from our eyes?

بَعتقد هيك ثأَملو تستقبلوهن هيك تعقّدو لما تدركنوعلى غلطهن
I believe that's how they hoped we would greet them. Look how they grew confused
when they realized their mistake.

هيك لبسنا الكوفية البيضاء و السوداء

That's how we wear the kufiya, the black and white kufiya.

صارو كلاب الزمان يلبسوها كموضة

They dogs of today started wearing it as a fashion accessory.

مهما إتفئنو فيها مهما غيّرو بلونها

No matter how creative they become,
no matter how they change its color,

كوفية عربية بتظلّها عربية

an Arab kufiya will remain Arab.

حطتنا بدهن إياها ثقافتنا بدهن إياها

Our kufiya: they want it. Our culture: they want it.

كرامتنا بدهن إياها كل شيء إلنا بدهن إياه

Our dignity: they want it. Everything that's ours: they want it.

لا ما راح نسكت لهن نسمح لهن

No, we won't be quiet for them. We won't permit them.

لا لا لبقلن

No, no. It suits them

يسرقواالشغلة مش إلهم ما خسن فيه

to steal something that isn't theirs, that has got nothing to do with them.

قلّدونا بيلتبسو لبس وهاالأرض بتكفيهنش

They mimic us in how they dress. This land is not enough for them.

طمعانين على القدس قدس اعرفو كيف تقولو بشر

They're greedy for Jerusalem, Jerusalem. Learn how to be humans

قبلما تلبسو الكوفية جينا نذكركن مين احنا

Before you wear the kufiya, we have come to remind you who we are.

و عصبان عن أبون هاي حطتنا

And whether you like it or not, this is how we wear it.[15]

Mansour's lyrics point to her anger at the Israeli appropriation of an object associated with Palestinian solidarity. Her presence is striking for a number of reasons: one, by being the "first lady of Arabic hip hop" in a very male-dominated rap culture, and another being her choice to rap in Arabic rather than English. She wears traditional Palestinian clothes when she performs, and as Polly Withers argues, genders the space she performs in. In some performative contexts, "she appears as the transmitter of a timeless Palestinian essence, in which women are responsible for repeatedly 'birthing' the nation" (Withers 2016, 255). In this music video, the regulatory "hegemonic national work ascribed to male and female bodies" (ibid.) is arguably coupled with the (male) gendered activity of rapping, at once disrupting and complicating gendered stereotypes. For those who do not understand Arabic, the rap delivery is nonetheless powerful with an underlying sense of urgency (as many YouTube comments attest),[16] her percussive style fuses well with Arabic language and gets to the heart of the anger she feels even when one does not understand the semantic meaning of the lyrics. For her, the language of hip-hop becomes shorthand for a type of resistant music in the mold of earlier US political rap groups like Public Enemy. Her background and experiences are alluded to in a later verse:

أنا شادية العرب لساني بيغوظ غاظ
I am the Shadia of the Arabs. My tongue stabs like a knife.

زلزالي بهزّ هزّ كلماتي حرف
My earthquake shakes uncontrollably. My words are a letter.

سجّل انا شادية منصور والحطة هويتي
Record it! I am Shadia Mansour and the kufiya is my identity.

من يوم ما خلقت سيدي والشعب مسؤوليتي
From the day I was born, Sir, and this people is my responsibility.

هيك انا ترئيت بين الشرق والغرب
That's how I was brought up—between the West and East,

بين لغتين بين البخيل و بين الفقير
between two languages, between the [rich] miser and the poor man.

شفت الحياة من الشكتين
I saw life from both sides.

بس أنا مثل الكوفية

But I'm like the kufiya.

كيفما لبستوني وينما شلحتوني بظلَّ على أصولي فلسطيني

No matter how you wear me, and wherever you take me off, I will remain as my
origin: Palestinian.

Having "seen life from both sides" seems to allude to her London upbringing while
she was able to visit her family in Palestine in the summers, and unlike Lowkey, was
able to see the inequalities first-hand. Like the kuffiyeh, Mansour considers her origins as Palestinian symbolized by the scarf she wears which she notes is symbolic of
her identity (see Figure 7.1).

"Terrorist?"

As we saw in the work of Riz MC, after 9/11 and the 7/7 bombings, the topic
of terrorism for London-based BAME rappers became a more pervasive part of
the rap landscape. In "Long Live Palestine," we have seen descriptions of Israel as
a "terror state." This concern with terrorism has both to do with the racial profiling of men and women of color in twenty-first-century Britain, but also those
who question the actions of Britain and the US in the Middle East and whether or
not that constitutes terrorism. In other words, Lowkey and others see the British,
Israeli, and US governments as the more dangerous terrorists, even though the

FIGURE 7.1 Shadia Mansour (feat. Dead Prez), "The Kufiyeh is Arab" (2011)

mainstream media does not frame it in this way. This has echoes of the "police are the biggest gang" trope in early American gangsta rap, for example "Who Protects Us from You?" by Boogie Down Productions, but the critique is arguably on an even larger level of nation-states and their governments.

Some the work of Lowkey may have been inspired by the Palestinian group D.A.M.'s song "Min irhabi?" (Who's the Terrorist?), which has been cited in multiple studies of the group (Equiq 2010; McDonald 2013a, 2013b; Maira and Shihade 2012, 1–26; Swedenberg 2013). The song opens:

> Who's the terrorist?
> I'm the terrorist?!
> How am I the terrorist when you've taken my land?
> Who's the terrorist?
> You're the terrorist!
> You've taken everything I owned while I'm living in my homeland

The song was downloaded more than a million times in less than a month in 2001, and reverses the perspective of the media image of Palestinians in the intifadas, throwing stones or suicide bombing as terrorists to trying to look at the Palestinian perspective as a group of people who have been occupied (and attacked) by an Israeli nation-state.

Lowkey explores a similar reversal of perspective in his song "Terrorist" from *Soundtrack to the Struggle* (produced by Red Skull). The opening of the track questions the labeling of terrorists in Britain, and uses the dictionary definition to explore the subjectivity of such a concept. The song opens with a spoken intro by Lowkey:

> So, we must ask ourselves, what is the dictionary definition of terrorism? The systematic use of terror especially as a means of coercion, but what is terror? According to the dictionary I hold in my hand, terror is violent or destructive acts, such as bombing committed by groups in order to intimidate a population, or government into granting their demands. So what's a terrorist?

He criticizes the media portrayals of Muslims as terrorists who would "Rather read the *Sun* than study all the facts," addressing an imagined (presumably white) right-wing Brit. His opening line in the verse states, "It seems like the Rag-heads and Paki's are worrying your dad / But your dad's favorite food is curry and kebab." This is a comment both on the racialization of Muslims post-9/11 and 7/7 as well as from an earlier era of '80s "Paki bashing" while noting the ironies of diverse tastes among such racists. They enjoy the contributions from those originally based in the former

Empire while espousing the sentiments of postcolonial melancholia. The irony sets up a stark duality between multiculturalism and anti-multiculturalism but also gets to the heart of the fact that identity is often complex and not one-dimensional, whether one is aware of it or not. "Your dad" in the lyrics sets up the addressee of the song: seemingly a young person who has not yet understood the wider global implications of UK and US foreign policy. The sung chorus states:

> They're calling me a terrorist
> Like they don't know who the terror is
> When they put it on me, I tell them this
> I'm all about peace and love
> They calling me a terrorist
> Like they don't know who the terror is
> Insulting my intelligence
> Oh how these people judge

Some of this critique involves an issue of scale. He raps, "Tell me, what's the bigger threat to human society / BAE Systems or home-made IED's? / Remote-controlled drones killing off human lives or man with home-made bomb committing suicide." IED stands for "improvised explosive device," such as the ones used in the 7/7 bombings. BAE systems is a British weapons company that kills thousands globally each year. He acknowledges that both are terrorism, but that we receive a lot of prejudice around Muslims in Britain based on these acts of terror while even larger acts of terrorism by his definition go unnoticed and uncriticized.

His second verse points to leaders Allende (Chile), Mosaddgeh (Iran), and Lumumba (Congo) who were democratically elected but overthrown with the help of the CIA and MI6 and replaced with more Western-friendly leaders, and points to non-Muslim leadership (Hugo Chavez, Fidel Castro) who also opposed imperialism. His final verse points to what he sees as acts of terrorism that go less criticized as such: Diego Garcia (an island in the Indian Ocean governed by the UK and used by the US for torture and interrogation), Contras (rebel groups opposing democracy in Nicaragua), the use of white phosphorous by the US army in Fallujah, Irgun and Stern Gang (Zionist groups responsible for killing Palestinians and British), and the atomic bombing of Hiroshima. When it is against the US or UK it is called terrorism, like Gerry Adams and the IRA or Timothy McVeigh and the Oklahoma City bombings. He ends the verse with "Everyday US —that is terrorism. Everyday UK —that is terrorism, everyday."

The music video depicts Lowkey as a prisoner who is being interrogated in a cell. Lowkey tries to persuade his interrogator through the verses of the song. After the song ends, the beat still loops with the words "Are these people the terrorists?" on the screen which accompanies graphic and disturbing images of dead and wounded (especially children) in the Middle East followed by "Are these people the terrorists?" with images of world leaders like George W. Bush, Tony Blair, Benjamin Netanyahu, and Barack Obama, as well as the now-infamous photos from Abu Ghraib prison. After being faced with this binary of who the real terrorists are, the words, "Let your humanity decide, not your prejudice" appear, urging us to make this decision in a perhaps less biased way than we are used to doing. The main point is that the concept of a "terrorist" is flexible depending on your vantage point, as echoed in verse 1 when Lowkey raps, "I guess it's all just dependent on who your nemesis is."

"Obama Nation"

While "Terrorist" looks globally at a number of case studies, "Obama Nation" homes in on the US in particular. Another spoken introduction presents the primary critique:

> This track is not an attack upon the American people.
> It is an attack upon the system within which they live.
> Since 1945 the US has attempted to overthrow more than fifty foreign governments.
> In the process the US has caused the end of life for several million people, and condemned many millions more to a life of agony and despair.

In the music video he says these words with the American flag waving in the background, subsequently showing images of casualties of war and others he is referencing. He points to the excessive consumption of America's "capitalism on steroids," treatment of Native Americans ("kept in casinos and reservations"), lack of reparations for slavery, and that the US is the "World's entertainer" as well as the "world's devastator." His main critique is that people felt, because of Obama's non-white status, he would help change US foreign policy ("I see imperialism behind your skin tone"). The lack of response to Gaza bombing in 2008 by Obama most likely has contributed to Lowkey's critique ("you morons were all wrong / I call Obama a bomber because those are your bombs"). Lowkey is also quick to point out in the song that he is not anti-America, "America is anti-me," which echoes a line from D.A.M.'s "Who's the terrorist?": "I'm not against peace / peace is against me."

Lowkey chants the chorus, "Is it Obama's nation or an abomination (x3) / doesn't make any difference when they bomb your nation." This chant is under the sung chorus which lyrically appropriates the US national anthem while melodically transforming it to the beat's harmony: "And the rocket's red glare / The bombs bursting in air / Gave proof through the night / that our flag was still there." Its melody differs greatly from the original, but this does not distract from identifying its lyrical source. Rather than being in a major mode like the original anthem, the song is in C minor with the chorus melody oscillating up and down (C–D–E♭–D–C–D–C–D–E♭–D–C–A♭). This change in both melodic and harmonic backdrop changes the context from the original 1812 war with Britain, to a more general description of US bombing of foreign countries.

One of the other related issues to the US and UK's involvement in Middle Eastern foreign policy is the de-humanization or demonization of Middle Eastern people in Anglo-British media in order to normalize such military behavior. Even prior to 9/11, film and television portrayed Arabs as either Sheiks in the desert or villains, often terrorists, barbaric, "misogynistic brutes with backward and mysterious customs" (Nittle 2018). Labeling Arabs as backward, or as terrorists, have a real effect not only on those in the MENA region but those in Britain and elsewhere. Lowkey attempts to humanize Arabs in his work, combating the "Arab as terrorist" stereotype. *Soundtrack to the Struggle* includes several "skit" sections with which this issue is brought to light. In "Skit 3" we have a clip from 2008 Republican presidential candidate John McCain who is responding to someone on the campaign trail who said she couldn't trust Obama because he was an Arab ("I can't trust Obama. I have read about him. He's not, he's not. He's an Arab"). McCain responds: "No, ma'am. He's a decent, family man citizen that I happen to have disagreements with on fundamental issues and that's what this campaign is all about. He's not. Thank you." "Skit 4" responds to this, in an interview with Ben Affleck who reflects on this exchange, pointing out that "Arab and good person are not antithetical to one another." These two skits highlight and reinforce the idea that Arab can be used as a slur in Western culture. Following D.A.M.'s lead, Lowkey unpicks the concept of a "terrorist," often related to the unjust profiling of Arab-based peoples, looking more closely at who may be more dangerously engaging in terrorist acts than such profiled groups (including our own governments).

Identity and Belonging: "The Who, What, Where, Why"

A large amount of academic attention has already been given to the topics of "belonging" and "identity," and yet such concepts are nevertheless an important topical point for rappers who feel outside the dominant culture. For them, the preoccupation comes from personal experience, either not being made to feel to belong based on ethnic categorizations or that they felt away from any mainstream sense of British identity. The two songs in this section and the next discuss these perspectives in varying yet interrelated ways. I want to look at two examples, one from Lowkey, whom we have already encountered, and the other from Persian-British rapper Shay D.

Spoken-word poet and rapper Shay D is from North London, and her parents were originally from Iran. She has rapped about feminism, class, inequality, materialism, and domestic abuse, and says she tries to "rep my community and try to better it" (Virtuous Media Attire 2018). In one interview, she mentions that she enjoys London for its art scene and that it is constantly reinventing itself and is more racially and religiously tolerant compared to the more rural areas of the UK. With that said, she also discussed her Persian roots and growing up with an immigrant single mother (her father left when she was six):

> I identify with my mother's culture, speak the language, eat the food, and brought up on a diet of Rumi and Hafiz so poetry has always had a heavy influence in my life. Being an only child to my mother I was alone a lot to keep myself busy and really identified with Hip Hop and its dialogue. Growing up, I had to defend my mother in a country where racism is passively quite rife and English was her second language, and seeing the struggle of poorer families in communities really pushed my passion for justice and I hated seeing people suffer. My mother and I were victims of gentrification, being evicted from our property that led us going through the homelessness system (covered in my song "Not the Chicken Shop Man"). (quoted in Dotiwala 2016)

Her 2016 debut album, *A Figure of Speech*, opens with the track "The Who, What, Why" (produced by Chairman Maf), which also has an accompanying music video directed by Oliver Whitehouse. The first verse opens:

> Are you a rapper or a poet
> Persian or you English
> Are you from Iran or do you class yourself as British
> If you were on trial and the lord was your witness
> Would you pray to God or do you listen to a spirit
> They asking all these questions trying to define you
> Categories and labels organising what's inside you
> To understand you better to comfort their own doubts
> Grab you by your branches from the root they pull you out

The video features various "characters" that we can assume to be facets of her own identity. Each character is played by Shay D through wearing different clothing and accessories and is shot in different locations. We first see the "poet" (see Figure 7.2), dressed in black clothing and a black beret and notebook just outside the SM:NM Supermarket. We then see a "rapper/hip hop head" reading in a bookstore, wearing a hip-hop appropriated trucker hat, gold chain, sunglasses, a blue bandana under her hat, and Los Angeles Lakers basketball jersey. There is the "London professional," in glasses and black suit jacket sitting on a couch in front of a graffiti mural. The "(Persian) Muslim" character is in a black veil, sitting next to fish in a fish and chip shop. Lastly, there is the "cosplay fan"/millennial with blue hair and flowing gray dress, as she might be dressed to attend an anime convention (see Figure 7.3). As

FIGURE 7.2 Shay D, "The Who, What, Why" (2015)

FIGURE 7.3 Shay D, "The Who, What, Why" (2015)

this character she raps primarily in front of Minster Court in the City of London (whose forecourt in Mincing Lane with three bronze horses sculpted by Althea Wynne). It is a set of office buildings which houses, among other things, the London Underwriting Centre, specializing in international insurance. The history of this area (Mincing Lane) was the world center for tea and spice trading in the nineteenth century, and we see the sign of Plantation Place (completed in 2004) flash during the music video. All of these characters have more than one dimension, for example, the London professional wears a necklace with Farsi letters on it (as do some of the others). Visually, we are encountering complex rather than stereotypical identities.

The first line of the song "Are you a rapper or a poet?" is visually accompanied by the rapper character image followed by the poet character. This is followed by the visual effect of a chalkboard with two boxes that can be ticked, poet or rapper. This boxes motif returns time and time again: Persian or British, God or spirit, true or false, and "Do you need to tick yes or no" to name a few. These chalkboard images seem to have a filter effect to make it look grainy and old (like an old home-movie VHS recording).[17] The grainy footage accompanying the chalkboard tick boxes provides the visual analogue for painting this thinking as outdated.

Early in the music video we see various books in the bookstore, including ones named *Street Art* and *100 Artists' Manifestos*, before we see her go to the plays / poetry / graphic novels section and she takes out (0:36 into the video) the graphic novel *Persepolis* by Marjaneh Satrapi. The novel is about the author growing up in Iran at the time of the revolution and about moving abroad and the experience of diaspora. It follows her six-year-old self as the daughter of two middle class Marxists, giving a window into daily life of a country at war with Iraq and becoming increasingly conservative under a fundamentalist regime. One can read this as a deliberate attempt for Shay D to engage with her parents' heritage, and relate in some respects to her mother's experience of diaspora, and her own coming-of-age in London.

A running theme in her work is questioning the promotion of hyper-sexualized women in mainstream hip-hop and criticism of hyper-capitalism and exploitation in the music industry as well as wider greed of the upper classes. Echoing the "capitalist villains" she raps about in the song, her millennial/anime character can be seen in a covered market not far from the "Gherkin" also in the City of London part of the capital (30 St. Mary Axe, a commercial skyscraper in London's financial district). She raps while young men (presumably bankers) in suits have pints outside and laugh (and almost mock) the out-of-place rapper. It speaks to both the white mainstream/minority ethnic dualities we find in some UK hip-hop, but also the "two city" nature of London, how tower blocks/council houses can rub against gentrified areas and posh residential streets. Though nothing about Shay D's video explicitly performs a lower- or working-class identity, rap is more often than not associated with providing a voice for underprivileged and invisible members of society. The bankers in the video can represent the embodiment of white British attitudes toward cultural "others," the performance of tick-box categories considering her out-of-place attire. It is a visual depiction of those who are seen to belong in the mainstream reacting against performances of difference in de facto semi-exclusive spaces. While the message of Shay D's video complicates any simple binary, the juxtaposition of her female, Middle Eastern, blue-haired identity against young white bankers in the City of London is a striking image of the ordinary/difference binary.[18]

The last verse includes critiques of capitalism ("They sweepin up communities / Capitalist villains and / Middle class citizens that forget about their privilege"), societal focus on outer appearance ("Keepin up appearances became too self obsessed / Mysogynistic world where we are sexual objects"), and the media. The last lines are as follows:

> Are we gonna take in everything that they televise
> Terrorise via free papers that just tell us lies
> Or are we gonna go the extra mile and read between the lines
> With my head in my books I push myself to get wise

Her final line instructs the audience to "push yourself and get wise," set against backdrop of shelves of books in the bookstore. The song and music video are a plea to accept the complexities of identity as well to "read between the lines," which admittedly is harder work than binary thinking. Her performing various personae brings home visually that people can express different thoughts and feelings without needing to be categorized in one fashion.

Sonically, there is a digitally sampled motif (it sounds sampled, at least) which is most likely two flutes (one wooden and one transverse) in unison as part of the basic beat. At least one of the flutes could be a Persian ney flute (made of wood), or designed to sound like one, in order to add an element of exoticism to the lyrical content. It is more prominent than the plucked instrument in the Mansour video, but like it, adds to this sense of cultural-sonic hybridity. The ney, however, is not simply for exoticism in a general sense, as it is a clear reference to her Persian heritage, an instrument which features prominently in the work of the thirteenth-century Persian poet, faqih, Islamic scholar, theologian, and Sufi mystic poet Jalāl ad-Dīn Muhammad Rumi.[19] There are various vocal lines which dip in and out of the beat (both individual and mass children's chorus on "ah" syllables), but they are lower in the mix. This sense of exoticism is not foreign to hip-hop more generally, of course, but in the context bolsters the lyrical content about identity. The beat helps to suture and anchor what is, visually, a rapid virtuosic display of multiple identities. It is the beat and its regularity which keeps it all together and allows us to understand all these identities as facets of the same person. Through her lyrics and video, Shay D is reflecting on her Persian/Iranian heritage in concert with her British (more specifically London-based) one, concluding by addressing to the listener that we should "get wise" beyond thinking reductively in tick boxes and to decolonize our own tick-box-thinking perceptions of racial and ethnic categories.

"Cradle of Civilization"

The last track I want to discuss fuses well-academically-trodden concepts such as "identity" and "belonging" alongside a critique of the Second Gulf War. Despite the large amount of attention, however, such themes are nevertheless an important topical point for rappers who feel outside the dominant culture. For them, the preoccupation comes from personal experience, not finding one's "place" within Britain.

Lowkey's "Cradle of Civilisation" (also from *Soundtrack to the Struggle*) is a personal response of behalf of those being bombed in his mother's country (literally and figuratively his motherland), yet feels removed since he has never been there himself. He discusses the freedom he has in Britain, but grieves for those still in Iraq, from the "cradle of civilization" which is in his blood and in his heart, but he has never visited ("the nationality I never felt"). He raps, "I never picked up a grenade in my garden / I never saw people I loved die starving . . . I never lost a friend to violence that was random." He also critiques the "liberation" of Iraq, questioning "1 million dead people doesn't equal liberation," and the role Britain and the US had in this. The chorus, sung in Arabic, means, "Oh, how beautiful is freedom" (something he tells us his mother would say to him). The female voice of Mai Khalil musically demonstrates the double-ness that Lowkey feels. Despite being born in London, he raps, "Still I feel like an immigrant, Englishman amongst Arabs and an Arab amongst Englishmen," perhaps demonstrating a "third space" which isn't quite the sum of its parts, but adds to a sense of ambivalence and placeless-ness. He ends the track with the line, repeated for emphasis, "In my sleep, in my dreams, Motherland I can still feel you calling me." One could argue this very much plays on the tradition of gendering Empire: "the colonized" historically feminized or infantilized, and one could read the piano lamenting figures as providing contrast sonically to the "harder," stereotypically-"masculine" sounds in his and his genre's oeuvre that amplify the song's rich metaphor for Motherhood. Mesopotamia is thought to have given birth to early civilization, a symbolic mother whose son Lowkey is now (and forever) separated. Like "Mother India" or "Mother Africa," we could see this as colonial-thinking and Lowkey may be looking at this through a Western lends, but on the other hand, his critique of the war complicates his relationship with lands carved through Empire and still suffering violent instability.

Lowkey is able to reflect on his dual position, as he raps in Arabic: "My mother is from Baghdad, and my father is from Dover, [then switches to English:] and that's the combination I carry on my shoulders." This powerful code switching is the sound of the postcolonial condition, the displacement brought about by capitalist power inequalities, greed, and exploitation that continues to rage on under neocolonialism. It is also an intensely personal song, one that gets to the heart of belonging, or not belonging, in the UK.[20] His mixed-race status, something which still needs more academic attention,[21] contributes in part to this sense of not belonging, in addition to being cut off from his mother's heritage.

The bilingualism serves a number of purposes in this context (and we have heard multilingualism as part of a global cypher in "Long Live Palestine Part 2"). The code-switching shows both virtuosic versatility, and an insider language that many listeners may not understand. For the English-speaking mainstream, it may give them a sense of what it's like to feel outside the culture, performing the otherness Lowkey often feels.[22]

The music video features Lowkey rapping in front of a large gate, no doubt symbolic of the barrier he feels between his home in Britain and his mother's homeland of Baghdad (see Figure 7.4). During the chorus, Mai Khalil sings in a physically separate location to Lowkey, in presumably another location, on a set of steps. Again, this seems to show the separateness of the two worlds, almost as if Khalil could represent a flashback of his mother when she lived in Iraq. The video also includes the

FIGURE 7.4 Lowkey, "Cradle of Civilisation" (2010)

fading in and out of footage from war-torn Iraq and elsewhere, bombing and death and violent protest to visualize/accompany the narrative.

The most prominent melodic or harmonic element in the basic beat is the looped piano line. In C#m, the piano plays downward three-note arpeggiated chords that roughly outline a C#m, A, B progression moves to A on the upbeat before beat three, and the B chord (VII) lands firmly on beat one of measure 2. This harmonic pattern is repeated throughout the song. The i–VI–VII never provides harmonic closure in the context of Western harmony since we never given the dominant chord, but the VII acts as a dominant in its place. Major thirds are played on the piano over the VII chord, and the piano pattern creates a sense of sadness, lamenting, and mourning, which matches the lyrical themes. A synthesized snare hits on beats two and four and the relationship between the bass's upbeat and snare backbeat propel the track forward rhythmically. The arpeggiated piano figure and its associations with sadness, or at least a reflective thoughtfulness (or plaintiveness), has its precedent in film and television soundtracks (The "Lonely Man Theme" from *The Hulk*, or Michael Nyman's score to *The Piano*, or the "new age" piano music of Yanni and Ludovico Einaudi). These loose generic associations and resonances, I would argue, are heard on the track given their widespread use in popular culture.

In addition to the survivor's guilt tied up with his political critique, there may be a sense of the Freudian uncanny (*Unheimliche*) which can be translated from the German as the "unhomely" or "un-housedness" (Huddart 2006, 80). It is unfamiliar yet familiar, not quite home yet comes back to haunt the subject. Colonialism itself, as Bhabha wrote, lies back at the origins of Western modernity, and is therefore an aspect of its "childhood." The bombing of the Middle East by Western powers could be seen as a neo-colonial return of the "repressed." As Kristeva wrote, echoing Fanon, foreignness as an uncanny trait serves to disrupt our own inner sense of being so that we can realize that we are also foreigners to ourselves (Huddart 2006, 84). It is this realization that can help enable us to live amongst others, and to cite Huddart, "The uncanny, in other words, opens a space for us to reconsider how we have come to be who we are" (2006, 83).

More often than not, to be BAME in Britain is to be Othered and/or to feel othered, and to quote Pickering in his book on stereotypes, "If, to be Other is to be torn in two, to be constructed as an object that denies you as a subject, then where can you belong? Otherness is a denial of belonging; it is the unrelenting sign of not belonging" (Pickering 2001, 79). Otherness and positive modes of belonging exist simultaneously and can form a double consciousness as well as a third space that falls in between multiple forms of identity consciousness, and many of these rappers discuss these personal issues openly in ways that more stereotypical mainstream rap avoids (notable exceptions being 2Pac and Eminem). Sonically, for Mansour, Lowkey, and

Shay D, the tracks I have highlighted strike a balance between working within the norms of the hip-hop genre, and adding some elements of sonic Otherness: whether it be Mansour and Khalil's singing style, the plucked instrument on "The Kuffiyeh Is Arab," or the flute in "The Who, What, Why," these elements give reminders of difference while working within a well-established sonic form.

Lowkey and Shay D's experience with identity politics should be treated on the level of the individual, but a pattern of sorts does emerge for many BAME rappers in terms of belonging to a society associated with whiteness. Here, I am not trying to homogenize the experience of growing up mixed-race or BAME in Britain, nor am I trying to characterize it as wholly positive or negative. Other intersectional considerations such as class and gender will also be a factor in these complex negotiations of identity (Bhopal and Preston 2012). What I think we can see, however, is that mixed-race Britons as well as second-generation immigrants (British-born children of immigrants), have a unique perspective from which to discuss belonging. From the few examples provided in this book, we can see different perspectives on "Doubleness": For Lowkey, it represents not fully belonging to one group of people, always made to feel like an immigrant in either camp (Arab or English). Pakistani-British Riz MC, who is not mixed race but still sees intersecting with British youth culture and with his parents as leading double lives, raps about being a double agent with echoes of DuBoisian "double consciousness," having to code switch when with his family or his friends ("Double Lives" from 2016). Akala sees ethnic categorization as an oversimplification of identity, not quite fitting the "boxes" of his background and wanting to do away with them altogether ("Find No Enemy" from 2010). For Shadia Mansour, growing up in Britain but visiting her family in Palestine provides a position of privilege where she has been able to see "life from both sides" and it gives her an important perspective from which to work. Algerian-British Jaz Kahina uses humor to discuss her ethnic identity: on "Round Ere" (2018) she raps "I'm from the land of the sands / ain't got a fuckin tan / but still kinda yellow like my liver needs a hand." David Vujanic uses humor to negotiate his "in between" status as Serbian and British. And Shay D encourages others to read between the lines of simple binaries of identity in order to move beyond them. Although these reflections all begin with some sort of binary or duality, the diversity of responses goes to show that a simple "third space" Bhabhaian reading of hybridity does not fully account for the variety of perspectives on British identity through rap in Britain.

In this way, the postcolonial melancholia of the mainstream has constructed second- or third-generation British citizens in imagined exile from a place that at once exists and does not exist. While not exiles in the strict sense, they are made to feel foreign and therefore carry baggage of the "broken history" (Said 2002, 177) of their colonized heritage. The salient and oft-quoted comment from Edward Said on exile hold a degree of truth for these rappers:

> Most people are principally aware of one culture, one setting, one home; exiles are aware of at least two, and this plurality of vision gives rise to an aware-ness of simultaneous dimensions, an awareness that—to borrow a phrase from music—is *contrapuntal*. (Said 2002, 186)

Said, in some sense like the rappers in this chapter, demonstrates his Western-ness through working within those frameworks and language while showing great aware-ness and sensitivity toward those affected negatively by colonialism, slavery, dis-placement, wars, and other abuses of power (often by the West). In this case, his use of counterpoint as a term, associated with Western art music, a set of codified rules, and linked in some ways to modernity and imperialism, goes uncritiqued. However, it does, like Bhabha and others, attempt to get to the heart of Otherness and belong-ing in the world. Perhaps ultimately it is the rap songs that get closest to the perfor-mance of these sentiments which are products of the postcolonial condition.

Conclusion: Resistance and Belonging for British-MENA Rappers

In thinking about how to study British musicians of the Middle Eastern diaspora, I initially looked to ethnographic studies of popular music in MENA regions. In such studies, there exist academic critiques of scholars who overuse terms and con-cepts around resistance and liberation to interpret music-making in, for example, Morocco (Moreno Almeida 2017), North Africa (Boum 2016), Palestine (Withers 2016), and Iran (Nooshin 2017). Echoing Nooshin in particular, oversimplifications of popular music making in these regions can be a product of filtering MENA activ-ity into a Western lens of understanding, and risks ignoring the artists' perspective or subtleties of how socio-cultural practices operate there. For example, should we read an Iranian popular song about love to be resistant to regimes less supportive of music, or should we hear it either on its own terms lyrically or inquire further about what the artist intended?

Rather than study non-Western rappers, however, my investigation of less-explored British-born rappers with Middle Eastern heritage adds at least one more layer of complication. Like Western ethnographers, these artists are arguably com-menting on the Middle East from a Western subject position and may use such (over-critiqued) frames as resistance ("Existence is Resistance") while also having a unique perspective on the situation given their personal connections to the region. They have grown up both with colonizer discourse of the UK mainstream and a heritage that makes more visible the perspective of the colonized. Echoing Said's comments on exile, their status as ethnically Othered may have contributed to the greater awareness of such counter-mainstream narratives. Such a simple narrative, however, is complicated by rappers like Lowkey having the full experience of their Othered heritage out of view, and mediated through the experience of growing up second-generation British.

For all the lyrical complexities that are reduced by academics in using tropes such as "resistance," we need to acknowledge and respect that the rappers themselves, in these contexts, use such terms as resistance in both lyrical content and extra-musical commentary on them. Simplifying arguments for the sake of narrative or getting messages across shares a commonality in most if not all forms of popular music. Lowkey himself says of rap that "you can use your voice as a form of resistance, as an *intifada*, an uprising against what is happening" (quoted in Lee 2010). Mansour echoes this with her sentiments on Arabic hip-hop, as do Akala and many other politically minded rappers (Immortal Technique, N.W.A., Public Enemy, and KRS-One in the US, for example). They rap about a variety of topics beyond politics and resistance,[23] and while the real contexts involve a complexity that would be impossible for an artist to portray fully (nor would they necessary want to), such reductions do not necessarily reduce the power of these political messages (Lowkey raps of the experience of displacement in "Children of Diaspora," for example, as "the type of pain that cannot be contained in a dissertation"). "Cradle of Civilization" shows, for example, an intensely personal account of (not) belonging coupled with a critique of the UK government's bombing of Iraq. In this way, and unlike grime or drill, a rapper like Lowkey becomes an ethnographer of a situation in which he may not fully be a participant.

It may not be a coincidence, then, that many of the rappers who tackle such political material have some sort of link to the history of those colonized by Empire, forming a "family of resemblances" regardless of ethnic affinities in multicultural London. Like Said's "reflections," these artists are aware of more than one culture in part due to the migrations (and/or estrangement) of one or more of their parents. In addition to the personal *as* political, for these rappers, it is also a case of the political (as in "real politics") never being far from the personal in their rap discourse. The personal and the political converge in their work, for example, how Iranian-British Reveal can couple a drug reference and a critique of NATO in the same line: "I blaze high grade [cannabis], you never hear the pop of a seed / Yo, the whole world's like Sodom and Gomorrah / NATO supply arms so countries can bomb each other harder / It's bad karma, what goes around comes around" ("What Estate You From?" 2002). These rappers from disparate countries can form "anticolonial alliances" (Drury 2017, 1) around identities that Nitasha Sharman has called "post-9/11 Brown" (Sharma 2015; Drury 2017). While not the only lens utilized, the frames of diaspora, exile, or displacement allow these rappers to explore the in-between spaces of personal and collective identity while critiquing the historical, social, and political conditions which contributed to this level of consciousness in the first place.

***

A short but important afterword: as a local resident of North Kensington, Lowkey witnessed the fire in Grenfell Tower which occurred on June 14, 2017 (Charles 2018). In response, he released the music video "Ghosts of Grenfell" on August 7, 2017. The video includes rapped verses and chorus material by Lowkey as lip-synced by Grenfell survivors and members of the community, painting a picture of multicultural London. Mai Khalil sings on chorus of the track, "Did they die or us?" while Lowkey chants "Ghosts of Grenfell, still calling for justice now hear em, now hear em scream" and "This corporate manslaughter will haunt you, now hear em scream." Khalil sings a bridge section as well in Arabic: "Tell me where I can go, people are burning at the hour of *sahoor* [the early morning meal before dawn during Ramadan], I feel as if I'm in another world, I feel as if I'm in another world" which is sung twice (see Figure 7.5).[24] This "other world" as symbolized in part through non-English language is now applied to a horrific tragedy while creating some sense of solidarity with the (largely) minority ethnic inhabitants of the tower. The figures in the video march around the tower, gathering in numbers before they arrive at a wall that is part memorial, part demand: "The Truth Will Not Be Hidden. The people's public inquest. First hand [*sic*] accounts, facts, testimonies. Grenfell tower

FIGURE 7.5 Lowkey, "Ghosts of Grenfell" (2017)

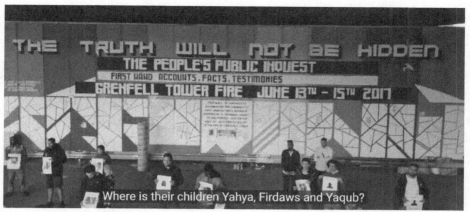

FIGURE 7.6 Lowkey, "Ghosts of Grenfell" (2017)

13–15 June 2017" and below these headings include accounts of the fire and missing persons posters (see Figure 7.6).

The song is a call to rally around the survivors and a plea for leaders to help. Given the fact that the cladding on the building had been a cheaper and more flammable option that failed to meet legal standard (Davies, Connolly, and Sample 2017; Symonds and Ellison 2018), some feel the tragedy could have been avoided, and that it was in part due to a lack of concern for the lower-classes and ethnically marginalized residents of the tower. This is made clear through Lowkey's plea to the "Queen's Royal Borough of Kensington and Chelsea," with its connotations of both the whiteness and upper-classness of the royal family as well as the affluence of the borough as a whole, contrasting with the multicultural makeup of those in the music video and the images of the burnt tower which features in the background at the end of the video. Lowkey is literally providing a voice for the voiceless in the video, and becomes the unifying force between those in the video (Lowkey does not feature in the video beyond providing his vocals). At the end of the song, each then-missing person was named ("Where is Deborah Campbell?" "Where is Majerie Vital and her son Ernie?" etc.) over the beat loop before the video ends with the song lyrics:

> The blood is on your hands
> There will be ashes on your graves
> Like a Phoenix we will rise.

"Ghosts of Grenfell" is reflective of Lowkey's concern with injustice toward marginalized peoples, their unjust deaths, and the displacement of the survivors. The bridge is sung in Arabic and, like the Arabic sung in "Cradle," performs a multifaceted bilingualism. At once, it signifies difference while providing a connection to a rapper's heritage, and in some ways attempts to normalize it. In other words, such a gesture linguistically demonstrates that Othered voices matter and should be represented. The performance of complex and marginalized identities can be heard in the lyrics of Lowkey, Shadia Mansour, and Shay D, and that these perspectives are informed to an extent by their complex heritage(s). We could also point to other examples of London-based rappers (Reveal, mic righteous, Jaz Kahina, Stylah), or indeed rappers further afield (other UK cities, Brazil, France, and the US in addition to the MENA), that lyrically demonstrate a connection with the Middle East and that such connections influence the perspectives they present. They use their voice as a method of exploring their own personal identity and as an instrument of critique to point out injustices carried out domestically and abroad.

Notes

1. The 2011 census marked 240,545 Arab British in England and Wales, and the National Association of British Arabs, noting some overlap in the categories, puts that number at 366,769 (NABA 2013). British people of Arab origin or with Arab ancestry are a demographic which has received little attention in academia, and even less has been given to their artistic/cultural output. This may be in part because the ethnic categorization "British Arab" did not exist until the 2011 census. The census reported London's population including 1.3% Arab members, with a high concentration Arabic-themed nightclubs and restaurants on Edgware Road. The term "Arab" is most commonly defined as belonging to the Semitic peoples, originating from the Arabian Peninsula and surrounding territories, and part of the Middle East and North Africa (MENA). Its diaspora covers the globe, and in the UK context, consists of a large number of Egyptians (who came in the 1940s) and those who fled the Lebanese civil war in the 1990s. One modern unifying force is that Arabic is the common language, including Arabic-speaking countries such as Iraq, Algeria, Egypt, Kuwait, Morocco, Lebanon, Saudi Arabia, and the region of Palestine. Latin America has the largest Arab population outside the Middle East, and France has the largest population in Europe.

2. Stylah is half Omani, half Moroccan and describes himself as a "black Arab," and was one of the members of Poisonous Poets (Fiasco 2006). Jaz Kahina is Algerian-British and both mic righteous and Lowkey are Iraqi-British.

3. I acknowledge that the term "Middle East" is itself a product of Empire, and use it with some reservation to refer to the Arab-majority world, including the Persian (Farsi speaking) diaspora as well as Arab nations. These boundaries and labels, as contested and problematic as they are, form a crucial part of the present argument that such a problematic history has had a direct effect on the culture and people of such diasporas now based in the UK.

4. Miri Song's study of mixed-race adolescents in Britain (2010a and 2010b) point to comments by one Arab (Egyptian)/white (Irish) mixed-race nineteen-year-old man who identified as British as a strategy for transcending racial categories. He explained: "It's wherever you're born. It's home for me . . . Um, I don't think colour is. . . It's if you speak the language, you're part of

the culture . . . there's a new culture emerging in London, Britain, just the youth culture, urban" (quoted in Song 2010a, 1203). Using hybrid influences from a number of cultures have helped to fuse multicultural London youth culture (and its music) into its own unique entity.

5. Arab countries once part of the British Empire include Bahrain, Egypt, Iraq, Jordan, Kuwait, Libya, Qatar, Yemen, and the UAE.

6. Comparatively, rappers of Arab descent in French hip-hop are more common than in English hip-hop, mirroring the higher Arab-based population there (six million), and were also more firmly part of the multicultural Parisian hip-hop scene in the 1990s.

7. Hip-hop is not the only genre used to further awareness of Palestine. One of the main examples is the British electronica and experimental artist Muslimgauze whose entire oeuvre was around the theme of Palestinian liberation (George and Piva 2010, 230). The final chapter of Polly Withers's thesis (2016, 240–276) focuses on Palestinian musicians performing in the UK (mostly London venues, and at festivals like WOMAD and the Shubbak Festival), which helps to show how these musicians are far from fixed geographically.

8. "For Palestine tears fall / In the middle of destruction, siege and poverty / Night is long and life is bitter / They killed Arafat Cheikh Yassine and Mohammed al-Dora / Still free, still with strong will / Still see children holding rocks and do not fear death / Martr here, bombing there and People shout 'Allah Akbar' . . . Arabs for their interest forsaken you / If you see us quiet it is not our fault / Our rulers have forgotten Islam / As long as night lasts, the light of dawn will rise" (Boum 2016).

9. A group called Existence is Resistance (founded in 2009 by Nancy Mansour Leigh and Mariam Aryai Rivera) began to lead hip-hop tours of the Occupied Territories to show hip-hop fans the contexts that led to the rise of hip hop in Palestine (George and Piva 2016, 525). The phrase "existence is resistance" is often associated with the Palestinian cause, and also used by politically minded rappers such as Akala ("Let it All Happen" from 2013 opens with the lines "Existence is resistance in a world that / Thinks the human instinct should be held back / And all of our wisdom we should sell that / Destroy the difference that we all have"). There is also a DJ School and Loop School in Nazareth and after-school clubs in Galilee and the Triangle offer hip-hop writing and dancing workshops (Equiq 2010, 57). Hip-hop is clearly seen as a force for good in Palestine, for education and to be used as resistance against injustice and social inequalities.

10. Lowkey says: "With my mum's background, the generation before her were quite heavily involved in politics—like her dad, his dad, her mum's dad, were all Arab Nationalist politicians. Whereas on my dad's side of the family, before him his dad was like a miner, and he grew up in Kent. It was interesting, the holidays, to be honest, because if I went to my dad's family where they live in Dover, it was like an estate in Dover, and there wasn't a brown face in sight. This was just a fact. Whereas when I went to my mum's side of the family, they had a beautiful house in UAE, and it's like just the contrast of living is crazy. I come from that. It was good, it was a good thing. Because in a lot of ways it doesn't give me the luxury of knowing where I stand on certain issues, because with me being born into this situation, I just can't look at any situation as 'Us and them.' Because, who am I in that situation? I have to find my own footing. Because I'm not born saying 'Okay, these guys are the good guys and these guys are the bad guys.' I'm just born with what I'm around, and I just have to make it" (McNally 2008).

11. Lowkey joined a group called Poisonous Poets with which was formed by rapper Reveal and released one self-titled mixtape in 2005. Poisonous Poets (sometimes known as Double P) also

consisted of Doc Brown, whom Lowkey met at Real Deal records, Reveal, Stylah, Tony D, and Therapist (Mehreen 2005).

12. For more on this see the campaign's pages ("Boycott Israel Campaign") as part of the *Innovative Minds* website.

13. mic righteous (Rocky Takalbighashi) is the son of a family that fled Iran during the 1979 revolution and is from Margate in Kent. His track "Don't it May You Wonder?" found on his album *Yob Culture* (2011) tells the story of a solider in Iraq who sees destruction and death everywhere ("All he sees is destruction, mud huts covered in bullet holes from the gunshots / Holes in the ground from where the bombs dropped / Soldiers stood there beside himself / That's when he heard the cries for help"). A little boy finds him whose parents were sent away and he tries to get the soldier to help his (dying and decaying) grandfather to be well again. The track ends, "Who's benefitting when the people dead, they speaking terrorism but I don't see no threat / All I see is innocent sisters and brothers die, what's the reason? Don't it make you wonder?"

14. Arabic hip-hop has become more popular in the '00s into the 2010s, and some give it a certain amount of credit for driving the Arab Spring and in countries such as Tunisia, Egypt, Libya, and Syria (Hebblethwaite 2011).

15. The lyrics and its translation originally come from *The Revolutionary Arab Hip-hop Blog* (http://revolutionaryarabraptheindex.blogspot.com/2011/11/shadia-mansour-and-m-1-arab-kufiya.html) and have been supplemented with translations from Kawa Morad, whom I thank graciously for providing a more nuanced translation for this book.

16. Some YouTube comments include "I'm from Europe, I've no idea what she's singing about, but she and her music are awesome, I'm stunned!" "This woman couldn't be more badass if she tried." "Shadia Mansour is the best rapper I've heard all year." "don't even know what she is saying, I know it's positive and that's all that matters." One user does provide an English translation in the YouTube comments section.

17. It looks like an old, black-and-white, chalkboard effect as the writing looks like a sharpie pen but had its colors inverted to be made to look like chalk through various effects. My thanks to Will Finch for pointing this out.

18. In one interview she discusses growing up on Crouch End Hill in Wat Tyler House: "I loved Crouch End . . . it got gentrified, I feel like it was one of the first places that really started . . . they got rid of the BT building, the phone boxes, the massage parlours . . . replaced by Marks and Spencers and Waitrose and coffee shops . . . the line of poverty and middle class is really close to each other there so it feels really shit when you come out of a shitty estate and then onto a posh road with nice houses" (Allcity TaxiTalk Show 2018).

19. The ney, itself the symbol of mysticism in Turkish and Persian music and culture, is featured at the beginning of Rumi's *Mathnawi*, his biggest opus (six volumes), where Rumi compares it to a human being: "ever since I was cut from the reed bed, I've made this crying sound," implying that we are cut from our source and only will be reunified in death. One of Rumi's poems may have been influential in the creation of Shay D's track: "All day I think about it, then at night I say it / Where did I come from, and what am I supposed to be doing? / I have no idea. / My soul is from elsewhere, I'm sure of that, / And I intend to end up there" (Rumi 1997, 2). Given she said she grew up "on a diet of Rumi" it is likely these connections are not mere coincidence. My sincere thanks to Michael Ellison for pointing these links out to me.

20. During the launch meeting of Kafa—Enough: A Campaign to defend Muslim communities on June 26, 2009, Lowkey states the following: "I would like to start off by saying one

thing—Nobody should expect Muslim people in this country to feel no affinity toward their brothers and sisters dying every single day in Iraq, towards no form of kinship for the 1.4 million people who have been made refugees in Pakistan by Obama's bombs, you cannot expect Muslim people to feel no kinship towards their brothers and sisters in occupied Palestine, and you cannot expect Muslim people to feel no affinity toward their brothers and sisters in Afghanistan. Now we cannot look at anything without taking into account its history. This room has a history. This [points down to the mic] has a history. This mic has a history, just like this country has a history. Just like France has a history. Now where were the two sources of extremely xenophobic comments coming from this week? In the form of Sarkozy in France and in the form of the *Daily Express* from Britain. Now, let us not forget that after the First World War that it was the British and the French who sliced up the Middle East and North Africa with no respect or empathy for the indigenous people of those lands. What we are talking about today is not a problem in Britain, it is a problem with the world. It is a problem of imperialism. It is a problem of a system which places importance and places priority on big business ahead of human life. Now it just so happens that the human lives we are talking about at the moment are predominantly Muslim. That is the case now . . . So colonization's not finished. Flags have just been replaced by huge, big corporations. This is what we are dealing with and we're not stupid and we should not fool ourselves about this."

21. Mixed-race studies as a field is still emerging, but some notable studies include Ifekwunigwe 2004; Song 2010a, 2010b; Song and Aspinall 2012; and the pioneering Wilson 1984. For a more journalistic account, see Alibhai-Brown 2001.

22. The inner sense of conflict, not feeling entirely English nor Arab, he sees as an important feature of some of his favorite artists. In a 2008 interview with James McNally, Lowkey discusses Gil Scott Heron and Lauryn Hill, saying he could relate to their work because "that's always been sort of almost built into me, as a human being, to constantly be in conflict with myself." He explains, "Naturally I can't relate to my mum and I can't relate to my dad. And I can't relate to her side of the family, and I can't relate to his side of the family . . . what real prototype do I have of existence? . . . [or] You could look at it like I'm just the type of person who'll never be satisfied, or content with what I have, and who always yearns for more. You could look at it like that. But, in a way, we are all like that" (McNally 2008). This also echoes the work of Franz Fanon who was able to articulate the self-as-othering and self-hatred that the colonized subject endures. For Lowkey, this self-othering reflects the two sides of his heritage—the resentment felt by those of the MENA region toward the British, and the Othering of Arabs in (especially post-7/7) Britain.

23. Polly Withers's (2016, 25–26) important work on Palestinian popular music making emphasizes that while scholars have looked at how musicians can perform "national-resistance work, we know less about the roles different musical, leisure, and consumption practices may or may not be playing in Palestine today" (25). Her work addresses this gap in the Middle Eastern context, but such a statement also applies to rappers associated with political or conscious hip-hop in the UK as well.

24. A sequel, "Ghosts of Grenfell 2," was released on the one-year anniversary of the tragedy, still calling for answers and for companies and politicians to be held accountable for the errors that led to the fire. Despite previous concerns of the residents, no action was taken by the Council in terms of residents' reservations regarding the £8.7 million refurbishments the year before. The governmental response, especially PM Theresa May visiting the site the following day but not meeting with any victims, has also received criticism. May called the fire a "failure of the State" and has since apologized for her failure of an adequate response (Nagesh 2017).

> Yo Theresa May where's the money for Grenfell?
> WHAT YOU THOUGHT WE JUST FORGOT ABOUT GRENFELL!?
> —STORMZY

CONCLUSION

British Rap in the Age of Grenfell and Brexit

THE FIRST CHAPTER of this book included an account of Kanye West's 2015 BRIT awards performance as an example of grime's mainstream and international recognition. I will end with another performance from the same awards show but in 2018. Grime artist Stormzy (who ended up winning two awards that night) performed his hits "Blinded by Your Grace Pt. 2" and "Too Big for Your Boots" with a freestyle in between the two songs. He was front and center stage, with simulated rain falling down on him from above (see Figure C.1). Behind him, dozens of singers sitting in balaclavas and hoodies on three tiers of long desks provide the choral background to his gospel-inflected opening song. After "Blinded," we hear a recorded speech as Stormzy takes his shirt off. What follows is a freestyle which includes Stormzy's plea to Prime Minister May about the money for Grenfell as quoted in this chapter's epigraph. He continues, "You're criminals and you got the cheek to call us savages / You should do some jail time, you should pay some damages / We should burn your house down and see if you can manage this / MPs sniff coke, we just smoke a bit of cannabis." After his freestyle he then goes into "Big for Your Boots," a catchy grime hook which also captures the braggadocio and calling out others exemplary of the genre.

The less-than-five-minute performance covered a range of emotions, from a humility reflective of his Christian values to scathing and angry critiques of the government and the little Englander values of the *Daily Mail*, and lastly, pointing

Brithop. Justin A. Williams, Oxford University Press (2021). © Oxford University Press.
DOI: 10.1093/oso/9780190656805.001.0001

FIGURE C.1 Stormzy at the BRIT Awards, 2018

out others who are getting "too big for their boots." Stormzy's set encapsulates the hybrid nature of UK hip-hop and many of its concerns, and as we have seen, Grenfell as a symbol for the British government's failures at the expense of some of its most vulnerable and forgotten people. His 2017 album, *Gang Signs and Prayer*, was the first grime album to reach number one, and Stormzy's success echoes a comment Gilroy wrote thirteen years earlier: "Given the extent of Britain's deepening economic and social divisions, it is perhaps surprising that the convivial metropolitan cultures of the country's young people are still a bulwark against the machinations of racial politics. This enduring quality of resistance of the young is no trivial matter" (Gilroy 2004, 132–33). The Ghanaian-British Stormzy, who was born in Croydon and grew up in South Norwood, demonstrates this while representing a bright future for the mainstreaming of grime and other UK MC cultures.[1]

Stormzy was also vocal in his support for Labour Party–leader Jeremy Corbyn, alongside others such as JME who put their support behind the leader in the 2017 general election. As Monique Charles writes, the Corbyn election provided "generation grime" (defined as "those predominantly under 30 who have grown up with it as a soundtrack to their lives") with an opportunity to engage with a political figure "whose values align more closely with their lived experience, personal values and aspirations. Corbyn's understanding of working-class issues, racial oppression and homelessness struck a chord" (Charles 2018, 40). Corbyn did not win the election, but the support of #Grime4Corbyn no doubt helped his success amongst the younger voters.

From its inception in the Bronx, hip-hop has provided a voice for lower-class racial minorities, a space for expression (dancing, graffiti writing, DJing, as well as MCing) under bleak socioeconomic conditions. As discussed in Chapter 6 and elsewhere, these associations are largely maintained globally through "anti-assimilationist expressions of minority difference" (Rollefson 2017, 3). Artists often become the ambassadors of the subaltern, often through personal experience one way or another or by adhering to a notion of a responsibility to do so. Hip-hop provides a "cultural citizenship" (Craft 2018) where other forms of belonging seem unavailable, and while rappers are more mixed and varied socioeconomically and have different points of access, many rappers are either speaking on behalf of those less privileged or are indeed from that subject position. In the UK context, the answer to "Can the subaltern speak?" is that when they *do* have the platform to speak, they often rap instead. As many have noted (Bramwell 2015; White 2017; Akala 2018; Hancox 2018), the rise of social media has broken down musical barriers (to a degree) so that young urban artists who normally would not have been given a platform to speak, now do so.

I have looked at several artists and groups from various UK regions, highlighting themes of nationalism, history, subculture/style, politics, humor, and diaspora/belonging. Big England and little England come together in hip-hop, and both need to be understood to embrace UK hip-hop's messages, to transform the nation's harmful stereotypes, and to help get us out of our postcolonial melancholia, looking toward a more honest future that embraces the diversity of its nation. While minority identity and resistance are arguably an overused concept academically, we cannot ignore that it is a primary theme of expression in UK hip-hop's politics. Language is crucial to the construction of our conceptions of society, and rap is no exception to this.[2] Britain has always been hybrid and multicultural, and rappers help us to understand our past and point toward our future.

Furthermore, looking at such artistic texts through a postcolonial lens creates a complex but important frame for interpretation. To quote Aaron and Williams in the Welsh context, postcoloniality "embraces concepts such as ambivalence (the mix of attraction and repulsion that may characterize relationships between imperial power and colony) and hybridity (the creation of 'transcultural' forms in the contact zone between the two) that raise many awkward questions" (2005, xvi). They are, however, questions that we should be asking.

Those featured in this book reflect a palette of sonic and cultural hybridity fused through hip-hop that was only made possible through Britain and British culture. Though an artist like Shadia Mansour now identifies herself as Palestinian, she was born and raised in London, growing up in a society that made possible such exploration of identities. The marriage between Lowkey's father from Dover and his middle-class Arab mother was made possible in Britain. Akala's third generation British mixed-race identity, with a British-Jamaican father and English-Scottish mother was a confluence of specific factors housed in Britain. Vujanic's Serbian-British identity no doubt informs his music and the "in between" worlds that he expresses through humor and excess.

Rappers in Britain are doing important work, not just through their music, but through their social work, working in prisons and schools, organizing womxn-centric club nights (Girls in Grime, Lyrically Challenged, and Ladies of Rage come to mind), holding youth workshops, and many other endeavors. One example includes Together in Pieces interactive CIC which is a community interest company based in Derry-Londonderry that aims to create social change through the exploration of hip-hop culture. This non-profit company led by Creative Director Eileen Walsh is literally transforming the lives of those in Northern Ireland and making it a better place through hip-hop. As ever, Britain's greatness is despite the lack of support these artists receive, and thus we find positive outcomes amid bleak socio-economic contexts, the high level of inequality, and the regrettable class system we have in this country.[3]

As these genres are given more value by academics, and given more monetary value by grant-giving institutions, how do we involve artists in productive, ethical, and non-exploitative ways? Our series of talks at ROPE-A-DOPE here in Bristol keeps fostering productive conversation between artist and scholar, and scholars like Rollefson have taken an ethical approach to fieldwork, and I think this is part of a wider conversation we should be having with funding councils, universities, schools, performance venues, record labels, media outlets, and our respective local and national governments for the purposes of policy making. As hip-hop and grime come of age, it is up to us to make sure it is given the cultural and financial importance it deserves, not least because some of the solutions to the country's problems may well be right before our ears if we know where to listen.

Fuck Brexit

On June 23, 2016, UK citizens voted narrowly (52%) to leave the European Union. Pro-Brexit campaigners like Nigel Farage used mass immigration from other EU countries as a scare tactic, and appealed to those who wanted more job opportunities, better funded NHS, and a general nostalgia for some older, idealized form of Britain that probably never existed in the first place (Gilroy's "postcolonial melancholia"). We might be tempted to say that postcolonial melancholia won out, that the referendum result was a reaction against such melancholia and turning toward the insular and arrogant exaggeration of Britain's place in the global order. It was also the product of our neoliberal era, and at the time of this writing, transnational corporations are leaving the country in search of more stable locales in the global financial system.

Although there are more explicit rap songs about Grenfell Tower than about Brexit, the social conditions which led to Brexit are lyrical fodder in more politically tinged UK hip-hop. Questions of belonging, national identity, racism, nostalgia are present in lyrics alongside critiques of neoliberalism, neocolonialism, and postcolonial melancholia. Akala, Lowkey, Stormzy, Plan B, Solareye, and many others demonstrate this while celebrating other, more positive aspects of their community.

There were some rap songs explicitly about Brexit, however, and for this I will return to the two case studies from Chapter 6 as they both wrote parody songs on the topic. Goldie Lookin Chain parodied The Streets "Dry Your Eyes Mate" into a song entitled "Auf Wiedersehen Mate." The music video for "Dry Your Eyes Mate" featured Mike Skinner with his pet dog, around various locations such as the bus stop, laundromat, the gym, pool hall, pub, and curry house, rapping about a recent breakup. Parodying the video, Rhys of GLC is seen in a pub, a car, supermarket, and café (see Figure C.2) rapping about the recent "breakup" with the EU. The chorus states: "Auf Wiedersehen Mate, I know it's hard to grasp this concept and idea. We're gonna say goodbye to IKEA. Adios mate, so I won't be driving a BMW or Mercedes. I'll have to drive a Rover. " He states he will miss the European Cup, Volvo, and Nutella, and

FIGURE C.2 Goldie Lookin Chain, "Auf Wiedersehen Mate" (2016)

beers like Kronenburg and "even Stella" (Stella Artois). "Keep your Edam, and give me back my cheddar," and laments no more parties in Ibiza and holidays in France for him. At the grocery store, he stares at the non-UK items he will have to let go of, sadly taking out a frozen chicken meal from the store freezer. His tone matches the sad, lamenting tone of the original version and essentially translates the "breakup song" genre into the context of national and international politics (something we also saw with Scottish independence media coverage and songs).

While The Streets celebrated the everyday nationalism of drinking Stella and Kronenburg, Goldie Lookin Chain points out that some of those aspects which defined white working-class British identity (albeit not "British" consumer products in their origin) might have to go. An exaggeration, but one that goes to show how non-UK products (and holidays) are an ingrained part of the idea of British culture, and that the everyday-ness of The Streets's style of hip-hop help to show the global nature of the signifiers of "national" identity. Like with the locality of "Cwmbran," McDonalds is as much part of the local landscape as is Wetherspoons and the local church hall.

Vujanic (as Bricka Bricka), alongside parody rapper "Original K" as "4N Boyz," uploaded a video entitled "Fuck Brexit" to YouTube on Mach 30, 2017. While "Hard in Da Paint" five years earlier showed an eighteen-year-old British-Serbian in his backyard in what felt like a home-made video, we now see Vujanic aged twenty-four, more confidently rapping on how these immigrants are "here to stay" (while still performing those problematic Eastern European stereotypes). Objects of labor are lyrically referenced and shown in the music video, as the two rap from a van which has a kitchen sink at the back. Bricka wears a high visibility jacket that many construction workers wear. Their "foreign" t-shirt logo deliberately references the Polish beer brand Tyskie in its design (see Figure C.3). Bricka states, "I wipe my ass with the *Daily Mail*" and plays on the immigrant-as-sexual-predator stereotype saying, "Got an English girl and her dad votes Tory / Sorry daddy but I make your daughter horny." Bricka raps on how sexy he is, and how he's "sorry not sorry" (a Beyoncé *Lemonade* reference) that he is taking people's jobs. Original K states, "Fuck Brexit we ain't gonna exit / squatting on a lambo [Lamborghini car], started in a bedsit . . . / we ain't going home, fuck the election." The chorus opens with, "Fuck Brexit, we are here to stay / Fuck Brexit, never going away / Fuck Brexit and fuck minimum wage / Fuck Brexit and Theresa May." While still apparently intended to be humorous, this feels more in line with the "voice to the voiceless" tropes of hip-hop ("greatest immigrants of all time!" Bricka states at the end), being overt about their visibility and importance to British society. With resemblances to "Immigrants (We Get the Job Done)" in *The Hamilton Mixtape* (Williams 2018), Bricka Bricka states, "You can hate all you want, you can vote Donald Trump, but you can't build a wall without immigrant."

FIGURE C.3 4N Boyz, "Fuck Brexit" (2017)

Just like "Englistan" discussed in Chapter 2, "Fuck Brexit," shows how hip-hop becomes an important form to say, "we are here," albeit through a more humorous medium than the former. Hip-hop yet again deftly navigates both resistance and belonging as a mouthpiece for counter-narratives and marginality around the globe, forming a family of resemblances that spans beyond the level of the national.

Realizing that UK rap and hip-hop are crucial parts of Britain's musical land-scape, and that "British music" as an academic field includes a wider range of people than academic writing has previous allowed; such an issue goes to the heart of what we value in music studies and perhaps in academia more generally. If art and cul-ture provide a lens into its society, to not value the artistic and cultural products of certain members means that not all members are valued. These rappers become ambassadors for the voiceless and ambassadors for a range of issues that have been neglected or overlooked in more mainstream pockets of society.

Diversifying mainstream arts and culture, through recent social media-led initia-tives by UK university students to "decolonize the curriculum" to include non-white playwrights and authors, is one such action that aims to represent multicultural Britain more accurately. Postcolonial melancholia is not just a condition felt to varying degrees by the British public, but it has real consequences: since the Brexit vote, hate crime has increased an average of 41%, and it has increased 326% against Muslims specifically (Ahmed 2017). If hip-hop can provide a cultural citizenship for those who feel marginalized, then placing the spotlight on them may go some way to promote inclusivity in the divisive times we are living in.

Lastly, to return to Gilroy, rappers may be instrumental in helping British soci-ety mourn its past healthily, which can only happen when we come to terms with it, accept it, not move on from it fully to the point of cultural amnesia, but see its ramifications in current society. Once the melancholia is replaced with mourning, we can "start to produce a new image of the nation that can accommodate its colonial dimensions" (Gilroy 2004, 115). Rap music in the UK can and does help in this process, working through important political and historical issues alongside its audiences. Time will tell, but the more attention we give to this art and artists, the greater chance we have of changing existing dynamics extra-musically beyond the boundaries of art and culture.

Notes

1. There have been other examples of detailed critiques of the UK government in grime, most notably, "Question Time" by the rapper Dave in 2017. To cite Monique Charles's work on the role of grime in the 2017 General Election: "Grime artists are unsung heroes. They use their position as organic intellectuals to engage with formal politics and push for change with the collective, for the collective. Although Labour did not win the election, this was a moment in history that has injected new energy into politics and massively increased political engagement amongst young people" (2018, 46).

2. Language shapes our values and shapes the cultures that we live in. Rap music is one manifestation of this and requires more attention to these ends. To quote from Ngugi wa Thing'o's *Decolonising the Mind*: "Language carries culture, and culture carries, particularly through orature and literature, the entire body of values by which we come to perceive ourselves and our place in the world. How people perceive themselves affects how they look at their culture, at their politics and at the social production of wealth, at their entire relationship to nature and to other human beings. Language is thus inseparable from ourselves as a community of human beings with a specific form and character, a specific history, a specific relationship to the world" (quoted in McLeod 2010, 21).

3. Akala writing on Grenfell is particularly relevant here: "The horrendous Grenfell Tower fire in June 2017, which claimed at least seventy-one lives and was undeniably caused by systematic contempt for the lives of poor people, was perhaps the ultimate and most gruesome tribute to austerity yet seen. The state's reaction, or total lack of reaction, in the days after the fire versus the overwhelming outpouring of public support was one of the strangest things I have ever seen with my own eyes. The slew of racist abuse and virulent hate that can be found in any thread online discussing the Grenfell victims—who happened to be disproportionately Muslims—and the conceptual linking of the dead families to the terrorists at London Bridge and Manchester in the previous months speaks loudly of how 'Muslim' has become a racialised, culturally essential category in twenty-first century Britain. At the time of this writing, seven months after the fire, most of the surviving families still have not been re-housed, even after the collection of millions of pounds of donations in their names and despite the fact that the local council is known to have £300 million in cash reserves. I lived on the same street as Grenfell for five years, but my building had sprinklers, working fire alarms, extinguishers and a maintenance man who came to check in every few months. Just a little bit of money can be the difference between life and death, even on the same London street" (Akala 2018, 20–21).

Chapter 5 Lyrics

Government Issue Music Protest News Reports

News Anchor in 2034 (Track 1 "The End")

This is an emergency government issue broadcast, live from parliament Ruin in the heart of New Glasgow. You join us as we witness bizarre scenes here at New Glasgow Tower, home to the country's professional class. The view from the slums is dramatic as we have learned a hijacker manning a government drone is encircling the massive, free-standing structure. Security personnel have been scrambling all around us, including the Royal Air Force, who, as we understand are concerned about attacking a craft in such a densely populated area. You can feel the fear on the ground here among the slum population, most of whom have never lived to witness an attack on British home soil. It really is like something out of a movie. Wait, we are seeing some activity on the craft, a door on the vessel seems to be opening yet we cannot get a glimpse of the pilot. People down here are gripped by panic as officials and security forces appeal to the people of New Glasgow to keep calm and carry on.

News Anchor (End of Track 1)

NHS stock has soared to the top of the FTSE 1000 after announcing it's working on a possible cure for a mysterious strain of dementia which attacks human beliefs.

News Anchor (Beginning of Track 2)

The government has announced plans to demolish the derelict Scottish parliament complex as part of the London Olympic celebrations in 2034. Organizers say the debris will become one of the UK's greatest tourist attractions. Parliament Ruin will open in 2034.

New Glasgow Central pillar that will house the city's professional class is almost complete at a cost of 2 trillion pounds. New Glasgow Tower, opening in September 2035, will be the tallest free-standing structure ever built and experts say it will help preserve culture form the dangers of the slum population.

Anchor (Track 3 "The Ghost of Sage Francis")

The government has issued new figures showing the number of missing children has dropped from 30,000 per year to 29,500. Ministers say authorities should be allowed to continue their investigations without hindrance from the press.

Anchor (End of Track 3)

Doctors are speculating that paganda virus, a strain of dementia which attacks human values, may be spreading through New Glasgow's wasp population. Wasps were genetically engineered and introduced into the MegaCity to pollinate plant life after the extinction of the bumblebee in 2025.

Anchor (Beginning of Track 4)

Z list weirdo Russell Brand has made a bizarre claim that undercover agents are trying to poison his food and drink with alcohol and drugs to prevent him from speaking about the threat of war with China.

Anchor (End of Track 6)

Former political firebrand Tommy Sheridan was admitted to New Glasgow General after being diagnosed with suspected paganda virus. Sources close to the socialist say he is forgetting who he was.

Anchor (Beginning of Track 7)

Emergency legislation outlawing retirement has been passed in Westminster. A Minister said, "People have an eternity to rest when they do so when we're still alive it's important to muck in and do our bit for this great nation. 10 million elderly citizens will return to work within the year, mostly taking up posts in government issue information centres."

Anchor (Track 8 "Veritas")

The refugee population of former Palestine continue roaming the globe looking for asylum as Israeli executive branch receive a Nobel Prize for promoting world peace.

Anchor (Track 13)

This news is just coming in so we are unable to confirm this report, but sources within New Glasgow are telling me that former socialist politician Tommy Sheridan is dead.

Anchor (Track 14)

Skirmishes continue to break out in the slums of New Glasgow. Security forces say they have the situation well under control.

Anchor (Track 15)

An investigation into a blaze in a mental institution in 2004 has found that the fire was started deliberately. Security forces are appealing for information from the only known survivor who was a baby at the time of the accident. Police are still unsure if the arsonist is still at large and are following up leads that the suspect may have adopted a new identity after going on the run.

Anchor (Track 16)

All studies show that the New Glasgow population are adjusting well to their new surroundings after many years of restless discontent. The government have attributed the findings to their social policies, some which were very unpopular. Officials say this evidence vindicates their arguments for law and order and that people will always adapt over time. Cases of crime, missing children and paganda virus are also down.

Bibliography

"Boycott Israel Campaign." *Innovative Minds.* 2012. http://www.inminds.co.uk/boycott-israel-2012.php.

"Multiculturalism: What Does it Mean?" *BBC News Magazine,* February 7, 2011. www.bbc.co.uk/news/magazine-12381027.

"State Multiculturalism Has Failed, Says David Cameron." *BBC News,* February 5, 2011. www.bbc.co.uk/news/uk-politics-12371994.

"Straight No Chaser." "Straight No Chaser: David Vujanic - Bricka Bricka, Brexit & Believing in Yourself!" September 18, 2016. *YouTube* interview. https://www.youtube.com/watch?v=6aqIuIH-wWU.

Aaron, Jane, and Chris Williams, eds. *Postcolonial Wales.* Cardiff: University of Wales Press, 2005.

Abbas, Tahir. "Muslim Minorities in Britain: Integration, Multiculturalism and Radicalism in the Post-7/7 Period. *Journal of Intercultural Studies* 28:3 (2007): 287–300.

Adams, Ruth. "The Englishness of English Punk: Sex Pistols, Subcultures and Nostalgia." *Popular Music and Society* 31:4 (2008): 469–88.

Adegoke, Yomi. "Grime, Afro Bashment, Drill . . . How Black British Music Became More Fertile Than Ever." *The Guardian,* June 1, 2018. https://www.theguardian.com/music/2018/jun/01/grime-afro-bashment-drill-how-black-british-music-became-more-fertile-than-ever.

Ahmad, Aijaz. "Jameson's Rhetoric of Otherness and the 'National Allegory.'" *Social Text* 17 (1987): 3–25.

Ahmed, Rizwan (Riz MC). "Channel 4 Diversity Speech." House of Commons, March 1, 2017. 2017. https://www.youtube.com/watch?v=36bcxDVNr1s.

Akala. BBC: BBAF Mandela Lecture. February 2014. https://www.youtube.com/watch?v=1wzUx8GEaIk.

Akala. *Natives: Race and Class in the Ruins of Empire.* London: Two Roads, 2018.

Alibhai-Brown, Yasmin. *Exotic England: The Making of a Curious Nation*. London: Portobello Books, 2015.

Alibhai-Brown, Yasmin. *Mixed Feelings: The Complex Lives of Mixed-Race Britons*. London: The Women's Press, 2001.

Alim, H. Samy. *Roc the Mic Right: The Language of Hip-Hop Culture*. London: Routledge, 2006.

Allcity TaxiTalk Show. "Interview with Shay D." January 28, 2018. https://www.youtube.com/watch?v=as9ygHf-e8U.

Allison, Lincoln. "Sport and Nationalism." In *Handbook of Sports Studies*, edited by Jay Coakley and Eric Dunning, 344–45. London: Sage, 2000.

Andersen, Janne Louise. "The Passion, Politics and Power of Shadia Mansour." *Rolling Stone*, September 4, 2011.

Anderson, Benedict. *Imagined Communities: Reflections on the Origins and Spread of Nationalism*. 2nd ed. London: Verso, 2006.

Anderson, Bridget. "The Politics of Pests: Immigration and the Invasive Other." *Social Research: An International Quarterly* 84:1 (2017): 7–28.

Andrews, Charlotte Richardson. "Hip-Hop and Folk Meet in a New Wave of Protest Music." *The Guardian*, November 6, 2012. http://www.theguardian.com/music/musicblog/2012/nov/06/hip-hop-folk-protest-music.

Andrews, Kehinde. "'Urban' Sounds: It's Time to Stop Using This Hackneyed Term for Black Music." *The Guardian*, August 14, 2018. https://www.theguardian.com/music/shortcuts/2018/aug/14/urban-time-stop-hackneyed-term-black-music.

Anonymous, Adam. "The Hip-Hop Scene in Wales." *BBC Wales Music*, September 15, 2009. http://www.bbc.co.uk/wales/music/sites/rap-hip-hop/pages/hio-hop-in-wales.shtml.

Apple, Michael. "The Absent Presence of Race in Educational Reform." *Race, Ethnicity and Education* 2:1 (1999): 9–16.

Augey, Arthur. *The British Question*. Manchester: Manchester University Press, 2013.

Bairner, Alan. *Sport, Nationalism, and Globalization: European and North American Perspectives*. Albany: SUNY, 2001.

Balandina, Alexandra. "Rap Music as a Cultural Mediator in Postconflict Yugoslavia." In *Hip-Hop at Europe's Edge: Music, Agency, and Social Change*, edited by Milosz Miszczynski and Adriana Helbig, 63–82. Bloomington: Indiana University Press, 2017.

Banks, Mark, and Jason Toynbee. "Race, Consecration and the 'Music Outside'?" In *Black British Jazz*, edited by Catherine Tackley, Jason Toynbee, and Mark Doffman, 91–110. Farnham: Ashgate, 2014.

Barrett, Jessica. "The Grime Symphony: Why the Uniquely British Urban Sound Is in the Middle of a Renaissance." *The Independent*, June 19, 2015. https://www.independent.co.uk/arts-entertainment/music/features/the-grime-symphony-why-the-uniquely-british-urban-sound-is-in-the-middle-of-a-renaissance-10331213.html.

Barron, Lee. "The Sound of Street Corner Society: UK Grime Music as Ethnography." *European Journal of Cultural Studies* 16:5 (2013): 531–47.

Bassett, Jordan. "'It's Reached UK domination': Author Dan Hancox Talks 'Inner City Pressure,' the Definitive Story of Grime." *NME*, May 19, 2018. https://www.nme.com/blogs/reached-uk-domination-author-dan-hancox-inner-city-pressure-definitive-grime-biography-2316923#ZBwh43t57q36YRPc.99.

Batey, Angus. "Home Grown." *The Times*, July 26, 2003.

Baycroft, Timothy. *Nationalism in Europe, 1789–1945*. Cambridge: Cambridge University Press, 2010.

BBC News. "BBC DJ Nihal Criticises Radio 1 Diversity." *BBC News Arts & Entertainment*, March 4, 2015. http://www.bbc.co.uk/news/entertainment-arts-31731397.

BBC News. "Election 2015: SNP Wins 56 of 59 Seats in Scots Landslide." *BBC News*, May 8, 2015. http://www.bbc.co.uk/news/election-2015-scotland-32635871.

BBC News. "Scottish Independence: Voters Say No." *BBC News*, September 19, 2014. http://www.bbc.co.uk/news/uk-scotland-29265698.

Beauchamp, Zack. "Brexit Isn't about Economics. It's about Xenophobia." *Vox*, June 24, 2016. https://www.vox.com/2016/6/23/12005814/brexit-eu-referendum-immigrants.

Bell, David. "Sleaford Mods: Austerity Dogs." *The Quietus*, November 26, 2013. http://thequietus.com/articles/13987-sleaford-mods-austerity-dogs-review.

Bennett, Andy, and Jon Stratton, eds. *Britpop and the English Musical Tradition*. Farnham: Ashgate, 2010.

Bennett, Andy. "Rappin' on the Tyne: White Hip Hop Culture in Northeast England – An Ethnographic Study." *The Sociological Review* 47 (1999): 1–24.

Bennett, Andy. "'Sitting in an English Garden': Comparing Representations of 'Britishness' in the Songs of the Beatles and 1990s Britpop Groups." In *The Beatles, Popular Music and Society: A Thousand Voices*, edited by Ian Inglis, 189–206. London: Palgrave Macmillan, 2000.

Bhabha, Homi. *The Location of Culture*. London: Routledge, 1994.

Bhain, Phil Mac Giolla. "Salmond's Civic Nationalism a Problem for the Westminster Elite." *Slugger O'Toole*, January 11, 2012. http://sluggerotoole.com/2012/01/11/salmonds-civic-nationalism-a-problem-for-the-westminster-elite/.

Bhopal, Kalwant, and John Preston. *Intersectionality and "Race" in Education*. London: Routledge, 2012.

Billig, Michael. *Banal Nationalism*. London: Sage, 1995.

Bizzle, Lethal (Maxwell Ansah). "David Cameron Is a Donut." *The Guardian*, June 8, 2006. http://www.theguardian.com/commentisfree/2006/jun/08/davidcameronisadonut.

bizzlevideos (Bizzle's YouTube channel). "LETHAL BIZZLE TALKS NDUBZ BEEF AND RADIO 1 PLAY." *YouTube*, February 12, 2012. https://www.youtube.com/watch?v=sdIX4UDyM8E.

Bloomfield, Craig. "Emmanuel Frimpong and Lethal Bizzle Release Range of Judi Dench Clothing." *Talksport*, November 30, 2011. http://talksport.com/magazine/features/2011-11-30/emmanuel-frimpong-and-lethal-bizzle-release-range-judi-dench-clothing#1EUiqLSl2SgYUsU8.99.

Boakye, Jeffrey. *Hold Tight: Black Masculinity, Millennials and the Meaning of Grime*. London: Influx Press, 2017.

Bone, Daniel. "Review: Loki With Becci Wallace: G.I.M.P." *Wordplay Magazine*, October 7, 2014. http://www.wordplaymagazine.com/2014/10/reviews/loki-becci-wallace-g-m-p/.

Boum, Aomar. "'Soundtracks of Jerusalem': YouTube, North African Rappers, and the Fantasies of Resistance." In *Modernity, Minority and the Public Sphere: Jews and Christians in the Middle East*, edited by Sasha R. Goldstein-Sabbah and Heleen L. Murre-van den Berg, 284–309. Leiden: Brill, 2016.

Braae, Nick. "We Don't Know How Lucky We Are: Masculine Humor in New Zealand Popular Music." In *The Routledge Companion to Popular Music and Humor*, edited by Thomas M. Kitts and Nick Baxter-Moore, 346–53. New York: Routledge, 2019.

Bradley, Lloyd. *Sounds like London: 100 Years of Black Music in the Capitol.* London: Serpent's Tail, 2013.

Bramwell, Richard, and James Butterworth. "'I Feel English as Fuck': Translocality and the Performance of Alternative Identities through Rap." *Ethnic and Racial Studies* 42:14 (2019): 2510–27.

Bramwell, Richard. *UK Hip-Hop, Grime and the City: The Aesthetics and Ethnics of London's Rap scenes.* London: Routledge, 2015.

Brinkurst-Cuff, Charlie. "Why is the History of Punk Music so White?" *Dazed*, November 12, 2015. http://www.dazeddigital.com/music/article/28372/1/why-is-the-history-of-punk-music-so-white.

Brøvig-Hanssen, Ragnhild. "Humor's Role in Mashups and Remixes: Similarities between Humor Structure and Remix Structure." In *On Popular Music and Its Unruly Entanglements*, edited by Nick Braae and Kai Arne Hansen, 189–207. New York: Palgrave Macmillan, 2020.

Buchowski, Michal. "Social Thought & Commentary: The Specter of Orientalism in Europe: From Exotic Other to Stigmatized Brother." *Anthropological Quarterly* 79:3 (2006): 463–82.

Bulut, Selim. "Heading for the British Asian Underground with Riz MC." *Dazed*, April 25, 2016. http://www.dazeddigital.com/music/article/30882/1/heading-for-the-british-asian-underground-with-riz-mc.

Burgess, Jean, and Joshua Green, eds. *YouTube: Online Video and Participatory Culture.* Cambridge: Polity Press, 2009.

Bury, Liz. "Lethal Bizzle Wants His Word 'Dench' in the Dictionary—But It's already There." *The Guardian*, September 12, 2013. http://www.theguardian.com/books/2013/sep/12/lethal-bizzle-dench-dictionary-campaign.

Bychawski, Adam. "Sleaford Mods: 'We're Not Fucking Communists.'" *NME*, April 5, 2015. http://www.nme.com/news/sleaford-mods/84232.

Caglar, Ayse, and Nina Glick Schiller. "Introduction." In *Migrants and City-Making: Multiscalar Perspectives on Dispossession*, 1–31. Durham, NC: Duke University Press, 2017.

Cameron, David. "You're Talking Rubbish, Lethal Bizzle . . . Lyrics about Guns and Knives Do Destroy Lives." *Daily Mail*, June 11, 2006. http://www.dailymail.co.uk/news/article-390139/Youre-talking-rubbish-Lethal-Bizzle--lyrics-guns-knives-destroy-lives.html#ixzz3uINSnUtD.

Campbell, Sean. "'Irish Blood, English Heart': Ambivalence, Unease and The Smiths." In *Why Pamper Life's Complexities? Essays on The Smiths*, edited by Sean Campbell and Colin Coulter, 43–64. Manchester: Manchester University Press, 2010.

Carpenter, Humphrey. *That Was the Satire That Was: The Satire Boom of the 1960s.* Faber and Faber, 2009.

Carr, Paul. "National Identity versus Commerce: An Analysis of Opportunities and Limitations within the Welsh Music Scene for Composers and Performing Musicians." *Popular Music History* 5:3 (2010): 265–85.

Cenciarelli, Carlo. "Dr Lecter's Taste for 'Goldberg,' or: The Horror of Bach in the Hannibal Franchise." *Journal of the Royal Musical Association* 137 (2012): 107–34.

Chang, Jeff. "Future Shock." *The Village Voice*, January 13, 2004. http://www.villagevoice.com/music/future-shock-6398102.

Channel 4 News. "Sleaford Mods on Jeremy Corbyn, Poverty and Language." *Channel 4 News*, September 11, 2015. https://www.youtube.com/watch?v=w4G_UYKoRkk.

Charles, Monique. "Grime Labour: Grime Politics Articulates New Forms of Cross-Race Working-Class Identities." *Soundings: A Journal of Politics and Culture* 68 (2018): 40–52.

Charles, Monique. "Hallowed by thy Grime?: A Musicological and Sociological Genealogy of Grime Music and Its Relation to Black Atlantic Religious Discourse." PhD diss., University of Warwick, 2016.

Chernilo, Daniel. "The Critique of Methodological Nationalism: Theory and History." *Thesis Eleven* 106:1 (2011): 98–117.

Cheshire, Jenny, and Paul Kerswill, Susan Fox, and Eivind Torgersen. "Contact, the Feature Pool and the Speech Community: The Emergence of Multicultural London English." *Journal of Sociolinguistics* 15:2 (2011): 151–96.

Clark, Laura. "'Jafaican' Is Wiping Out Inner-City English Accents." *Daily Mail*, April 12, 2006.

Cloonan, Martin. "Pop and the Nation-State: Towards a Theorisation." *Popular Music* 18:2 (1999): 193–207.

Cloonan, Martin. "State of the Nation: 'Englishness,' Pop and Politics in the Mid-1990s." *Popular Music and Society* 21:2 (1997): 47–70.

Collins, Hettie, and Olivia Rose. *This is Grime*. London: Hodder & Stoughton, 2016.

Collinson, Ian. "Devopop: Pop-Englishness and Post-Britpop Guitar Bands." In *Britpop and the English Musical Tradition*, edited by Andy Bennett and Jon Stratton, 163–77. Farnham: Ashgate, 2010.

Collinson, Ian. "Dis Is England's New Voice': Anger, Activism & the Asian Dub Foundation." In *Sonic synergies: music, technology, community, identity*, edited by Gerry Bloustien, Margaret Peters, & Susan Luckman, 105–14. Hampshire, UK: Ashgate, 2008.

Condry, Ian. *Hip-hop Japan: Rap and the Paths of Cultural Globalization*. Durham: Duke University Press, 2006.

Covach, John. "Stylistic Competencies, Musical Humor, and 'This Is Spinal Tap.'" In *Concert Music, Rock and Jazz Since 1945: Essays and Analytical Studies*, edited by Elizabeth West Marvin and Richard Hermann, 402–24. Rochester: University of Rochester Press, 1995.

Coward, Henry. *Choral Technique and Interpretation*. New York: H. W. Gray, 1914.

Craft, Elizabeth Titrington. "Headfirst into a Political Abyss: The Politics and Political Reception of *Hamilton*." *American Music* 38:4 (2018): 429–47.

Critchley, Simon. *On Humour*. London: Routledge, 2002.

Cronin, Mike. *Sport and Nationalism in Ireland: Gaelic Games, Soccer, and Irish Identity since 1884*. Dublin: Four Courts Press, 1999.

crownsoundvids. "Crownsound presents "Breaking the Barrier final." 2015. *YouTube*, April 2, 2015. https://www.youtube.com/watch?v=gHjHt9vhp3Y.

Daisley, Stephen. "Essay: What Is Scottish Nationalism, What Is It Not, What Could It Be?" *Stv News*, June 12, 2015. http://news.stv.tv/scotland-decides/analysis/1322184-essay-stephen-daisley-on-the-snp-and-the-politics-of-nationalism/.

Dalmonte, Rossana. "Towards a Semiology of Humor in Music." *International Review of the Aesthetics and Sociology of Music* 26:2 (1995): 167–87.

Davies, Rob, Kate Connolly, and Ian Sample. "Cladding for Grenfell Tower Was Cheaper, More Combustible Option." *The Guardian*, June 16, 2017. https://www.theguardian.com/uk-news/2017/jun/16/manufacturer-of-cladding-on-grenfell-tower-identified-as-omnis-exteriors.

Day, Timothy. "Cultural History and a Singing Style: The English Cathedral Tradition." In *The Oxford Handbook of Singing*, edited by Graham Welch, David M. Howard, and John Nix, n.p. New York: Oxford University Press, 2019.

De Lacey, Alex. "Deeper Than Rap: Grime Is Not a Subgenre of Hip-Hop." *Pigeons and Planes*, November 3, 2015. https://pigeonsandplanes.com/in-depth/2015/11/grime-hip-hop.

De Paor Evans, Adam. *Provincial Headz: British Hip Hop and Critical Regionalism.* Sheffield: Equinox, 2020.

De Paor Evans, Adam. "From Broken Glass to Ruf Diamonds: Manchester Hip Hop." In *Sounds Northern*, edited by Ewa Mazierska, 155–73. Sheffield: Equinox, 2018.

Dickinson, Kay. *Arab Cinema Travels: Transnational Syria, Palestine, Dubai and Beyond.* London: Palgrave/BFI, 2016.

Donnison, Jon. "British Palestinian Rapper Conducts a 'Musical Intifada.'" *BBC News*, September 7, 2010. https://www.bbc.co.uk/news/world-middle-east-11215298.

Dossena, Marina. "'And Scotland Will March Again.' The Language of Political Song in 19th- and 20th-Century Scotland." In *After the Storm: Papers from the Forum for Research on the Languages of Scotland and Ulster triennial meeting*, edited by Janet Cruickshank and Robert McColl Millar. Aberdeen: Forum for Research on the Languages of Scotland and Ireland, 2013.

Dossena, Marina. "Power to the Singers: Scots, English, Politics and Policies." *The Bottle Imp* 9 (2011). http://www.arts.gla.ac.uk/ScotLit/ASLS/SWE/TBI/TBIIssue9/Dossena.pdf.

Dotiwala, Jasmine. "Rappers Shay D and Kingpin are London's 'Love Jones.'" *The Source*, July 13, 2016. http://thesource.com/2016/07/13/rappers-shay-d-and-kingpin-are-londons-love-jones/.

Drummond, Rob. "Maybe It's a Grime [t]ing: th-Stopping among Urban British Youth." *Language in Society* 47:2 (2018): 171–96.

Drummond, Rob. "(Mis)interpreting Urban Youth Language: White Kids Sounding Black?" *Journal of Youth Studies* 20:5 (2017): 640–60.

Drury, Meghan. "Counterorienting the War on Terror: Arab Hip Hop and Diasporic Resistance." *Journal of Popular Music Studies* 29 (2017): 1–11.

Duncombe, Stephen, and Maxwell Tremblay, eds. *White Riot: Punk Rock and the Politics of Race.* London: Verso, 2011.

Duncum, Paul. "Youth on YouTube as Smart Swarms." *Art Education* 67:2 (2014): 32–36.

Dunn, Kevin C. "Never Mind the Bollocks: The Punk Rock Politics of Global Communication." *Review of International Studies* 34 (2008): 193–210.

Durand, Alain-Philippe. *Black, Blanc, Beur: Rap Music and Hip-Hop Culture in the Francophone World.* Lanham: Scarecrow Press, 2002.

Dynarowicz, Ewa. "Stereotypes as Source of Subcultural Capital: Poland and the Polish in the Auto-Representation Project of the Dutch Rapper, Mr. Polska." *Popular Music* 37:3 (2018): 466–86.

Eaton-Lewis, Andrew. "Scottish Rapper Loki: Vote No, Get This." *The Scotsman*, October 25, 2014. http://www.scotsman.com/lifestyle/culture/music/scottish-rapper-loki-vote-no-get-this-1-3583861.

Edensor, Tim. *National Identity, Popular Culture and Everyday Life.* Oxford: Berg, 2002.

Edwards, Simone Elesha. "Interview: Akala at Hyperlink Festival." *MOBO*, April 30, 2013. http://www.mobo.com/news-blogs/interview-akala-hyperlink-festival.

El Hamamsy, Walid, and Mounire Soliman. *Popular Culture in the idle East and North Africa: A Postcolonial Outlook*. London: Routledge, 2013.

Ellis, Amelia. "Interview with the Sleaford Mods." *Nottingham Post*, September 9, 2014. http://www.nottinghampost.com/Interview-Sleaford-Mods/story-22897417-detail/story. html#ixzz3XDWQiatr.

Encarnacao, John. *Punk Aesthetics and New Folk*. Farnham: Ashgate, 2013.

Eqeiq, Amal. "Louder than the blue ID: Palestinian Hip-hop in Israel." In *Displaced at Home: Ethnicity and Gender Among Palestinians in Israel*, edited by Rhoda Ann Kanaaneh and Isis Nusair, 53–74. Albany: State University of New York Press, 2010.

English, Paul. "Independence Referendum: Scots Musicians Stage Yes Campaign Concert in Edinburgh ahead of Thursday's Vote." *Daily Record*, September 15, 2015. http://www.dailyrecord.co.uk/news/politics/independence-referendum-scots-musicians-stage-4260497.

Eyerman, Ron, and Andrew Jamison. *Music and Social Movements. Mobilizing Movements in the Twentieth Century*. Cambridge: Cambridge University Press, 1998.

Fanon, Frantz. *The Wretched of the Earth*. Translated by Constance Farrington. London: Penguin, 1967.

Fiasco. "Stylah [interview]" *Hip-Hop Game*, September 14, 2006. hiphopgame.co.uk/site/interviews/artists/stylah.

Forman, Murray. *The 'Hood Comes First: Race, Space, and Place in Hip-hop*. Middletown: Wesleyan University Press, 2002.

Floyd, Samuel. *The Power of Black Music*. New York: Oxford University Press, 1995.

Fox, Killian. "Akala: The Thieves Banquet – review." *The Guardian*, May 26, 2013. https://www.theguardian.com/music/2013/may/26/akala-the-thieves-banquet-review.

Fox, Susan, Arfaan Khan, and Eivind Torgersen. "The Emergence and Diffusion of Multicultural English." In *Pan-Ethnic Styles of Speaking in European Metropolitan Areas*, edited by Friederike Kern and Margret Selting, 19–44. Amsterdam: Benjamins, 2011.

Freud, Sigmund. *The Joke and its Relation to the Unconscious*. London: Penguin Classics, 2003.

Garner, Steve, and Sher Selod. "The Racialization of Muslims: Empirical Studies of Islamophobia." *Critical Sociology* 41:1 (2015): 9–19.

Garrett, Charles Hiroshi. "'Pranksta Rap': Humor as Difference in Hip-Hop." In *Rethinking Difference in Music Scholarship*, edited by Olivia Blocechl, Melanie Lowe, and Jeffrey Kallberg, 315–37. Cambridge: Cambridge University Press, 2015.

Garside, Juliette. "BBC under Fire for 'Censoring' Palestine Lyric." *The Guardian*, May 13, 2011. https://www.theguardian.com/media/2011/may/13/bbc-palestine-lyric-mic-righteous.

Gates, Henry Louis, Jr. *The Signifying Monkey*. New York: Oxford University Press, 1988.

Gelbart, Matthew. "A Cohesive Shambles: The Clash's 'London Calling' and the Normalization of Punk." *Music and Letters* 92:2 (2011): 230–72.

Gellner, Ernest. *Nations and Nationalism*. 2nd ed. Oxford: Wiley-Blackwell, 2006.

George, Edward, and Anna Piva. "A Musical Intifada: Palestine and Electronica and Hip Hop." In *The Palgrave Encyclopedia of Imperialism and Anti-Imperialism*, edited by Immanuel Ness and Zak Cope, 525–35. London: Palgrave, 2016.

Gieben, Bram E. "Like a Boss: Hip-Hop Scottish Prodigy Loki Returns." *The Skinny*, July 12, 2013. http://www.theskinny.co.uk/music/interviews/like-a-boss-scottish-hip-hop-prodigy-loki-returns.

Gieben, Bram E. "Scottish Hip-Hop: Renaissance in Extremis." *Medium*, November 16, 2018. https://medium.com/@bram_e/scottish-hip-hop-renaissance-in-extremis-fcd3c47abe33.

Gillota, David. *Ethnic Humor in Multiethnic America*. Newark: Rutgers University Press, 2013.

Gilroy, Paul. *After Empire: Melancholia or Convivial Culture?* London: Routledge, 2004.

Gilroy, Paul. "Art of Darkness: Black Art and the Problem of Belonging in England." *Third Text* 4 (1990): 45–52.

Gilroy, Paul. *The Black Atlantic*. London: Verso, 1993.

Gilroy, Paul. *There Ain't no Black in the Union Jack*. London: Hutchinson, 1987.

Gilroy, Paul. "Why Harry's Disoriented about Empire." *The Guardian*, January 18, 2005. https://www.theguardian.com/uk/2005/jan/18/britishidentity.monarchy.

Giuffre, Liz, and Philip Hayward, eds. *Music in Comedy Television*. London: Routledge, 2017.

Glick Schiller, Nina, and Linda Basch, and Cristina Blanc-Szaton, eds. *Toward a Transnational Perspective on Migration: Race, Class, Ethnicity, and Nationalism Reconsidered*. New York: The New York Academy of Sciences, 1992.

Glick Schiller, Nina, and Ayse Caglar. "Locality and Globality: Building a Comparative Analytical Framework in Migration and Urban Studies." In *Locating Migration: Rescaling Cities and Migrants*, edited by Nina Glick Schiller and Ayse Caglar, 73–95. Ithaca: Cornell University Press, 2011.

Glick Schiller, Nina, and Ayse Caglar. "Towards a Comparative Theory of Locality in Migration Studies: Migrant Incorporation and City Scale." *Journal of Ethnic and Migration Studies* 35:2 (2009): 177–202.

Glick Schiller, Nina, and Ulrike Hanna Meinof. "Singing a New Song? Transnational Migration, Methodological Nationalism and Cosmopolitan Perspectives." *Music and Arts in Action* 3:3 (2011): 21–39.

Gosa, Travis. "The Fifth Element: Knowledge." *The Cambridge Companion to Hip-Hop*, edited by Justin A. Williams, 56–70. Cambridge: Cambridge University Press, 2015.

Greenberg, Ela. "'The King of the Streets': Hip Hop and the Reclaiming of Masculinity in Jerusalem's Shu'afat Refugee Camp." *Middle East Journal of Culture and Communication* 2 (2009): 231–50.

Grice, Andrew. "Damning Report Accuses Government of Stoking Anti-Immigrant Sentiment as Hate Crime Rises." *The Independent*, August 25, 2017. https://www.independent.co.uk/news/uk/politics/theresa-may-immigration-hate-crimes-brexit-rhetoric-language-blame-report-a7911241.html.

Griffiths, Dai, and Sarah Hill. "Postcolonial Music in Contemporary Wales: Hybridities and Weird Geographies." In *Postcolonial Wales*, edited by Jane Aaron and Chris Williams, 215–33. Cardiff: University of Wales Press, 2005.

Grove, Sophie. "The Olympics—A Triumph for Multicultural Britain." *monocle*, August 14, 2012. https://monocle.com/monocolumn/affairs/the-olympics-a-triumph-for-multicultural-britain/.

Guerra, Paula, and Andy Bennett. "Never Mind the Pistols? The Legacy and Authenticity of the Sex Pistols in Portugal." *Popular Music and Society* 38:4 (2015): 500–521.

Gulliver, Trevor. "Banal Nationalism in ESL Textbooks." *Canadian Journal of Education* 34:3 (2011): 119–35

Hall, Richard. "How the Brexit Campaign Used Refugees to Scare Voters." *Global Post*, June 24, 2016. http://abovewhispers.com/2016/06/28/how-the-brexit-campaign-used-refugees-to-scare-voters/.

Hammer. "Welsh Sheep Jokes." Message Board. *Visor Down*, December 2, 2007. http://www.vis-ordown.com/forum/crap-jokes/welsh-sheep-jokes.

Hancox, Dan. *Inner City Pressure: The Story of Grime*. London: William Collins, 2018.

Hancox, Dan. "Rap Responds to the Riots: 'They Have to Take Us Seriously.'" *The Guardian*, August 12, 2011. http://www.theguardian.com/music/2011/aug/12/rap-riots-professor-green-lethal-bizzle-wiley.

Hancox, Dan. "Was Kanye Patronising or Boosting Grime with His Brits Performance?" *The Guardian*, March 2, 2015. https://www.theguardian.com/music/musicblog/2015/mar/02/was-kanye-patronising-or-boosting-grime-with-his-brits-performance.

Harding, Nick. "Why Are so Many Middle-Class Children Speaking in Jamaican Patois? A Father of an 11-Year-Old Girl Laments a Baffling Trend." *The Daily Mail*, October 11, 2013. https://www.dailymail.co.uk/femail/article-2453613/Why-middle-class-children-speaking-Jamaican-patois-A-father-11-year-old-girl-laments-baffling-trend.html.

Harries, Dan. *Film Parody*. London: BFI, 2000.

Heawood, Sophie. "When Hood Meets Fringe." *The Guardian*, May 5, 2006. http://www.theguardian.com/music/2006/may/05/popandrock.

Hebblethwaite, Cordelia. "Is Hip Hop Driving the Arab Spring?" *BBC News*, July 24, 2011. https://www.bbc.co.uk/news/world-middle-east-14146243.

Hebdige, Dick. *Subculture: The Meaning of Style*. London: Routledge, 1979.

Hickey, Roberta. "Don't Just Call It Grime." *GRM Daily*, August 3, 2017. http://grmdaily.com/dont-just-call-it-grime.

Hill, Sarah. *'Blerwythirhwng?' The Place of Welsh Pop Music*. Farnham: Ashgate, 2007.

Hoberman, John. *Sport and Political Ideology*. London: Heinemann, 1984.

Hobsbawm, Eric. *Nations and Nationalism Since 1780*. 2nd ed. Cambridge: Cambridge University Press, 2012.

Hobsbawm, Eric, and Terence Ranger. *The Invention of Tradition*. 2nd ed. Cambridge: Cambridge University Press, 2012.

Hook, Dave. "An Autoethnography of Scottish Hip-Hop: Identity, Locality, Outsiderdom and Social Commentary." PhD diss., Edinburgh Napier University, 2018.

hooks, bell. *Talking Back: Thinking Feminist, Thinking Black*. New York: South End Press, 1989.

Hopkins, Katie. "Rescue Boats? I'd Use Gunships to Stop Migrants." *The Sun*, April 17, 2015. Transcript available at: http://www.gc.soton.ac.uk/files/2015/01/hopkins-17april-2015.pdf.

Huddart, David. *Homi K. Bhabha*. London: Routledge, 2006.

Hugill, Stan. *Shanties from the Seven Seas: Shipboard Work-Songs and Songs used as Work-Songs from the Great Days of Sail*. London: Routledge & Kegan Paul, 1966.

Hussain, Yasmin, and Paul Bagguley. "Securitized Citizens: Islamophobia, Racism and the 7/7 London Bombings." *The Sociological Review* 60 (2012): 715–34.

Hutcheon, Linda. *A Theory of Parody: The Teachings of Twentieth-Century Art Forms*. Urbana and Chicago: University of Illinois Press, 2000.

Hutten, Rebekah, and Lori Burns. "Beyoncé's Black Feminist Critique: Multimodal Intertextuality and Intersectionality in 'Sorry.'" In *Beyoncé in the World: Finding Meaning with Queen Bey in Troubled Times*, edited by Christina Baade and Kristin McGee. Middletown, CT: Wesleyan University Press, forthcoming, 2021.

Hyder, Rehan. *Brimful of Asia: Negotiating Ethnicity on the UK Music Scene*. Farnham: Ashgate, 2004.

Iandoli, Kathy. "The Special Relationship: Grime and America." *Boiler Room*, April 24, 2015. https://boilerroom.tv/the-special-relationship-grime-and-america/.

Ifekwunigwe, Jayne O., ed. *"Mixed Race" Studies: A Reader*. London: Routledge, 2004.

Isherwood, Gustav. "The Hip-hop Resistance: Forging Unity in the Arab Diaspora." *Romes* 48:1–2 (2014): 24–33.

Jameson, Fredric. "Third-World Literature in the Era of Multinational Capitalism." *Social Text* 15 (1986): 65–88.

Jeffries, Miles. *It's Wales: Welsh XXX Jokes*. Talybont: Y Lolfa Cyf, 2004.

Johnston, Ian. "Brexit: Anti-Immigrant Prejudice Major Factor in Deciding Vote, Study Finds." *The Independent*, June 22, 2017. https://www.independent.co.uk/news/uk/politics/brexit-racism-immigrant-prejudice-major-factor-leave-vote-win-study-a7801676.html.

Jones, Owen. *Chavs: The Demonization of the Working Class*. London: Verso, 2011.

Jones, Rhys, and Peter Merriman, "Hot, Banal and Everyday Nationalism: Bilingual Road Signs in Wales." *Political Geography* 28 (2009): 164–73.

Kahf, Usama. "Arabic Hip Hop: Claims of Authenticity and Identity of a New Genre." *Journal of Popular Music Studies* 19:4 (2007): 359–85.

Kajikawa, Loren. *Sounding Race in Rap Songs*. Berkeley: University of California Press, 2015.

Kanaanah, Rhoda Ann, and Isis Nusair, eds. *Displaced at Home: Ethnicity and Gender among Palestinians in Israel*. Albany: State University of New York Press, 2010.

Kärjä, Antti-Ville. "Humour and Parody as Strategies of Securing the Ethnic Other in Popular Music." In *Migrating Music*, edited by Jason Toynbee and Byron Dueck, 78–91. London: Routledge, 2011.

Kärjä, Antti-Ville."N-Songs in Multicultural Finland." In *Researching Music Censorship*, edited by Annemette Kirkegaard, Jonas Otterbeck, Helmi Järviluoma, and Jan-Sverre Knudsen, 243–66. Cambridge: Cambridge Scholars Publishing, 2017.

Kärjä, Antti-Ville. "The Joiking Injuns: Interpreting (Multi)Cultural Politics of Parody in the Music of the Finnish Western Film." *Journal of Scandinavian Cinema* 4:3 (2014): 215–30.

Kay, Peter. "Music and Humor: What's so Funny?" *Music Reference Services Quarterly* 10:1 (2006): 37–53.

Kennedy, Maev. "Prince Will Find Familiar Friends in Victorian Nudes as he Reopens Tate." *The Guardian*, October 30, 2001. https://www.theguardian.com/uk/2001/oct/30/arts.monarchy.

Kerswill, Paul. "Identity, Ethnicity and Place: The Construction of Youth Language in London." In *Space in Language and Linguistics: Geographical, Interactional, and Cognitive Perspectives*, edited by Peter Auer, Martin Hilpert, Anja Stukenbrock, and Benedikt Szmrecsanyi, 128–64. Berlin: de Gruyter, 2013.

Kerswill, Paul. "The Objectification of 'Jafaican': The Discoursal Embedding of Multicultural London English in the British Media." In *Mediatization and Sociolinguistic Change*, edited by Jannis Androutsopoulos, 428–55. Berlin: De Gruyter, 2014.

Krims, Adam. *Rap Music and the Poetics of Identity*. Cambridge: Cambridge University Press, 2000.

Kumar, Krishnan. "English and British National Identity." *History Compass* 4:3 (2006): 428–47.

Kumar, Krishnan. "Negotiating English Identity: Englishness, Britishness and the Future of the United Kingdom." *Nations and Nationalism* 16:3 (2010): 469–87.

Kuus, Kerje. *Geopolitics Reframed: Security and Identity in Europe's Eastern Enlargement*. London: Palgrave Macmillan, 2007.

Lacasse, Serge. "Intertextuality and Hypertextuality in Recorded Popular Music." In *The Musical Work: Reality or Invention?*, edited by Michael Talbot, 35–58. Liverpool: University of Liverpool Press, 2000.

Laing, Dave. *One Chord Wonders: Power and Meaning in Punk Rock*. Milton Keynes: Open University Press, 1985.

Lawrence, Tim. *Life and Death on the New York Dance Floor, 1980–1983*. Durham, NC: Duke University Press, 2016.

Leach, Anna. "Scotland Referendum: Who Voted YES?" *The Daily Mirror*, September 19, 2014. http://www.mirror.co.uk/news/ampp3d/scotland-referendum-who-voted-yes-4286743.

Lee, Iara, dir. *Cultures of Resistance*. 2010.

Lhamon, W. T., Jr. *Raising Cain: Blackface Performance from Jim Crow to Hip Hop*. Cambridge: Harvard University Press, 2000.

Lipsitz, George. *Dangerous Crossroads: Popular Music, Postmodernism and the Poetics of Place*. London: Verso, 1997.

Lockyer, Sharon, and Michael Pickering. *Beyond a Joke: The Limits of Humour*. New York: Palgrave Macmillan, 2009.

Loki. "Government Issue Music Protest: The Why of GIMP and details of the project." *Lokithegimp* Blogspot, January 11, 2014a. http://lokithegimp.blogspot.co.uk/.

Loki. "Hip Hop and Scottish Independence." *National Collective*, February 10, 2014b. http://nationalcollective.com/2014/02/10/loki-hip-hop-and-scottish-independence/.

Long, Paul, and Tim Wall. "Constructing the Histories of Popular Music: The Britannia Series." In *Popular Music and Television in Britain*, edited by Ian Inglis, 11–26. London: Routledge, 2010.

Lott, Eric. *Love and Theft: Blackface Minstrelsy and the American Working Class*. New York: Oxford University Press, 1993.

Lovink, Geert, and Sabine Niederer, eds. *Video Vortext Readers: Responses to YouTube*. Amsterdam: Institute of Network Cultures, 2008.

Lowe, Melanie. "Claiming Amadeus: Classical Feedback in American Media." *American Music* 20 (2002): 102–19.

Lynskey, Dorian. "How the Mainstream Finally Came to Grime." *GQ*, July 18, 2018.

M'charek, Amade, Katharina Schramm, and David Skinner. "Technologies of Belonging: The Absent Presence of Race in Europe." *Science, Technology & Human Values* 39:4 (2014): 459–67.

Maira, Suniana, and Magid Shihade, "Hip Hop from '48 Palestine: Youth, Music and the Present/Absent." *Social Text* 30:3 (2012): 1–26.

Marsden, Richard. "The Real Reason Yes Scotland Avoids Braveheart Nostalgia." *The Conversation*, September 5, 2014. http://www.scotsman.com/scottish-independence/richard-marsden-the-real-reason-yes-scotland-avoids-braveheart-nostalgia/.

Mathieu, Felix. "The Failure of State Multiculturalism in the UK? An Analysis of the UK's Multicultural Policy for 2000–2015." *Ethnicities* 18:1 (2018): 43–69.

Mbembe, Achille. "The Banality of Power and the Aesthetics of Vulgarity in the Postcolony." *Public Culture* 4:2 (1992): 1–30.

McAlpine, Fraser. "Lethal Bizzle, 'Babylon's Burning the Ghetto.'" *BBC Radio 1 Chart Blog*, July 12, 2007. http://www.bbc.co.uk/blogs/chartblog/2007/07/lethal_bizzle_babylons_burning.shtml.

McCrone, David. *Understanding Scotland: The Sociology of a Nation*. 2nd ed. London: Routledge, 2001.

McCrone, David, and Frank Bechhofer. "Claiming National Identity." *Ethnic and Racial Studies* 33:6 (2010): 921–48.

McDonald, David A. "Imaginaries of Exile and Emergence in Israeli Jewish and Palestinian Hip Hop." *The Drama Review* 57:3 (2013a): 69–87.

McDonald, David A. *My Voice is My Weapon: Music, Nationalism, and the Poetics of Palestinian Resistance*. Durham, NC: Duke University Press, 2013b.

McGarvey, Darren (Loki). *Poverty Safari: Understanding the Anger of Britain's Underclass*. Edinburgh: Luath Press Limited, 2017.

McLaren, James. "Urban Edge in Newport: The Welsh Grime Quest Continues." *BBC Wales Music*, July 13, 2012. http://www.bbc.co.uk/blogs/walesmusic/2012/07/urban-edge-newport-grime-charlie-sloth.shtml.

McLeod, John. *Beginning Postcolonialism*. 2nd ed. Manchester: Manchester University Press, 2010.

McNally, James. "Panic Stricken: Hip-Hop and London, 1987–1988." Paper Presented at *It's Not Where You're From, it's where You're At* Hip-hop Conference. Cambridge University. June 2016.

McNally, James. "The Formation of Hip-Hop in London, 1982–84: A Cultural History." PhD diss., Goldsmith's College, 2015.

McNally, James. "Unpublished interview with Lowkey for *Hip-hop Connection*." 2008.

McRobbie, Angela. "But Is It Art?" *Marxism Today*, November–December 1998. 55–57.

Mearon, Siobhan. "Grime, Revival or Renaissance?" *University Observer*, October 14, 2016. https://universityobserver.ie/grime-revival-or-renaissance/.

Meer, Nasar, and Tariq Modood. "Multiculturalism: A Resilient Category in Britain." *Political Insight*, April 8, 2014. https://www.psa.ac.uk/insight-plus/blog/multiculturalism-resilient-category-britain.

Mehreen. "Poisonous Poets Interview." *Original UK Hip-hop* blog, April 22, 2005. https://web.archive.org/web/20120223222022/http://www.ukhh.com/features/oldinterviews/poisonous_poets/index.html.

Meleady, Rose, Charles R. Seger, and Marieke Vermue. "Examining the Role of Positive and Negative Intergroup Contact and Anti-Immigrant Prejudice in Brexit." *British Journal of Social Psychology* 56:4 (2017): 799–808.

Melegh, Attila. *On the East-West Slope: Globalization, Nationalism, Racism and Discourses on Central and Eastern Europe*. Budapest: Central European University Press, 2006.

Mera, Miguel. "Is Funny Music Funny?: Contexts and Case Studies of Film Music Humour." *Journal of Popular Music Studies* 14:2 (2002): 91–113.

Mercer, Kobena. "Art That is Ethnic in Inverted Commas." *Frieze*. Issue 25. November–December 1995. 39–41.

Meredith, Fionola. "Belfast City Breakers: 'Instead of Violence, We Were Dancing.'" *The Irish Times*, August 4, 2018. https://www.irishtimes.com/life-and-style/people/belfast-city-breakers-instead-of-violence-we-were-dancing-1.3584270.

Miller, Alex. "Back to Bizznezz." *NME*, July 13, 2007. http://www.nme.com/reviews/lethal-bizzle/8794.

Miller, Laura. "Fresh Hell." *The New Yorker*, June 14, 2010. http://www.newyorker.com/magazine/2010/06/14/fresh-hell-2.

Mitchell, Tony. "Doin' Damage in my Native Language: The Use of 'Resistance Vernaculars' in Hip Hop in France, Italy, and Aotearoa/New Zealand." *Popular Music and Society* 24 (2000): 41–54.

Mitchell, Tony, ed. *Global Noise: Rap and Hip Hop Outside the USA*. Middletown, CT: Wesleyan University Press, 2001.

Modood, Tariq and John Salt, eds. *Migration, Ethnicity and Britishness*. London: Palgrave Macmillan, 2011.

Moore, Allan F. "Singer-Songwriters and the English Folk Tradition." In *The Cambridge Companion to the Singer-Songwriter*, edited by Katherine Williams and Justin A. Williams, 55–66. Cambridge: Cambridge University Press, 2016.

Moreno Almeida, Christina. *Rap Beyond "Resistance": Staging Power in Contemporary Morocco*. London: Palgrave Macmillan, 2017.

Moylan, Tom. *Scraps of the Untainted Sky: Science Fiction, Utopia, Dystopia*. Oxford: Westview Press, 2000.

Musić, Goran, and Predrag Vukčević. "Diesel Power: Serbian Hip Hop from the Pleasure of the Privileged to Mass Youth Culture." In *Hip- Hop at Europe's Edge: Music, Agency, and Social Change*, edited by Milosz Miszczynski and Adriana Helbig, 85–108. Bloomington: Indiana University Press, 2017.

Myers, Matt. "Scottish Independence: Why Didn't the Working-Class Yes Vote Win the Day?" *rs21*, September 23, 2014. http://rs21.org.uk/2014/09/23/scottish-independence-why-didnt-the-working-class-yes-vote-win-the-day/.

NABA (National Association of British Arabs). Report on the 2011 census. May 2013. https://web.archive.org/web/20140529130456/http://naba.org.uk/library/reports/census_2011.html.

Nagesh, Ashitha. "Theresa May Apologises for Failures in the Wake of the Grenfell Tower Tragedy." *Metro*, June 21, 2017. https://metro.co.uk/2017/06/21/theresa-may-apologises-for-failures-in-the-wake-of-the-grenfell-tower-tragedy-6725032/.

Ngũgĩ wa Thiong'o. *Decolonising the Mind: The Politics of Language in African Literature*. London: Heinemann, 1986.

Ngũgĩ wa Thiong'o. *Devil on the Cross*. Translated by Ngũgĩ wa Thiong'o. London: Heinemann, 1987

Nielsen, Steen Kaargard. "Wife Murder as Child's Game: Analytical Reflections on Eminem's Performative Self-Dramatization." *Danish Yearbook of Musicology* 34 (2006): 31–46.

Nittle, Nadra Kareem. "Common Muslim and Arab Stereotypes in TV and Film." *ThoughtCo.*, July 12, 2018. https://www.thoughtco.com/tv-film-stereotypes-arabs-middle-easterners-2834648.

Nkrumah, Kwame. *Neo-Colonialism, the Last Stage of Imperialism*. London: Thomas Nelson & Sons, 1965.

No author. "Sheep Jokes." 2013. http://www.sheepjokes.co.uk/short-jokes/.

No author. "Welsh Jokes." http://hahas.co.uk/welsh/.

No author. "Why Is Adidas so Popular Among Russians?" *Weird Russia*, April 1, 2015. http://weirdrussia.com/2015/01/04/why-is-adidas-so-popular-among-russians/.

Nooshin, Laudan. "Whose Liberation? Iranian Popular Music and the Fetishization of Resistance." *Popular Communication* 15:3 (2017): 163–91.

O'Keefe, Alice. "Rapper Asks BBC to Play 9/11 Song." *The Guardian*, April 9, 2006. https://www.theguardian.com/media/2006/apr/09/radio.arts.

O'Keefe, Alice. "What Happened to MC Riz." *The Guardian*, April 16, 2006. https://www.theguardian.com/uk/2006/apr/16/theobserver.uknews.

O'Toole, Fintan. "Brexit Is Being Driven by English Nationalism. And It Will End in Self-Rule." *The Guardian*, June 19, 2016. https://www.theguardian.com/commentisfree/2016/jun/18/england-eu-referendum-brexit.

Olusoga, David. "The History of British Slave Ownership Has Been Buried: Now Its Scale Can Be Revealed." *The Guardian*, July 12, 2015. https://www.theguardian.com/world/2015/jul/12/british-history-slavery-buried-scale-revealed.

Palmer, Jerry. *Taking Humour Seriously*. London: Routledge, 1993.

Palmer, Roy. *Boxing the Compass: Sea Songs & Shanties*. Todmorden: Herron, 2001.

Partridge, Kenneth. "Americans Were Bound to Hate The Streets' *Original Pirate Material*." *A.V. Club*, February 17, 2015. http://www.avclub.com/article/americans-were-bound-hate-streets-original-pirate--214890.

Peddie, Ian. "Playing at Poverty: The Music Hall and the Staging of the Working Class." In *Music and Protest*, edited by Ian Peddie, 129–50. Farnham: Ashgate, 2012.

Peddie, Ian, ed. *Music and Protest: The Library of Essays on Music, Politics and Society*. Farnham: Ashgate, 2012.

Peddie, Ian, ed. *The Resisting Music: Popular Music and Social Protest*. Farnham: Ashgate, 2006.

Persley, Nicole Hodges. "Hip-Hop Theater and Performance." In *The Cambridge Companion to Hip-Hop*, edited by Justin A. Williams, 85–98. Cambridge: Cambridge University Press, 2015.

Petridis, Alexis. "Review: Lethal Bizzle, *Back to Bizznizz*." *The Guardian*, July 20, 2007. http://www.theguardian.com/music/2007/jul/20/urban.shopping.

Phillips, Dilwyn. *Welsh Jokes (It's Wales)*. Talybont: Y Lolfa, 2002.

Picker, John M. *Victorian Soundscapes*. Oxford University Press, 2003.

Pickering, Michael. *Blackface Minstrelsy in Britain*. London: Routledge, 2008.

Pickering, Michael. *Stereotyping: The Politics of Representation*. New York: Palgrave Macmillan, 2001.

Pierce, Helen. *Unseemly Pictures: Graphic Satire and Politics in Early Modern England*. New Haven, CT: Yale University Press, 2008.

Piterberg, Gabriel. "Erasures." *New Left Review* 10 (2001): 31–42.

Pittock, Murray. *The Road to Independence? Scotland Since the Sixties*. London: Reaktion Books, 2008.

Plunkett, John. "BBC DJ Criticises 'All White' Radio 1 and 'All Black' 1Xtra 'Silos.'" *The Guardian*, March 4, 2015. http://www.theguardian.com/media/2015/mar/04/bbc-dj-criticises-all-white-radio-1-all-black-1xtra-silos-nihal.

Pompova, Izabela. "European Migrants: Burden or Benefit for the British Economy? The Depiction of EU Migrants in the UK and Its Consequences. *Migrants & Society* 2015, University of Nottingham Human Rights Law Centre. https://www.nottingham.ac.uk/hrlc/documents/student-conference-2015/izabela-pompova-paper.pdf.

Potter, Russell. *Spectacular Vernaculars: Hip-Hop and the Politics of Postmodernism*. New York: SUNY Press, 1995.

Procter, James. *Stuart Hall*. London: Routledge, 1994.

Ramsey, Guthrie P. "Who Hears Here? Black Music, Critical Bias, and the Musicological Skin Trade." *The Musical Quarterly* 85:1 (2001): 1–52.

Red Train Blog, The. "Invisible Britain." December 6, 2015. http://redtrainblog.blogspot.co.uk/2015/12/invisible-britain.html?m=1.

Reinhardt-Byrd, Brenna. "Stylized Turkish German as the Resistance Vernacular of German Hip-Hop." In *The Cambridge Companion to Hip-Hop*, edited by Justin A. Williams, 292–300. Cambridge: Cambridge University Press, 2015.

Rhys, Steffan. "19 Welsh Jokes That Are Pretty Much the Best Ones Ever Told." *WalesOnline*, July 1, 2015. http://www.walesonline.co.uk/lifestyle/fun-stuff/19-welsh-jokes-pretty-much-9562314.

Rimmer, Jonathan. "The Hip Hop Artists: How Rappers Were Turned on by the IndyRef." *The National*, November 28, 2015. http://www.thenational.scot/culture/the-hip-hope-artists-how-rappers-were-turned-on-by-the-indyref.10519.

Roderick, John. "Punk Rock is Bullshit." *Seattle Weekly*. March 06, 2013.

Rollefson, J. Griffith. *Flip the Script: European Hip Hop and the Politics of Postcoloniality.* Chicago: University of Chicago Press, 2017.

Rollefson, J. Griffith. "'He's Calling His Flock Now': Black Music and Postcoloniality from Buddy Bolden's New Orleans to Sefyu's Paris." *American Music* 33 (2015): 375–97.

Rollefson, J. Griffith. "Musical (African) Americanization: The Case of Aggro Berlin." In *Crosscurrents: American and European Music in Interaction, 1900–2000*, edited by Felix Meyer, Carol J. Oja, Wolfgang Rathert, and Anne C. Schreffler, 472–88. Oxford: Boydell Press, 2014.

Rollefson, J. Griffith. "The 'Robot Voodoo Power' Thesis: Afrofuturism and Anti-Anti-Essentialism from Sun Ra to Kool Keith." *Black Music Research Journal* 28:1 (2008): 83–109.

Rose, Margaret A. *Parody: Ancient, Modern and Post-Modern.* Cambridge: Cambridge University Press, 1993.

RT. "8 Reasons Why Scotland Voted 'No' to Independence." *RT*, September 19, 2014. https://www.rt.com/uk/188952-why-scotland-vote-no/.

Rumi. *The Essential Rumi.* Translated by Coleman Barks. New York: Castle Books, 1997.

Rymajdo, Kamila. "Grime Beyond Borders: Manchester and Beyond." *The Skinny*, August 18, 2017. https://www.theskinny.co.uk/music/interviews/grime-beyond-borders.

Rzepnikowska, Alina. "Racism and Xenophobia Experienced by Polish Migrants in the UK before and after Brexit Vote." *Journal of Ethnic and Migration Studies* 45:1 (2019): 61–77.

Saeed, Amir. "The Politics of Hip Hop and Cultural Resistance: A British-Asian Perspective." In *Postcolonial Media Culture in Britain*, edited by Rosaline Brunt and Rinella Cere, 14–26. New York: Palgrave Macmillan, 2011.

Said, Edward. "Reflections on Exile." In *Reflections on Exile and Other Essays*, 176–86. Cambridge: Harvard University Press, 2002.

Samson, Valerie. "Music as Protest Strategy: The Example of Tiananmen Square." In *Ashgate Library of Music and Protest*, edited by Ian Peddie. Farnham: Ashgate, 2012.

Sandy Boots. "Best Welsh Jokes." Message Board. *Army Rumour Service*, August 10, 2007. https://www.arrse.co.uk/community/threads/best-welsh-jokes.65286/.

Saving Grace. "Interview with DJ MK." *Saving Grace.* http://www.saving-grace.co.uk/interview/dj-mk/.

Schloss, Joseph. *Making Beats: The Art of Sample-Based Hip-Hop.* Middletown, CT: Wesleyan University Press, 2004.

Schneider, Rebecca. "Gesture to Opera: Yinka Shonibare's *Un Balllo in Maschera.*" *The Opera Quarterly* 31:3 (2015): 155–69.

Scots Language Centre. "Political and Protest Song." http://www.scotslanguage.com/Scots_Song_uid65/Types_of_Scots_Song/Political_and_Protest_Songs.

Seippel, Ørnulf. "Sports and Nationalism in a Globalized World." *International Journal of Sociology* 47:1 (2017): 43–61.

Shabi, Rachel. "Chequered History." *The Guardian*, September 22, 2008. https://www.theguardian.com/lifeandstyle/2008/sep/22/fashion.middleeast.

Sharma, Nitasha. "Rap, Race, Revolution: Post-9/11 Brown and a Hip Hop Critique of Empire." *Audible Empire: Music, Global Politics, Critique*, edited by Ronald Radano and Tejumola Olaniyan, 292–313. Durham, NC: Duke University Press, 2015.

Shukla, Nikesh, ed. *The Good Immigrant*. London: Unbound, 2016.

Skey, Michael. *National Belonging and Everyday Life: The Significance of Nationhood in an Uncertain World*. Basingstoke: Palgrave Macmillan, 2011.

Skinner, Mike. *The Story of the Streets*. London: Corgi Press, 2013.

Slater, Mark. "Timbre and Non-Radical Didacticism in the Streets' *A Grand Don't Come for Free*: A Poetic-ecological Model." *Music Analysis* 30:2–3 (2011): 360–95.

Slater, Tom, and Ntsiki Anderson. "The Reputational Ghetto: Territorial Stigmatisation in St. Paul's, Bristol." *Transactions of the Institute of British Geographers* 37:4 (2012): 530–46.

Sleaford Mods. "Sleaford Mods Criticise UKIP and Cereal 'Jesters' in Alternative Christmas Queen's Speech for NME." *NME*, December 25, 2014. http://www.nme.com/news/sleaford-mods/81928.

Smith, Anthony D. *The Ethnic Origins of Nations*. Oxford: Blackwell, 1986.

Smith, Anthony D., ed. *Nationalism: Theory, Ideology, History (Key Concepts)*. Cambridge: Polity, 2001.

Snickers, Pelle, and Patrick Vonderau, eds. *The YouTube Reader*. London: Wallflower Press, 2009.

Song, Miri. "Is There 'a' Mixed Race Group in Britain? The Diversity of Multiracial Identification and Experience." *Critical Social Policy* 30:3 (2010a): 337–58.

Song, Miri. "What Happens after Segmented Assimilation? An Exploration of Intermarriage and 'Mixed Race' Young People in Britain." *Ethnic and Racial Studies* 33:7 (2010b): 1194–213.

Song, Miri, and Peter Aspinall. "Is Racial Mismatch a Problem for Young 'Mixed Race' People in Britain? The Findings of Qualitative Research." *Ethnicities* 12:6 (2012): 730–53.

Speers, Laura. *Hip-Hop Authenticity and the London Scene*. London: Routledge, 2017.

Spisak, April. "What Makes a Good . . . Dystopian Novel?" *The Horn Book Magazine*, May 2012. http://www.hbook.com/2012/04/choosing-books/recommended-books/what-makes-a-good-ya-dystopian-novel/#_.

Spivak, Gayatri Chakravorty. "Subaltern Studies. Deconstructing Historiography." In *The Spivak Reader*, edited by Donna Landry and Gerland MacLean, 203–36. London: Routledge, 1996.

Stormzy, and Jude Yawson. *Rise Up: The #Merky Story So Far*. London: Merky Books, 2018.

Stratton, Jon, and Nabeel Zubieri, eds. *Black Popular Music Since 1945*. Farnham: Ashgate, 2014.

Stratton, Jon. "'Police on My Back' and the Postcolonial Experience." *Social Identities: Journal for the Study of Race, Nation and Culture* 19:5 (2013): 536–51.

Swedenburg, Ted. "Palestinian Rap: Against the Struggle Paradigm." In *Popular Culture in the Middle East and North Africa*, edited by Walid El Hamamsy and Mounire Soliman, 17–32. London: Routledge, 2013.

Symonds, Tom, and Claire Ellison. "Grenfell Tower Cladding Failed to Meet Standard." *BBC News*, April 5, 2018. https://www.bbc.co.uk/news/uk-43558186.

Tawil-Souri, Helga. "Where Is the Political in Cultural Studies? In Palestine." *International Journal of Cultural Studies* 14:5 (2011): 467–82.

Thapar, Ciaran. "The Hard Knock Life of British Multiculturalism." *New Statesman*, December 18, 2014. https://www.newstatesman.com/politics/2014/12/hard-knock-life-british-multiculturalism.

Thompson, Stacy. "Punk Cinema." *Cinema Journal* 43:2 (2004): 47–66.

Tijmstra, Sylvia A. R. "Uniquely Scottish? Placing Scottish Devolution in Theoretical Perspective." *Environment and Planning C: Government and Policy* 27 (2009): 732–46.

Tolia-Kelly, Divya, and Andy Morris. "Disruptive Aesthetics?: Revisiting the Burden of Representation in the Art of Chris Ofili and Yinha Shonibare." *Third Text* 18 (2004): 153–67.

Torgersen, Eivid, and Szakay Anita. "An Investigation of Speech Rhythm in London English." *Lingua* 122 (2012): 822–40.

Torgersen, Eivid. "A Perceptual Study of Ethnicity and Geographical Location in London and Birmingham." In *Dialectological and Folk Dialectological Concepts of Space*, edited by Sandra Hansen, Christian Schwartz, Philipp Stoeckle, and Tobias Streck, 75–95. Berlin: Mouton De Gruyter, 2012.

Torrance, David. "Curious Case of SNP's Shift from Ethnic Nationalism." *Herald Scotland*, April 14, 2014. http://www.heraldscotland.com/opinion/13155444.Curious_case_of_SNP_s_shift_from_ethnic_nationalism.

Toynbee, Jason, Catherine Tackley, and Mark Doffman. *Black British Jazz: Routes, Ownership and Performance*. Farnham: Ashgate, 2014.

Traber, Daniel S. "L.A.'s 'White Minority': Punk and the Contradictions of Self-Marginalization. In *White Riot: Punk Rock and the Politics of Race*, edited by Stephen Duncombe and Maxwell Tremblay, 82–99. London: Verso, 2011.

Turner, Katherine L., ed. *The Sound of Irony: Music, Politics and Popular Culture*. Farnham: Ashgate, 2015.

Tyler, Imogen. "'Being Poor Is Not Entertainment': Class Struggles against Poverty Porn." *Social Action & Research Foundation*, November 16, 2014. http://www.the-sarf.org.uk/being-poor-is-not-entertainment-class-struggles-against-poverty-porn-by-imogen-tyler/.

Vernallis, Carol. "Audiovisual Change: Viral Web Media and the Obama Campaign." *Cinema Journal* 50:4 (2011): 73–97.

Virtuous Media Attire. "Shay D Interview." April 11, 2018. https://www.vmattire.co.uk/shayd/.

VogueVideo. "Vogue Meets the Brit-Hop Generation." *Vogue*, September 15, 2017. https://www.vogue.co.uk/video/vogue-meets-the-brit-hop-generation.

Waldron, Daniel, and Sanwar Ali. "Toxic Anti-UK Visa and Immigration Rhetoric Fuelled by Government Says Report." *Workpermit.com*, September 9, 2017. https://workpermit.com/news/toxic-anti-uk-visa-and-immigration-rhetoric-fuelled-government-says-report-20170919.

Weaver, Robin. "Identity and Post-Referendum Scotland." *National Collective*, February 6, 2015. http://nationalcollective.com/2015/02/06/identity-post-referendum-scotland/#sthash.8faV7PSr.dpuf.

Weaver, Simon, and Piotr Ozieranski. "New European Tricksters: Polish Jokes in the Context of European Union Labour Migration." *International Journal of Cultural Studies* 19:5 (2016): 577–91.

Welsh, Irvine. *Trainspotting*. London: Secker and Warburg, 1993.

White, Joy. "Grime—A Very British Musical Genre." *Prospect*, July 24, 2018. https://www.prospectmagazine.co.uk/arts-and-books/grime-a-very-british-musical-genre.

White, Joy. *Urban Music and Entrepreneurship: Beats, Rhymes and Young People's Enterprise*. London: Routledge, 2017.

Wiley. "Wiley on Why Kanye West's Brit Awards Salute to Grime Was Empowering Not Patronising." *NME Blog*, March 4, 2015. https://www.nme.com/blogs/nme-blogs/wiley-on-why-kanye-wests-brit-awards-salute-to-grime-was-empowering-not-patronising-759925.

Williams, Chris. "Problematizing Wales." In *Postcolonial Wales*, edited by Jane Aaron and Chris Williams, 3–17. Cardiff: University of Wales Press, 2005.

Williams, Justin. "The Construction of Jazz Rap as High Art in Hip-hop Music." *Journal of Musicology* 27:4 (2010): 435–59.

Williams, Justin. "'We Get the Job Done': Immigrant Discourse and Mixtape Authenticity in *The Hamilton Mixtape*." *American Music* 36:4 (2018): 487–506.

Williams, Justin. "Soweto's War: Race, Class and Jazz/Hip-Hop Hybridities." In *Black British Jazz: Routes, Ownership, Performance*, edited by Jason Toynbee, Catherine Tackley, and Mark Doffman, 133–49. Farnham: Ashgate, 2014.

Williams, Justin. *Rhymin' and Stealin': Musical Borrowing in Hip-Hop*. Ann Arbor: University of Michigan Press, 2013.

Williams, Justin, ed. *The Cambridge Companion to Hip-Hop*. Cambridge: Cambridge University Press, 2015.

Williams, Raymond. *The Sociology of Culture*. New York: Schocken Books, 1982.

Williams, Zoe. "Katie Hopkins Calling Migrants Vermin Recalls the Darkest Events of History." *The Guardian*, April 19, 2015. https://www.theguardian.com/commentisfree/2015/apr/19/katie-hopkins-migrants-vermin-darkest-history-drownings.

Wilson, Anne. "'Mixed Race' Children in British society: Some Theoretical Considerations." *British Journal of Sociology* 35:1 (1984): 42–61.

Wimmer, Andreas, and Nina Glick Schiller. "Methodological Nationalism, the Social Sciences, and the Study of Migration: An Essay in Historical Epistemology." *The International Migration Review* 37:3 (2003): 576–610.

Withers, Polly. "Performing Alterity: The Translocal Politics of an Urban Youth Music Scene in Post-Oslo Palestine." PhD diss., University of Exeter, 2016.

Wolff, Larry. *Inventing Eastern Europe*. Stanford: Stanford University Press, 1994.

Yegorov, Oleg. "Criminals or Just Misunderstood: Who Are Russia's 'Gopniks'?" *Russia Beyond*, March 29, 2016. https://www.rbth.com/politics_and_society/2016/03/29/criminals-or-just-misunderstood-who-are-russias-gopniks_580121.

Young, Robert. *Postcolonialism: A Very Short Introduction*. Oxford: Oxford University Press, 2003.

Youngs, Ian. "Is UK on Verge of Brithop Boom?" *BBC News*, November 21, 2005. http://news.bbc.co.uk/1/hi/entertainment/4455862.stm.

Zahova, Kalina. "Intercultural Reception as Manifested in Popular Music." *Situating popular musics: IASPM 16th International Conference Proceedings*, 2011, 287–94.

Zamora, Lois. *The Usable Past*. Cambridge: Cambridge University Press, 1997.

Zubieri, Nabeel. "'New Throat Fe Chat': The Voices and Media of MC Culture." In *Black Music in Britain Since 1945*, edited by Jon Stratton and Nabeel Zubieri, 185–201. Farnham: Ashgate, 2014.

Zubieri, Nabeel. *Sounds English: Transnational Popular Music*. Urbana-Champaign: University of Illinois Press, 2001.

Zubieri, Nabeel. "Worries in the Dance: Post-Millennial Groove and Sub-Bass Culture." In *Britpop and the English Music Tradition*, edited by Andy Bennett and Jon Stratton, 179–92. Farnham: Ashgate, 2010.

Zumkhawala-Cook, Richard. "'Aye or Die!': Hip Hop Scotland and the New Sound of Nationalism." Paper Presented at the Annual International Association for the Study of Popular Music. Louisville, KY. February 21, 2015.

Zumkhawala-Cook, Richard. *Scotland as We Know It: Representations of National Identity in literature, Film and Popular Culture*. London: McFarland, 2008.

Index